Passing the ITIL® Foundation Ex
2011 Edition

Other publications by Van Haren Publishing

Van Haren Publishing (VHP) specializes in titles on Best Practices, methods and standards within four domains:
- IT management
- Architecture (Enterprise and IT)
- Business management and
- Project management

Van Haren Publishing offers a wide collection of whitepapers, templates, free e-books, trainer material etc. in the **Van Haren Publishing Knowledge Base**: www.vanharen.net for more details.

Van Haren Publishing is also publishing on behalf of leading organizations and companies: ASLBiSL Foundation, CA, Centre Henri Tudor, Gaming Works, Getronics, IACCM, IAOP, IPMA-NL, ITSqc, NAF, Ngi, PMI-NL, PON, Quint, The Open Group, The Sox Institute, Tmforum.

Topics are (per domain):

IT (Service) Management / IT Governance	Architecture (Enterprise and IT)	Project/Programme/ Risk Management
ABC of ICT	Archimate®	A4-Projectmanagement
ASL	GEA®	ICB / NCB
BiSL	SOA	MINCE®
CATS CM®	TOGAF®	M_o_R®
CMMI		MSP™
CoBIT	**Business Management**	P3O®
Frameworx	Contract Management	PMBOK® Guide
ISO 17799	EFQM	PRINCE2®
ISO 27001	eSCM	
ISO 27002	ISA-95	
ISO/IEC 20000	ISO 9000	
ISPL	ISO 9001:2000	
IT Service CMM	OPBOK	
ITIL®	Outsourcing	
ITSM	SAP	
MOF	SixSigma	
MSF	SOX	
SABSA	SqEME®	

For the latest information on VHP publications, visit our website: www.vanharen.net.

Passing the ITIL® Foundation Exam

2011 EDITION

David Pultorak

Jon E Nelson

Vince Pultorak

Van Haren
PUBLISHING

Colofon

Title:	Passing the ITIL® Foundation Exam, 2011 Edition
Authors:	David Pultorak, Jon E Nelson, Vince Pultorak
Editor:	Jane Chittenden
Publisher:	Van Haren Publishing, Zaltbommel, www.vanharen.net
ISBN hardcopy:	978 90 8753 664 0
ISBN eBook:	978 90 8753 912 2
Print:	First edition, first impression, January 2012
Design and Layout:	CO2 Premedia bv, Amersfoort – NL
Copyright:	© Van Haren Publishing 2012

For any further enquiries about Van Haren Publishing, please send an e-mail to: info@vanharen.net

Foreword

Since the late 1980s many IT professionals have participated in ITIL training and have gone on to sit the examinations. The challenge with exams is that many of us are out of practice in sitting them. What is needed is assistance in studying that covers the material completely but succinctly, and that makes the concepts memorable. This study guide provides the structure, key details and study tips to assist you in passing your ITIL exam. It puts context around key ITIL ideas and provides memory aids to help you recall key points.

You are taking the first step towards taking ITIL – training and obtaining the qualifications. Once the education and examination are complete you next step is to apply what you have learned to your work. When you do, I ask you to consider the mistakes other organizations have made so that you avoid repeating them. These include claiming to use ITIL, but forgetting to educate IT staff; not using ITIL to drive out metrics and measure performance; and not engendering adoption of common vision and terminology, putting service provision at risk.

I would be remiss if I didn't mention the current sea change in IT – the advent of cloud computing – especially as ITIL plays a key role in leveraging this new world of work for IT professionals. Cloud computing is another great leap forward in what IT makes possible, and with that possibility, IT becomes more sophisticated, and demands and expectations from customers wanting IT Service delivered faster, cheaper and with continuous availability reach new heights. To seize the opportunity of on and off premise cloud computing, organizations will need to bridge the globe, integrate many cultures and have standardized processes integrated with the virtualization technology. What it will take for this to happen is capable IT professionals with a shared code of good practice in mind to manage, organize, conduct processes, share knowledge and develop people along a path that makes the most of the opportunities with the cloud. Without such shared thinking and action, the opportunity will be lost for some organizations, a gain for competitors and newcomers who do rise to the challenge. It is therefore critical that you integrate ITIL with your technology, educate your organization on the benefits of ITIL, and instill a culture of Continuous Service Improvement so you can meet the challenges of the cloud and future strategies in IT.

It is important to remember that with cloud computing, as with any new technology, the people and process aspects of IT, those supported and enabled by ITIL, are vital to ensuring the new technology translates into better, faster and cheaper IT services. I wish you the best of luck in this, the first step in your journey to support, enable and leverage what has arrived and comes next in IT: the age of cloud computing.

Kathleen Wilson
August 8, 2011, Mississauga, Ontario, Canada

Acknowledgements

The goal of this publication is to provide a concise set of ITIL information at the Foundation level, and to provide the practical tips, examples and provoking questions that are necessary to help the reader grasp the critical ITIL concepts required to pass the ITIL Foundation certification examination.

Van Haren Publishing would like to thank the Authors of this book and acknowledge the hard work it took to achieve this work. David Pultorak, Jon E. Nelson and Vince Pultorak spent many hours drafting, redrafting and checking this work so that it meets the high standard required. The Publishers thank them for their expertise, courtesy and patience.

Many colleagues and contributors helped to review and validate the content of this study guide. Special thanks go out to the following who kindly spent valuable time checking the material:

- Claire Agutter, ITIL Training Zone

- Pierre Bernard, Pink Elephant

- Ton Bondi, Microsoft Corporation

- Rob van der Burg, Microsoft

- Edleen Guanko, Pultorak & Associates Ltd

- Kevin Holland, Service Management Consultant Specialist

- Donna Knapp, ITSM Academy

- Ali Makahleh, Microsoft Corporation

- Joyce Parker, Microsoft Corporation

- Peter Quagliariello, Pultorak & Associates Ltd

- Mart Rovers, Interprom

- Joel Smith, Microsoft Corporation

- Howard Williams, Microsoft Corporation

- Kathleen Wilson, Microsoft Corporation

Preface

While the ITIL books contain all the content required to pass the Foundation examination, two things are missing for those who seek to study and pass the examination and apply what they have learned back on the job.

The first and most important for you, the examination-takers, is content presented in a way that helps make the terminology, principles, and models in the framework memorable. We have endeavored to provide that here, in the form of examples, key questions, checklists, stories, anecdotes, metaphors, mnemonics and so on – anything that helps you grasp the concepts vividly so they are at the ready in your mind when you sit the examination.

The second is content that helps you get started on applying what you have learned back on the job. It is likely that you are taking the exam to demonstrate your knowledge of the concepts, with the goal of transferring that knowledge into effective and efficient action back in your job. The pedagogical elements mentioned above are also intended to drive applicability home, to help you answer the question for yourself: "Okay, I get it. Now what? What is most important to do when I get back to my workplace? How can I make the most of what I have learned to make a difference for myself, for my team, for the organization overall, and for my suppliers, customers, and end users?" Thinking through how to apply the concepts learned back at your organizations sets the stage for later application and also can help make the concepts "stick" in your mind, useful when you sit the examination.

Any study aids that are used in addition to the source materials must make it easy to cross-reference the source materials to make it easy to traverse the materials and to ensure the learning of full coverage of content. Accordingly, we have aligned this little book to the ITIL Foundation syllabus and indexed its content against it, so that you can be sure of comprehensive coverage that is easily navigated between this book, ITIL books, and the syllabus.

We wish you luck in your examination preparation and success in the application of the concepts learned back on the job.

David Pultorak, Jon E Nelson, Vince Pultorak

August 8, 2011, Philadelphia, PA USA

Table of contents

Introduction

This study guide provides the reader with a tool for preparing for the ITIL® Foundation 2011 Edition Foundation certification examination. It includes the core material required for the examination as defined in the course syllabus, along with practical questions, tips and examples to reinforce concepts learned and facilitate the application of learning at individual, team, and organizational levels. This guide is intended for candidates preparing to take the ITIL® Foundation 2011 Edition certification course and examination.

Readers can also use the publication *Foundations of ITIL V3* or the ITIL Core volumes (Service Strategy, Service Design, Service Transition, Service Operation, and Continual Service Improvement) for more detailed context and guidance.

Using this Study Guide

This study guide is based on The ITIL Foundation Certificate in IT Service Management SYLLABUS v5.3. Where there are gaps in syllabus reference sequence numbers in this publication, for example, there is an ITILFND02-02-2 but no 02-1, an ITILFND03-03-21 and 03-24 but no 03-22 and 03-23, these are not errors, as these gaps exist in the syllabus and this book is intended to precisely map to the syllabus.

Where the syllabus specifies "understand" as a verb for a learning objective, strongly recommend that students should not only be able to 'understand'; but also be able to 'explain' as it is a skill that can be demonstrated. Syllabus entries have also been modified make sense standing alone, without reference to superordinate or subordinate materials, and to preserve completeness and traceability back to the syllabus and source publications when viewed in isolation. For example, they have been prefixed with their corresponding unit number, for example, entry 01-1 has been prefixed with ITILFND01 (the unit number), and where syllabus entries contain sub-bullets, these entries have been combined into a single syllabus reference. In some cases for readability of section headings, acronyms have been used (for example CSI for continual service improvement).

For each unit, the timing (for example, 90m for ITILFND01) refers to the minimum study period recommended by the syllabus. Where no minimum study period is recommended, it is because the content is recommended to be covered as part of other units.

What is ITIL?

The Information Technology Infrastructure Library (ITIL) offers a systematic approach to the delivery of quality IT service. ITIL was developed in the 1980s and 1990s by the UK government Central Computer and Telecommunications Agency (CCTA), later the Office of Government Commerce (OGC) and now subsumed into the Cabinet Office, under contract to the UK Government, with the objective of ensuring better use of IT services and resources. Since it was introduced, ITIL has provided not only a best practice framework, but also the approach and philosophy shared by the people who work with it in practice. ITIL was updated the first time in 2000-2002 (V2), again in 2007 (ITIL V3), and then in 2011 (ITIL® 2011 edition)

The ITIL® 2011 edition updates to the 2007 edition ITIL publications were released 29 July 2011. The ITIL® 2011 edition publications were designed to be easier to read and understand, to relate more clearly to one another and to correct issues to provide more clarity, consistency, correctness and completeness. The ITIL® 2011 edition updates did not change core ITIL process areas and principles significantly, as the focus of the updates was on clarity and not on introducing new concepts.

The publication (and therefore, the course and examination) most impacted by the ITIL® 2011 edition updates is the ITIL Service Strategy publication, as this is where much of the focus for the 2011 edition updates was placed.

New syllabi and examinations based on the 2011 Edition publications were made available 8 August 2011. Existing certificate holders need not recertify.

Several organizations are involved in promoting the adoption of the best practices described in ITIL and associated examination schemes.
- *The UK Government Cabinet Office* – Owner of ITIL, promoter of best practices in numerous areas including IT Service Management.
- *itSMF (IT Service Management Forum)* – A global, independent, internationally recognized not-for-profit organization dedicated to support the development of IT Service Management, e.g. through publications in the ITSM Library series. It consists of a growing number of national chapters (40+), with itSMF International as the controlling body.
- *APM Group* – In 2006, OGC contracted the management of ITIL rights, the certification of ITIL examinations, and accreditation of training organizations to the APM Group (APMG), a commercial organization. APMG defines the certification and accreditation schemes for the ITIL examinations, and publishes the associated certification scheme.
- *Examination institutes* – To support the worldwide delivery of the ITIL examinations, APMG has accredited ten examination institutes as of the time of publication: APMG-International, BCS-ISEB, CERT-IT, CSME, DANSK-IT, DF Certifiering AB, EXIN, Loyalist Certification Services, PEOPLECERT Group, and TÜV SÜD Akademie. For more information, see http://www.itil-officialsite.com/ExaminationInstitutes/ExamInstitutes.aspx

- *Publishing organizations* – TSO publishes the Core ITIL framework within 5 titles. A number of publishers also produce derivative works based on the framework under licence.

ITIL examinations

There are four qualification levels:
- *ITIL Foundation* – aimed at basic knowledge of, and insight into, the core principles and processes of ITIL. This qualification is positioned at the same level as ITIL V2 Foundation examination.
- *ITIL Intermediate* – based on two workstreams, one based on the Service Lifecycle, and one based on practitioner capabilities.
- *ITIL Expert* –aimed at those individuals who are interested in demonstrating a high level of knowledge in ITIL in entirety
- *ITIL Master* - aimed at people that are experienced in the industry – typically, but not exclusively, senior practitioners, senior consultants, senior managers or executives, with five or more years' relevant experience. All candidates must hold the ITIL Expert qualification.

For each element in the scheme a number of credits can be obtained that can be used to obtain the ITIL Expert qualification. Further information on the actual status of this system can be found at the ITIL Official Site: http://www.itil-officialsite.com/.

Structure of this study guide

This study guide provides you with a tool for preparing for the ITIL Foundation certification examination. It includes the examinable content required for the examination as defined in the official course syllabus.

Using this Study Guide

The text is organized in Units deliberately to help the students: for clarity it does not follow the sequential texts of the core ITIL titles. For the most part, this study guide is structure with two facing pages. The left facing page contains the ITIL content that the syllabus requires the Foundation examination to cover, including a syllabus reference and the associated definitions, concepts and models from ITIL materials. Definitions are denoted with a colored box, for example:

Business case (SS)
Justification for a significant item of expenditure. The business case includes information about costs, benefits, options, issues, risks and possible problems. See also cost benefit analysis.

In many cases, the right facing page contains examples, memory aids and practical guidance developed by IT Service Management Practitioners. The purpose of this content is to drive the ITIL concepts home, to make them memorable so that you can recall them for the exam, and to provide some ideas as to how to get started applying the concepts once back on the job.

In some cases, mostly in the section that covers the ITIL processes, there is no right-facing page; this is due to the volume of generic material that is required to be covered for that topic by the syllabus.

Throughout this guide references to the ITIL Foundation syllabus are included so that you can map what is covered here back to the syllabus, and through the syllabus reference, back to the ITIL books themselves. For example:

ITILFND01-01-1 Describe the concept of best practices in the public domain (SS 2.1.7)

This is a reference to section to unit ITILFND01, topic 01-1 of the syllabus, which covers the concept of good practice; this syllabus entry references the Service Strategy (SS) book, section 2.1.7 for further information. Syllabus references use acronyms for each book, as follows:
- Service Strategy (SS)
- Service Design (SD)
- Service Transition (ST)
- Service Operation (SO)
- Continual Service Improvement (CSI)

This study guide illustrates each syllabus topic in capsule form, along with a relevant example or mnemonic or other device to help make the topic stick; syllabus references are provided so you can trace them back to the full ITIL book coverage of the topic for more information.

This study guide and the syllabus references included here are written to align to the ITIL Foundation syllabus version 5.3.

How to use this study guide

This guide is intended for candidates preparing to take the ITIL Foundation certification course and examination. It can be used as ready reference to learn more about specific topics, or can be read cover to cover for comprehensive examination preparation.

CHAPTER 1
ITILFND01 SERVICE MANAGEMENT AS A PRACTICE (90M)

The purpose of this unit is to help you to define the concept of a service, and to comprehend and explain the concept of service management as a practice.

ITILFND01-01-1 Describe the concept of best practices in the public domain (SS 2.1.7)

BEST PRACTICES IN THE PUBLIC DOMAIN

Best practice is defined as proven activities or processes that have been successfully used by multiple organizations. ITIL is an example of best practice.

Organizations benchmark themselves against peers and seek to identify and close gaps in capabilities to become more competitive. One way to close such gaps is to adopt best practices. There are several sources for best practice including public frameworks, standards and the proprietary knowledge of organizations and individuals.

ITIL is the most widely recognized and trusted source of best practice guidance in the area of ITSM.

Publicly available frameworks and standards such as ITIL, LEAN, Six Sigma, COBIT, CMMI, PRINCE2®, PMBOK®, ISO 9000, ISO/IEC 20000 and ISO/IEC 27001 are attractive compared to proprietary knowledge for the following reasons:

Proprietary knowledge	Public frameworks and standards
Deeply embedded in organizations and therefore difficult to adopt, replicate or even transfer with the cooperation of the owners; often in the form of tacit knowledge which is inextricable and poorly documented.	Validated across a diverse set of environments and situations rather than the limited experience of a single organization.
Customized for the local context and the specific needs of the business to the point of being idiosyncratic. Unless the recipients of such knowledge have matching circumstances, the knowledge may not be as effective in use.	Subject to broad review across multiple organizations and disciplines, and vetted by diverse sets of partners, suppliers and competitors.
Owners expect to be rewarded for their investments. They may make such knowledge available only under commercial terms through purchases and licensing agreements.	The knowledge of public frameworks is more likely to be widely distributed among a large community of professionals through publicly available training and certification. It is easier for organizations to acquire such knowledge through the labor market.

Ignoring public frameworks and standards can needlessly place an organization at a disadvantage. Organizations should cultivate their own proprietary knowledge on top of a body of knowledge based on public frameworks and standards. Collaboration and coordination across organizations become easier on the basis of shared practices and standards. Further information on best practice in the public domain is provided in Appendix D of the SS publication.

ITILFND01-01-1 Describe the concept of best practices in the public domain (SS 2.1.7)

There are certain things you would expect to see in any well-run run organization: purpose, outcomes, goals, objectives, roles, activities, deliverables, and tools. There are other things that you might expect to see, but the gist here is that a well-run organization will have the right ones, and those 'right ones' that are generally accepted are known as best practices.

Think about a soccer team for a minute. If they didn't have the objective of winning games, you would certainly think something was amiss. And if there was no manager, or keeper, or the approach to these roles was inadequate or ill-defined, there would be issues. If there was no practice, or practice was conducted irregularly or out of step with ways that improve performance, you would be right to worry about the prospects of the team. And if basic things like goals and balls and gloves were not in evidence or not adequate, you would have further cause for worry about the team's capability to perform.

The same goes for IT organizations. While IT is continually evolving, there are basics you would expect to see in a well-run organization, like basic change management practices in evidence, functions for managing technology, applications, service desk and IT operations.

Why is it that two organizations given roughly the same set of resources will get wildly different results? The answer is capability. The whole idea with best practices and proprietary knowledge is that they give you a competitive advantage, a higher capability.

One sensible approach for leveraging best practices and proprietary knowledge to increase capability is to consider adopting and leveraging as much of what is proven and commoditized before moving on to developing your own methods. In other words, it is usually best to avoid 'reinventing the wheel' when the commonly accepted wheel will do.

Think about your organization. What best practices are in evidence? For the best practices you see, what is positive that is happening in the organization because they are in place? For those that are missing or inadequate, what is the negative impact of this? What proprietary knowledge is in use that is providing competitive advantage?

ITIL is presented as best practice. That is why for those with IT experience, many concepts in ITIL are familiar, although terminology may vary from what they are used to.

Adopting and adapting generally accepted frameworks like ITIL can give you a ready-made basis for organizing IT. It can make what you do more defensible to regulators and auditors, as you are in step with the industry. It can make it easier for you to onboard new staff and suppliers, as it is more likely that you will have a shared view of expected outcomes, practices, and terminology.

ITIL is a framework and is not prescriptive ('how to do'), and is therefore descriptive ('what to do'): the art in applying ITIL successfully is figuring out which areas provide the most benefit for your organization, and driving changes from the top down and the bottom up.

ITILFND01-01-2 Describe and explain why ITIL is successful (SS 1.3)

Why is ITIL so successful?

ITIL embraces a practical approach to service management – do what works. And what works is adapting a common framework of practices that unite all areas of IT service provision towards a single aim – that of delivering value to the business. The following list defines the key characteristics of ITIL that contribute to its global success:

Vendor-neutral	• Applicable in any IT organization as it is not based on any particular technology platform or industry type • Owned by the UK government and is not tied to any commercial proprietary practice or solution
Non-prescriptive	• Offers robust, mature and time-tested practices with applicability to all types of service organization • Continues to be useful and relevant in public / private sectors, internal / external service providers, small, medium, large enterprises, any technical environment
Best practice	• Represents the world's best-in-class service providers' learning experiences and thought leadership

ITIL is successful because it describes practices that enable organizations to deliver benefits, return on investment and sustained success. ITIL is adopted by organizations to enable them to:

- Deliver value for customers through services
- Integrate the strategy for services with the business strategy and customer needs
- Measure, monitor and optimize IT services and service provider performance
- Manage the IT investment and budget
- Manage risk
- Manage knowledge
- Manage capabilities and resources to deliver services effectively and efficiently
- Enable adoption of a standard approach to service management across the enterprise
- Change the organizational culture to support the achievement of sustained success
- Improve the interaction and relationship with customers
- Coordinate the delivery of goods and services across the value network
- Optimize and reduce costs

ITILFND01-01-2 Describe and explain why ITIL is successful (SS 1.3)

In our work over the years, some of the top reasons why we see organizations turn to ITIL include:

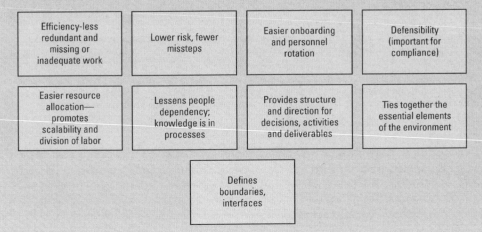

We find that ITIL provides the basis for effective action by helping organizations shape and align themselves in a structured way as they drive towards their key outcomes, as follows.

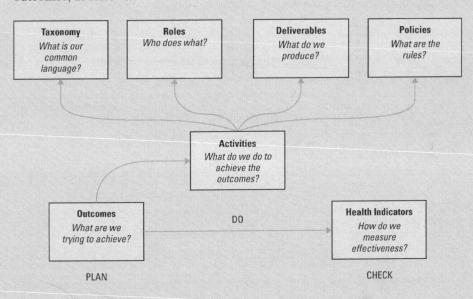

The Concept of a Service

Service A means of delivering value to customers by facilitating outcomes customers want to achieve without ownership of specific costs and risks

IT service A service provided by an IT service provider made up of information technology, people and processes. A customer-facing IT service directly supports business processes of one or more customers and its service level targets should be defined in an SLA; other IT services (supporting services) are not directly used by the business but are required by the service provider to deliver customer-facing services.

Services facilitate outcomes by enhancing the performance of associated tasks and reducing the effect of constraints. These constraints may include regulation, lack of funding or capacity, or technology limitations. The result is an increased probability of desired outcomes. While some services enhance task performance, others perform the task itself.

Customers seek outcomes but do not wish to have accountability or ownership of all the associated costs and risks. Customers will be satisfied with a service when they judge it a good value based on a comparison of cost or price and reliability with the desired outcome.

Services can be discussed in terms of how they relate to one another and their customers, and can be classified as core, enabling or enhancing.

Core services	Deliver the basic outcomes desired by customers, represent the value the customer wants and is willing to pay for, anchor the value proposition for the customer and provide the basis for their continued utilization and satisfaction.
Enabling services	'Basic factors' required for the 'real' (core) service to be delivered, they are not perceived as services by customers even though they may be visible to them.
Enhancing services	Services added to a core service to make it more exciting or enticing to the customer, unessential to the delivery of a core service, added to a core service as 'excitement' factors to encourage customers to use the core service more (or to choose the service over that of its competitors).

Most service providers will follow a strategy where they can deliver a set of more generic services to a broad range of customers, thus achieving economies of scale and competing on the basis of price and a certain amount of flexibility. One way of achieving this is by using service packages. A service package is a collection of two or more services that have been combined to offer a solution to a specific type of customer need or to underpin specific business outcomes. A service package can consist of a combination of core services, enabling services and enhancing services.

Where a service or service package needs to be differentiated for different types of customer, one or more components of the package can be changed, or offered at different levels of utility and warranty, to create service options. These different service options can then be offered to customers and are sometimes called service level packages.

ITILFND01-01-3 Define and explain the concept of a service (SS 2.1.1)

Why do customers buy IT services, and when they do, what value do they see? Understanding this starts with visiting why you buy and see value in services.

An example may help illustrate: we recently moved in to a 50 year old house and the lawn sprinklers were not working properly. Some didn't come on at all; others just dribbled water.

I went about the job in what I thought was a good, systematic fashion: I got out some graph paper and noted the location of each of the sprinkler heads; I looked at each one and wrote down the type; I dug one of them out and unscrewed it to see the size of the connector so I'd be sure to get the right type at the home store. Once at the home store I got the sprinkler heads, plus a number of other tools for digging them out, screwing and unscrewing them on, as well as adaptors in case I needed them.

I spent more than I thought I would, then went home and started digging out the rest of the sprinkler heads, then unscrewing them one at a time, and replacing them; all was good until I got to the third one, which broke off the steel pipe it was attached to below the thread. Now I had another problem – affixing plastic sprinkler head somehow to a busted rusted metal pipe. In addition I noted that I didn't have the correct sprinkler head inserts for the spray pattern I needed to cover the lawn. So back to the home store.

After a couple more weekends of similar issues and still no sprinklers working, encouraged by my lovely wife, I finally gave in and called a sprinkler installer. The installer showed up with his truck chock full of the right tools, all the right fittings and workarounds, and experience dealing with the precise kinds of issues I was facing; he had the sprinklers up and running in less than two hours.

The moral of the story is that I should have factored in the costs (my time in buckets, all the various parts, including ones I never used and paid for, tools I didn't have that I had to get to use one) and risks (due to the fact that I didn't have knowledge and experience). I should have called the sprinkler person out of the gate. Why? Why for the same reason as defined by ITIL as the concept of a service – that he could do it cheaper, with less risk, than me doing it myself. So in the end it's a higher value. Keep this in mind when considering your services to your customer – do you have the skills and tools and experience to provide a value higher at less risk than them doing it themselves? How about as compared to another IT service provider? You had better – having that value edge is the only sustainable reason for using your services.

Think about an instance where it made sense to choose a service versus doing it yourself. How did this result in better confidence to control costs and risks?

For an example of core, enabling and enhancing services you need look no further than your mobile phone service – core services include being able to place calls and text messages, enabling services include the wireless network that underpin voice and data services, and enhancing services are 'sweeteners' such as video calling and family mapping.

ITILFND01-01-4 Define and explain the concept of internal and external customers (SS 3.2.1.2)

Internal and external customers

There is a difference between customers who work in the same organization as the IT service provider (internal customers), and customers who work for another organization (external customers). Both must be provided with the agreed level of service, with the same levels of customer service.

customer Someone who buys goods or services. The customer of an IT service provider is the person or group who defines and agrees the service level targets.
internal customer A customer who works for the same business as the IT service provider.
external customer A customer who works for a different business from the IT service provider.

The table below, adapted from SS Table 3.1, compares internal and external customers.

	Internal customers	External customers
Funding	Provided internally – IT is a cost to be recovered.	Funded directly by external customers in the form of revenue. IT becomes a generator of income for the organization. The cost of the service, plus a margin, must be recovered from the customer.
Strategy and objectives	Provider and customer share the overall organizational objectives and strategy.	The objectives and strategies of the service provider and the customer are different.
Accounting	The cost of service is the primary driver; the aim of providing services is an optimal balance of service cost and quality supporting achieving organizational objectives.	The price of the service is the primary driver; the aim of providing services to external customers is to maximize profitability while still remaining competitive with pricing.
Service design role	Internal customers tend to be involved in detailed design specifications.	External customers typically buy predefined services and are not involved in design.
Involvement in service transition and operation	Internal customers are often involved in building, testing and deploying services, assessing and authorizing changes, and defining deployment procedures, mechanisms and schedules.	Involvement in change management is clearly documented in the contract. Customers assess requests for change based on impact and price. Deployment involvement is often carefully scripted.
Drivers for improvement	Improvements are driven by impact on the business, specifically balancing cost and quality and the ability to help business units meet their objectives.	Improvements are driven by the need to retain customers that contribute to the profitability of the service provider, and to remain competitive in the market.

ITILFND01-01-4 Define and explain the concept of internal and external customers (SS 3.2.1.2)

Internal customer example	External customer example
The marketing department is an internal customer of the IT organization because it uses IT services. The head of marketing and the CIO both report to the chief executive officer (CEO). If IT charges for its services, the money paid is an internal transaction in the organization's accounting system – i.e. not real revenue.	An airline might obtain consulting services from a large consulting firm. Two-thirds of the contract value is paid in cash, and one-third is paid in air tickets at an equivalent value.

It is important to distinguish first between a user (someone who uses services) and a customer (someone who pays for services and defines and agrees service level targets). Like all distinctions in ITIL, this isn't mere terminology for its own sake – each term is defined and distinguished against others because it is something worth management consideration. Said another way, if you are not recognizing and labeling something in your environment, it is very likely that no one is managing it. So for example, if you don't really distinguish between customers and users, it may be the case that you have systems in place to ensure great user satisfaction, but are completely missing any systematic way to identify customers and keep them happy. This is a grave error of omission – unrecognized stakeholders represent one of the greatest risks to a services enterprise.

Conversely, you might recognize and work for customer satisfaction systematically, but have nothing or little in place to tend to users. So you see this is not mere terminology – it is a set of labels and distinctions made to define what is important and worth managing.

And so it goes with the distinction between the internal and external customers: one is inside your business (internal), the other is outside. You may in fact not have external customers for your IT services, in which case you can skip the discussion. But if you do, you need to distinguish between internal and external customers because they are fundamentally different in nature and, as a result, the practices needed to be effective in dealing with them are fundamentally different as well. A lack of understanding of these dynamics is what causes friction due to under and over and improperly serviced customers. Given scarce resources, you need to apportion them appropriately, both in quantity and quality, and that starts with understanding and distinguishing between types of customers and their characteristics.

ITILFND01-01-5 Define and explain the concept of internal and external services (SS 3.2.2.3)

Internal and external services

Just as there are internal and external customers, there are internal and external services.

Service A means of delivering value to customers by facilitating outcomes customers want to achieve without the ownership of specific costs and risks.

- **Internal service** A service delivered between departments or business units in the same organization.
- **External service** A service delivered to external customers.

Business service A service delivered to business customers by business units; for example, delivery of financial services to customers of a bank, or goods to the customers of a retail store. Successful delivery of business services often depends on one or more IT services.

IT service A service provided by an IT service provider, made up of a combination of information technology, people and processes. A customer-facing IT service directly supports the business processes of one or more customers and its service level targets should be defined in a service level agreement. Other IT services, called supporting services, are not directly used by the business but are required by the service provider to deliver customer-facing services.

Three types of IT services

1. **Supporting service** An IT service that is not directly used by the business, but is required by the IT service provider to deliver customer-facing services (for example, a directory service or a backup service). There can be no service level agreements for supporting services as they are all internal to the same department. Instead, the performance of supporting services should be managed by operational level agreements.
2. Internal customer-facing service An IT service that directly supports a business process managed by another business unit – for example, sales reporting service, enterprise resource management. Internal customer-facing services are managed according to service level agreements.
3. External customer-facing service An IT service that is directly provided by IT to an external customer – for example, internet access at an airport. These services are managed using a contract – even a simple online agreement constitutes a contract of sale and purchase with terms and conditions.

We differentiate between internal and external services to delineate services that support an internal activity and those that actually achieve business outcomes. The difference between internal and external services is significant because internal services have to be linked to external services before their contribution to business outcomes can be understood and measured. This is especially important when measuring the return on investment of services.

ITILFND01-01-5 Define and explain the concept of internal and external services (SS 3.2.2.3)

Business services questions
- Can you list the *business services* your firm provides?
- Can you list, for each business service, the IT services that enable its outcomes to be met?

Internal customer-facing services questions
- Can you list the *internal customer-facing services* in your organization?
- Can you list the customer(s) for each?
- Would you say for each those customers are highly aware, aware, or unaware of the services?
- For which of these services are service level agreements defined, agreed and used?
- If you have this in place, or if it is missing or inadequate, what is happening in your organization because of it?

External customer-facing services questions
- Can you list the *external customer-facing services* in your organization?
- Can you list the customer(s) for each?
- Would you say for each those customers are highly aware, aware, or unaware of the services?
- For which of these services are contracts defined, agreed and used?
- If you have this in place, or if it is missing or inadequate, what is happening in your organization because of it?

Supporting services questions
- Can you list *supporting services* that underpin your IT services and cite how they relate?
- Can you identify which support internal and external services only, and which are shared?
- For which of these services are operational level agreements defined, agreed and used?

ITILFND01-01-6 Define and explain the concept of service management (SS 2.1.2)

Service Management

Service management A set of specialized organizational capabilities for providing value to customers in the form of services

Service provider An organization supplying services to one or more internal or external customers

Capability the ability of an organization, person, process, application, Configuration Item or IT service to carry out an activity

Resource a generic term that includes IT infrastructure, people, money or anything else that might help to deliver an IT service

Service asset any resource or capability used by a service provider to deliver services to a customer

Performance a measure of what is achieved or delivered by a system, person, team, process, or IT service

Customer asset any resource or capability used by a customer to achieve a business outcome

Business outcome the results as seen by the business

The more mature a service provider's capabilities are, the greater the ability to consistently produce quality services that meet the needs of the customer in a timely and cost-effective manner. The act of transforming capabilities and resources into valuable services is at the core of service management. Without these capabilities, a service organization is merely a bundle of resources that by itself has relatively low intrinsic value for customers.

Service management is more than just a set of capabilities. It is also a professional practice supported by an extensive body of knowledge, experience and skills. A global community of individuals and organizations in the public and private sectors fosters its growth and maturity. Formal schemes exist for the education, training and certification of practicing organizations, and individuals influence its quality. Industry best practices, academic research and formal standards contribute to and draw from its intellectual capital.

The origins of service management are in traditional service businesses such as airlines, banks, hotels and phone companies. Its practice has grown with the adoption by IT organizations of a service-oriented approach to managing IT applications, infrastructure and processes. Solutions to business problems and support for business models, strategies and operations are increasingly in the form of services. The popularity of shared services and outsourcing has contributed to the increase in the number of organizations that behave as service providers, including internal IT organizations. This in turn has strengthened the practice of service management while at the same time imposed greater challenges.

ITILFND01-01-6 Define and explain the concept of service management (SS 2.1.2)

Given a similar set of resources, why would one IT service provider be better at service provision than another? The answer lies in capability.

Think about it this way for a minute: Let us say a TV station came into your workplace and asked everyone on your immediate team to make an omelet. The omelet would be judged by a famous chef and the person who made the best omelet would win $100,000 and a kitchen makeover. Who would make the best omelet, and why? Note that part of the rules is that everyone starts with precisely the same ingredients, in the same kitchen, using the same tools.

Well the winner probably is one of the best if not the best organized. They know their way around the kitchen, how each implement is used properly – they have knowledge and experience applying that knowledge. They apply specific techniques and a set of steps that are proven to routine parts of making an omelet, and when faced with an issue, like a stove that doesn't get quite hot enough, they can work around and adapt.

The same goes for IT service providers. The difference in the 'omelet' they produce for their customers does of course depend on resources – the factors of production that go into service provision. So these must be as they should be. But as important is their capabilities – their ability to manage, organize, the knowledge, skill and experience of their people. In a word, in their capability, and for a services firm, that capability is known as IT service management.

Think about it: if most companies have the same basic 'ingredients' (resources) for running IT (networks, ERP applications, servers, data centers, etc.), why do some organizations achieve better results than others? The answer is in their capabilities (management, organization, processes, knowledge, and people), which are the abilities of an organization, person, process, application, Configuration Item or IT service to carry out an activity. Capabilities are intangible assets of an organization.

ITILFND01-01-7 Define and explain the concept of IT service management (SS 2.1.3)

IT service management

Now that we've defined service management, we move on to **IT** service management. Understanding this concept requires first understanding the different perspectives of and meanings assigned to IT: IT as a:

1. Collection of systems, applications and infrastructures
2. Organization with its own set of capabilities and resources
3. Category of services utilized by business
4. Category of business assets

Every IT organization should act as a service provider, using the principles of service management to ensure that they deliver the outcomes required by their customers.

IT service management (ITSM) The implementation and management of quality IT services that meet the needs of the business. IT service management is performed by IT service providers through an appropriate mix of people, process and information technology.

A service level agreement (SLA) is used to document agreements between an IT service provider and a customer. An SLA describes the IT service, documents service level targets, and specifies the responsibilities of the IT service provider and the customer. A single agreement may cover multiple IT services or multiple customers.

IT service provider A service provider that provides IT services to internal or external customers.

ITSM must be carried out effectively and efficiently. Managing IT from the business perspective enables organizational high performance and value creation.

A good relationship between an IT service provider and its customers relies on the customer receiving an IT service that meets its needs, at an acceptable level of performance and at a cost that the customer can afford. The IT service provider needs to work out how to achieve a balance between these three areas, and communicate with the customer if there is anything which prevents it from being able to deliver the required IT service at the agreed level of performance or price.

ITILFND01-01-7 Define and explain the concept of IT service management (SS 2.1.3)

With IT service management we are going to:
1. Organize around IT services as the fundamental organizing concept and focal point for management
2. Carry out and improve best practices processes that underpin the effective and efficient support and delivery of IT services
3. Grow the maturity of our organization and processes and the knowledge and skills of our people
4. Adopt common terminology and practices
5. Insist on a core set of tools required to carry out our profession

It's ironic, really that other professions, like accounting, have had standard terminology, generally accepted processes and principles, and tools for quite some time now. While these evolve over time, it isn't the case (or shouldn't be!) that you walk in to one firm and talk to a particular accountant, and she doesn't use or recognize the terms "liabilities" and "owner's equity", that she doesn't expect the firm to have fairly standard accounts payable and receivable processes, etc. Questions like, "what is the ROI on your general ledger?" if posed would seem ludicrous – an accountant needs the general ledger as a basic tool for doing her work.

On the other hand, look at the "state of the state" in many organizations for the IT profession. "What is the ROI on your CMDB?" is a common question, yet a strong CMDB and CMS underpin (or should!) just about every questions and decision you can make in IT, if you want to work on the basis of facts (and you should!). Terminology is all over the place – one person says "fault", another says, "error", another says, "incident", another, "problem" and they all think they're talking about the same thing and they are not. The overhead of all this translation and miscommunication is frightening, needless, and happily, curable.

IT service management helps us get on the same page with defined terminology definitions and distinctions, key principles and models for managing and organizing. It is a holistic approach for recognizing and managing what is important, and in the end, a worldview – a self-concept for IT services – not the only one, but the one ITIL is suggesting is most effective: "We are here to provide a service to a customer. Everything we do is organized around those services, and we adopt common best practices so we can be as capable as possible given limited resources."

In the end, the big bet with ITIL, as with all management frameworks, is that relatively small changes in thinking and acting can make a huge difference in results. Sure you can throw resources at the problem, but resources alone won't cut it – you need capability. So... what are you doing to improve your IT service management capability, and improve your results?

CMDB - Configuration management data base
CMS - Content management System

ITILFND01-01-8 Define and explain the concept of stakeholders in service management (SS 2.1.5)

Stakeholders in service management

Stakeholders have an interest in an organization, project or service etc. and may be interested in the activities, targets, resources or deliverables from service management. Examples include organizations, service providers, customers, consumers, users, partners, employees, shareholders, owners and suppliers.

Stakeholder A person who has an interest in an organization, project, IT service etc. Stakeholders may be interested in the activities, targets, resources or deliverables. Stakeholders may include customers, partners, employees, shareholders, owners etc.
Customers Those who buy goods or services. The customer of an IT service provider is the person or group who defines and agrees the service level targets. This term is also sometimes used informally to mean a user – for example, 'This is a customer-focused organization.'
Users Those who use the service on a day-to-day basis. Users are distinct from customers, as some customers do not use the IT service directly.
Suppliers Third parties responsible for supplying goods or services that are required to deliver IT services. Examples of suppliers include commodity hardware and software vendors, network and telecom providers, and outsourcing organizations.

The term 'organization' is used to define a company, legal entity or other institution. It is also used to refer to any entity that has people, resources and budgets – for example, a project or business. Within the service provider organization there are many different stakeholders including the functions, groups and teams that deliver the services.

There is a difference between customers who work in the same organization as the IT service provider, and customers who work for other organizations. They are distinguished as follows:

Internal customers work for the same business as the IT service provider. For example, the marketing department is an internal customer of the IT organization because it uses IT services. The head of marketing and the chief information officer both report to the chief executive officer. If IT charges for its services, the money paid is an internal transaction in the organization's accounting system, not real revenue.	**External customers** work for a different business from the IT service provider. External customers typically purchase services from the service provider by means of a legally binding contract or agreement.

ITILFND01-01-8 Define and explain the concept of stakeholders in service management (SS 2.1.5)

Stakeholders can have a huge positive or negative impact on your results. Unidentified stakeholders represent one of the biggest risks to an IT service provider. So, can you list:

- Who your key stakeholders are?
- What their stake is, for each?
- What systems you have in place to identify and satisfy key stakeholders? To help them help you achieve outcomes of interest to them?
- Which stakeholders are internal and external customers?
- For each stakeholder, can you identify where they are now and where they want to be against the outcomes they have a stake in?
- Where are your risks relative to stakeholders? Where are they under-represented, served or challenged? Where is there friction or resistance in critical areas?
- What strategies are in play for communicating with stakeholders, anticipating their reactions, ensuring their expectations are met?
- How are you making sure what you are doing is based on real stakeholder needs, and not simply just the perception of those needs?

ITILFND01-01-9 Define processes and functions (SS 2.2.2, 2.2.3.1)

Processes and functions

Note: processes and functions are defined here to contrast them and treated further in the next section.

Processes and functions are not the same. A process is a set of activities; a function is a set of people.

process A structured set of activities designed to accomplish a specific objective. A process takes one or more defined inputs and turns them into defined outputs.

The four key characteristics of a process are:

1. **Measurability** We are able to measure the process in a relevant manner. It is performance-driven. Managers want to measure cost, quality and other variables while practitioners are concerned with duration and productivity.
2. **Specific results** The reason a process exists is to deliver a specific result. This result must be individually identifiable and countable.
3. **Customers** Every process delivers its primary results to a customer or stakeholder. Customers may be internal or external to the organization, but the process must meet their expectations.
4. **Responsiveness to specific triggers** While a process may be ongoing or iterative, it should be traceable to a specific trigger

Function A team or group of people and the tools or other resources they use to carry out one or more processes or activities – for example, the service desk.

- In larger organizations, a function may be broken out and performed by several departments, teams and groups, or it may be embodied within a single organizational unit (e.g. the service desk); In smaller organizations, one person or group can perform multiple functions – for example, a technical management department could also incorporate the service desk function

ITIL Service Operation describes four functions in detail:

1. Service Desk
2. Technical Management
3. IT Operations Management
4. Applications Management

An organization will need to clearly define the roles and responsibilities required to undertake the processes and activities involved in each lifecycle stage. These roles will need to be assigned to individuals, and an appropriate organization structure of, groups, teams, departments, and divisions – be sure to know the definitions and distinctions between these (see the ITIL glossary for help with this).

ITILFND01-01-9 Define processes and functions (SS 2.2.2, 2.2.3.1)

ITIL 2011 Edition specifies 26 processes and 4 functions, as follows:

Service Strategy Processes (5)
1. *Strategy management for IT services (New to 2011 Edition)**
2. Service portfolio management
3. Financial management for IT services
4. Demand management
5. *Business relationship management (New to 2011 Edition)*

Service Design Processes (8)
1. *Design coordination (New to 2011 Edition)*
2. Service catalogue management
3. Service level management
4. Availability management
5. Capacity management
6. IT service continuity management (ITSCM)
7. Information security management
8. Supplier Management

Service Transition Processes (7)
1. Transition planning and support
2. Change management
3. Service asset and configuration management
4. Release and deployment management
5. Service validation and testing
6. *Change evaluation (Renamed in 2011 Edition)*
7. Knowledge management

Service Operation Processes (5)
1. Event management
2. Incident management
3. Request fulfillment
4. Problem management
5. Access management

Continual Service Improvement Processes (1)
1. Seven-step improvement process

Service Operation Functions (4)
1. Service Desk
2. Technical Management
3. IT Operations Management
4. Application Management

ITILFND01-01-10 Explain the process model and the characteristics of processes
(SS 2.2.2, Figure 2.5)

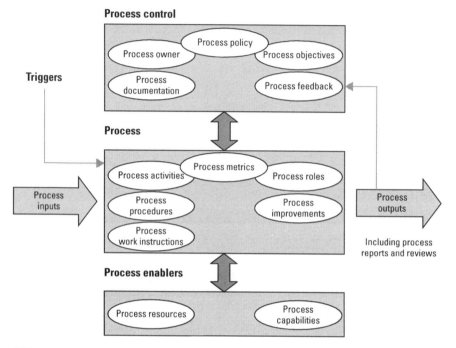

SS Figure 2.5: Process model

© Crown copyright 2011. Reproduced under license from the Cabinet Office.

A process is organized around a set of objectives, with outputs driven by the
objectives and should include process measurements (metrics), reports and process
improvement. The output must conform to operational norms derived from business
objectives for the process to be considered effective. If the activities of the process
are carried out with a minimum use of resources, the process can also be considered
efficient. Inputs are data or information used by the process and may be the output
from another process. A process, or an activity within it, is initiated by a trigger such
as the arrival of an input or other event. A process may include roles, responsibilities,
tools and management controls required to deliver outputs reliably, and define
policies, standards, guidelines, activities and work instructions needed. Processes,
once defined, should be documented and controlled so they can be repeated and
managed. Measurement and metrics can be built into the process to control and
improve the process. Analysis, results and metrics should be incorporated in regular
management reports and process improvements.

ITILFND01-01-10 Explain the process model and the characteristics of processes
(SS 2.2.2, Figure 2.5)

This model is a straightforward – use the mnemonic POETIC to remember it. Think about our omelet-making example:
1. Process - cooking in the kitchen
2. Outputs - meals served
3. Enablers – kitchen gadgets, cooking know-how
4. Triggers – teenager is hungry
5. Inputs - ingredients for omelet
6. Control – kitchen timer, knob on stove to adjust heat

You must be able to recall the components of the process model. You must know, for example, that a process will not kick in without a specific trigger. Think about, for example, your incident management process – what triggers it? A call from a user, an event trapped in the infrastructure.

It is helpful to know what is included within each component, for example:
- In process control, we see that processes are controlled by assigning a process owner, by having documentation and policies to follow, by having a process objective that functions as a 'north star' outcome for the process, and by having a feedback loop; these are just some of the mechanisms that can keep a process on track – can you think of others? If not, it may be easier to list a couple of key ways processes get off track, and some ideas on mechanisms for preventing it from happening – these are process control mechanisms
- The process itself – typically a set of stepwise activities (highest level), procedures (middle level of detail) and work instructions (finest level of detail), metrics for the process, roles (who is doing the activities needs to be clear), and an improvement loop built right into the process
- In process outputs, we see that it's not just "the omelet" that is produced as output, but also reports and reviews, "mom, I made an omelet for my little brother today, and he said it was delicious!"
- Process enablers – these are the assets (resources and capabilities) used by the process, as distinguished from process inputs

CHAPTER 2
ITILFND02 THE
ITIL SERVICE
LIFECYCLE (60M)

The purpose of this unit is to help you understand the value of the ITIL service lifecycle, how the processes integrate with each other, throughout the lifecycle and explain the objectives, scope and business value for each phase in the lifecycle. The syllabus recommends that this content is covered within other units.

The structure of the itil service lifecycle

The ITIL core consists of five lifecycle publications corresponding to the five stages of the service lifecycle. Each provides part of the guidance necessary for an integrated approach as required by the ISO/IEC 20000 standard specification. The Introduction to the ITIL Service Lifecycle provides an introduction to the core. Complementary publications such as an Introductory Overview of ITIL help you apply the core in a diverse range of environments.

ITIL Service Strategy provides guidance on how to view service management not only as an organizational capability but as a strategic asset. It describes the principles underpinning the practice of service management which are useful for developing service management policies, guidelines and processes across the ITIL service lifecycle.

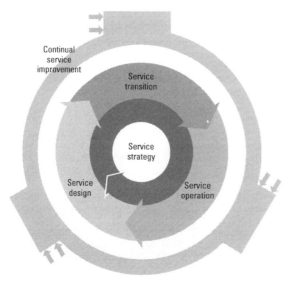

ITIL Service Design provides guidance for the design and development of services and service management practices. It covers design principles and methods for converting strategic objectives into portfolios of services and service assets.

ITIL Service Transition provides guidance for the development and improvement of capabilities for introducing new and changed services into supported environments. It describes how to transition an organization from one state to another while controlling risk and supporting organizational knowledge for decision support. It ensures that

SS Figure 1.1 The ITIL service lifecycle

© Crown copyright 2011. Reproduced under license from the Cabinet Office.

the value(s) identified in the service strategy, and encoded in service design, are effectively transitioned so that they can be realized in service operation.

ITIL Service Operation describes best practice for managing services in supported environments. It includes guidance on achieving effectiveness and efficiency in the delivery and support of services to ensure value for the customer, the users and the service provider.

ITIL Continual Service Improvement provides guidance on creating and maintaining value for customers through better strategy, design, transition and operation of services. It combines principles, practices and methods from quality management, change management and capability improvement.

ITILFND02-02-2 Describe the structure of the ITIL service lifecycle (SS 1.2, Figure 1.1)

Here is another view in to the five lifecycle phases and what they cover:

Service Strategy	Defines the perspective, position, plans and patterns that a service provider needs to execute to meet an organization's business outcomes
Service Design	Includes the design of the services, governing practices, processes and policies required to realize the service provider's strategy and to facilitate the introduction of services into supported environments
Service Transition	Ensures that new, modified or retired services meet the expectations of the business as documented in the service strategy and service design stages of the lifecycle
Service Operation	Coordinates and carries out the activities and processes required to deliver and manage services at agreed levels to business users and customers
Continual Service Improvement	Ensures that services are aligned with changing business needs by identifying and implementing improvements to IT services that support business processes

Remember the lifecycle phases by the mnemonic TDOCS (technical documentation), that is, transition, design, operation, continual improvement, and strategy.

These five ITIL core publications are intended to provide more universal and timeless principles (things that don't change that often and are more generally applicable across a variety of environments and situations). Complementary publications are meant to supplement the core for emerging areas like public and private clouds, and for other areas of specific concern, for example, application in a specific industry vertical, or in a specific kind of environment, for example, regulated.

If you don't have a copy of the handy itSMF publication, you should get it – the itSMF published, "an Introductory Overview of ITIL" pocket book as a free, downloadable PDF. Van Haren also publishes an excellent pocket book, distinguished by its more detailed coverage of processes within the lifecycle, as well and a number of additional complementary publications.

ITILFND02-02-3 Account for the purpose, objectives and scope of service strategy
(SS 1.1.1, 1.1.2)

Service strategy purpose, objectives and scope

Purpose
To define the perspective, position, plans and patterns that a service provider needs
to be able to execute to meet an organization's business outcomes

Objectives to provide:
- An understanding of what strategy is

- A clear identification of the definition of services and the customers who use them

- The ability to define how value is created and delivered

- A means to identify opportunities to provide services and how to exploit them

- A clear service provision model, that articulates how services will be delivered and
  funded, and to whom they will be delivered and for what purpose

- The means to understand the organizational capability required to deliver the
  strategy

- Documentation and coordination of how service assets are used to deliver services,
  and how to optimize their performance

- Processes that define the strategy of the organization, which services will achieve
  the strategy, what level of investment will be required, at what levels of demand,
  and the means to ensure a working relationship exists between the customer and
  service provider

Scope
- Generic principles and processes of service management
  - ♦ These generic principles are applied consistently to IT service management
- Intended for use by both internal and external service providers, and includes
  guidance for organizations which are required to offer IT services as a profitable
  business, as well as those which are required to offer IT services to other business
  units within the same organization – at no profit
- Two aspects of strategy:
  1. Defining a strategy whereby a service provider will deliver services to meet a
     customer's business outcomes
  2. Defining a strategy for how to manage those services

ITILFND02-02-3 Account for the purpose, objectives and scope of service strategy
(SS 1.1.1, 1.1.2)

Service Strategy provides guidance on how to view service management not only
as an organizational capability but as a strategic asset. It describes the principles
underpinning the practice of service management which are useful for developing
service management policies, guidelines and processes across the ITIL service
lifecycle.

Topics covered include
- the development of market spaces
- characteristics of internal and external provider types
- service assets
- the service portfolio
- strategy implementation through the service lifecycle
- business relationship management
- demand management
- financial management
- organizational development
- strategic risks

Service Strategy processes are as follows:
1. Strategy management for IT services
2. Service portfolio management
3. Financial management for IT services
4. Demand management
5. Business relationship management

ITILFND02-02-4 Briefly explain what value service strategy provides to the business (SS 1.1.4)

Service Strategy's Value to the business

- ☑ Selecting and adopting the best practice as recommended in the service strategy publication will assist organizations in delivering significant benefits. Adopting and implementing standard and consistent approaches for service strategy will:
- ☑ Support the ability to link activities performed by the service provider to outcomes that are critical to internal or external customers
- ☑ Enable the service provider to have a clear understanding of what types and levels of service will make its customers successful and then organize itself optimally to deliver and support those services
- ☑ Enable the service provider to respond quickly and effectively to changes in the business environment, ensuring increased competitive advantage over time
- ☑ Support the creation and maintenance of a portfolio of quantified services that will enable the business to achieve positive return on its investment in services
- ☑ Facilitate functional and transparent communication between the customer and the service provider, so that both have a consistent understanding of what is required and how it will be delivered
- ☑ Provide the means for the service provider to organize itself so that it can provide services in an efficient and effective manner

ITILFND02-02-4 Briefly explain what value service strategy provides to the business
(SS 1.1.4)

Perspective, position, plans, and patterns are four of the five aspects of strategy
defined by Henry Mintzberg, in "Five Ps for Strategy" in The Strategy Process, pp
12-19, H Mintzberg and JB Quinn eds., 1992, Prentice-Hall International Editions,
Englewood Cliffs NJ.
1. **Plan** – what is our intended strategy, our conscious, purposeful course of action
   and guidelines for action?
2. **Pattern** – what is our strategy-in-action, the patterns of behavior that are realizing
   our strategy?
3. **Position** – what is our desired position in the market for our services?
4. **Perspective** – what is our shared worldview as to who we are and where we want to
   go and why in the market for our services?

The general idea with the strategy stage is to apply well-established ideas about
strategy in business to an IT service provider. ITIL started in the late 1980s as the
big idea that we should not just care and feel for technology, but we should think of
ourselves and position ourselves and present ourselves to our customers as service
providers, taking care that the processes were in place to properly support and deliver
services. The next logical question is: "How are these services designed, and how do
you know that this design is aligned to what the business needs?" The answer to the
second part of that question is Service Strategy.

Said as simply as possible, in the ideal situation the services the IT service provider
provides are 100% in alignment with an overall strategy about who they want to be
as a service provider (what position they want in the market), 100% understanding
of who they serve, and the services provided are 100% a direct hit for what the
business that is supported needs to support their business objectives, with a clear
value proposition in the mind of the business. Getting to this Nirvana state requires
first having an understanding of the market, of the customer's vital business functions
and patterns, etc. This is followed by an understanding of current services and how
the align with and support (or not) the customer. Said another way, if your service is
currently creating super-high-quality buggy whips, but your customer doesn't need
buggy whips, you are in the wrong business. The whole idea with service strategy is
to get in (and stay in, through change) the right business, with the right set of services
with the right value proposition. A second aspect is ensuring that you don't just have
the right services, but you also have a strategy and structure (architecture, really) for
consistently delivering and supporting those services so that customers see value in
what you do and you see profit in doing it. This is where the principles, processes,
concepts and models of IT service management are invaluable.

So… having a look at these value statements, and considering your service strategy
processes, how does your organization stack up? What is working well, and what does
it look like in your organization when it does? What is missing or inadequate, and
what does it look like in your organization as a result?

ITILFND02-02-5 Account for the purpose, objectives and scope of service design
(SD 1.1.1, 1.1.2)

Service DESIGN purpose, objectives and scope

Purpose
To design IT services, together with the governing IT practices, processes and policies, to realize the service provider's strategy and to facilitate the introduction of these services into supported environments ensuring quality service delivery, customer satisfaction and cost-effective service provision

Objective
To design IT services so effectively that minimal improvement during their lifecycle will be required

Scope
- Provides guidance for the design of appropriate and innovative IT services to meet current and future agreed business requirements
  - Describes the principles of service design and looks at identifying, defining and aligning the IT solution with the business requirement
  - Introduces the concept of the service design package and looks at selecting the appropriate service design model
  - Covers the methods, practices and tools to achieve excellence in service design
  - Discusses the fundamentals of the design processes and attends to what are called the 'five aspects of service design'
- Enforces the principle that the initial service design should be driven by a number of factors, including the functional requirements, the requirements within service level agreements (SLAs), the business benefits and the overall design constraints

ITILFND02-02-5 Account for the purpose, objectives and scope of service design
(SD 1.1.1, 1.1.2)

Service Design provides guidance for the design and development of services and
service management practices, including design principles and methods for converting
strategic objectives into portfolios of services and service assets.

The scope of Service Design is not limited to new services, but includes the changes and
improvements necessary to increase or maintain value to customers over the lifecycle
of services, the continuity of services, achievement of service levels, conformance to
standards and regulations, and guidance on how to develop design capabilities for
service management.

Service Design processes are as follows:
1. Design coordination
2. Service catalogue management
3. Service level management
4. Availability management
5. Capacity management
6. IT service continuity management
7. Information security management
8. Supplier management

The value service design provides to the business

Selecting and adopting best practice as recommended in the Service Design publication will assist organizations in delivering significant benefits. With good service design, it is possible to deliver quality, cost-effective services and ensure business requirements are consistently met. Adopting and implementing standard and consistent approaches for service design will:

Reduce total cost of ownership (TCO)	Cost of ownership can only be minimized if all aspects of services, processes and technology are designed properly and implemented against the design.
Improve quality of service	Both service and operational quality will be enhanced through services that are better designed to meet the required outcomes of the customer.
Improve consistency of service	This will be achieved by designing services within the corporate strategy, architectures and constraints.
Ease the implementation of new or changed services	Integrated and full service designs and the production of comprehensive service design packages will support effective and efficient transitions.
Improve service alignment	Involvement of service design from service concept will ensure new or changed services match business needs, designed to meet service level requirements.
Improve service performance	Performance will be enhanced if services are designed to meet specific performance criteria and if capacity, availability, IT service continuity and financial plans are recognized and incorporated.
Improve IT governance	By building controls into designs, service design can contribute towards the effective governance of IT.
Improve effectiveness of service management and IT processes	Processes will be designed with optimal quality and cost effectiveness.
Improve information and decision-making	Comprehensive and effective measurements and metrics enable better decision-making and continual improvement of services and service management practices throughout the service lifecycle.
Improve alignment with customer values and strategies	For organizations committed to concepts like green IT or strategies such as use of cloud technologies, service design will ensure all areas of services and service management are aligned with the values and strategies.

ITILFND02-02-6 Briefly explain what value service design provides to the business (SD 1.1.4)

It is not enough to have the right strategy for services; that strategy has to be realized in actual services, and that requires design.

Resources are scarce in most IT organizations, so it is important that you get something back when you allocate resources, and all other things being equal, you make the best investment in scarce resources that you can. So why invest in Service Design?

Better designs should implement the strategy you have set out, and thereby align better to support the customer's business. Said another way, poor design chips away at both the perception and reality of value. Costs get out of control because of patches, fixes, and workarounds required to get the service to perform. Each issue is yet another opportunity for customer dissatisfaction. As costs go up and service levels go down, the value equation goes out of whack and the customer starts to fume. This is not where you want to be.

Good design sets you up for the strategic – services designed deliver on some portion of the customer's "big bets" and have the right characteristics and therefore are valued – as well as the tactical and operational.

Here's what we mean by this: one of the authors has a VW New Beetle. To change the headlamp requires a special (expensive) tool or a visit to the dealer (also expense). This is usually discovered after purchasing a new headlamp, attempting to put it in, and fiddling with it unsuccessfully for hours (an opportunity for dissatisfaction). This is a design flaw that could have been avoided by a better understanding of the customer, what maintenance they might expect to do themselves, and design for operability and maintainability.

The real lesson here is that the more you get right upstream (strategy, design, transition) the less trouble you'll have downstream (operation). Getting strategy for services right is important, but precisely how that strategy is realized in design is both an art and science that can pay huge dividends downstream, where it counts, where value is created and seen by the customer, where most services spend the vast majority of their lives: in operation.

So… having a look at these value statements, and considering your service design processes, how does your organization stack up? What is working well, and what does it look like in your organization when it does? What is missing or inadequate, and what does it look like in your organization as a result?

ITILFND02-02-7 Account for the purpose, objectives and scope of service transition
(ST 1.1.1, 1.1.2)

Purpose

To ensure that new, modified or retired services meet the expectations of the business as documented in the service strategy and service design stages of the lifecycle.

Objectives

- Plan and manage service changes efficiently and effectively
- Manage risks relating to new, changed or retired services
- Successfully deploy service releases into supported environments
- Set correct expectations on performance and use of new or changed services
- Ensure that service changes create the expected business value
- Provide good-quality knowledge and information about services and service assets

Scope

- Provides guidance for the development and improvement of capabilities for transitioning new and changed services into supported environments, including release planning, building, testing, evaluation and deployment
- Considers service retirement, transfer of services between service providers
- Focuses on how to ensure that the requirements from service strategy, developed in service design, are effectively realized in service operation while controlling the risks of failure and subsequent disruption
- Includes the transition of changes in the service provider's service management capabilities that will impact on the ways of working, the organization, people, projects and third parties involved in service management

ITILFND02-02-7 Account for the purpose, objectives and scope of service transition
(ST 1.1.1, 1.1.2)

Service Transition provides guidance for the development and improvement of capabilities for introducing new and changed services into supported environments. It describes how to transition an organization from one state to another while controlling risk and supporting organizational knowledge for decision support; it ensures value identified in service strategy and encoded in service design are effectively transitioned to be realized in service operation.

The Service Knowledge Management system is a key topic.

Service strategy processes are as follows:
1. Transition planning and support
2. Change management
3. Service asset and configuration management
4. Release and deployment management
5. Service validation and testing
6. Change evaluation
7. Knowledge management

ITILFND02-02-8 Briefly explain what value service transition provides to the business (ST 1.1.4)

The value service transition provides to the business

Selecting and adopting the best practice as recommended in the Service Transition publication will assist organizations in delivering significant benefits. It will help readers to set up service transition and the processes that support it, and to make effective use of those processes to facilitate the effective transitioning of new, changed or decommissioned services.

Adopting and implementing standard and consistent approaches for service transition will:
- ☑ Enable projects to estimate the cost, timing, resource requirement and risks associated with the service transition stage more accurately
- ☑ Result in higher volumes of successful change
- ☑ Be easier for people to adopt and follow
- ☑ Enable service transition assets to be shared and re-used across projects and services
- ☑ Reduce delays from unexpected clashes and dependencies
- ☑ Reduce effort on managing service transition test and pilot environments
- ☑ Improve expectation setting for all stakeholders involved in service transition including customers, users, suppliers, partners and projects
- ☑ Increase confidence that the new or changed service can be delivered to specification without unexpectedly affecting other services or stakeholders
- ☑ Ensure that new or changed services will be maintainable and cost-effective
- ☑ Improve control of service assets and configurations

ITILFND02-02-8 Briefly explain what value service transition provides to the business (ST 1.1.4)

It is important to get strategy and design right to ensure that, in the end, when the service is released into production and begins the longest part of its journey in life, it is successful, because it is a strategic fit for what the customer needs and has been designed for operation.

The stage after design is transition, our topic here. After all the effort to get the strategy and design right, it is important to make sure the process for introducing the service into production is good. A good service transition process minimizes surprises, emergency changes, delays, etc. You know the process is not good when a flurry of changes is required to get any service into production (part of the issue here would lie in design also), estimates can't be counted on, and the organization goes "tilt" when more than a few complex changes need to go in at once.

A controlled transition process prevents individual changes, releases, projects, etc. from stepping all over each other; it makes sure dependencies are clear and honored in the schedule, and it seeks to minimize effort required due to lack of planning.

So... having a look at these value statements, and considering your service transition processes, how does your organization stack up? What is working well, and what does it look like in your organization when it does? What is missing or inadequate, and what does it look like in your organization as a result?

ITILFND02-02-9 Account for the purpose, objectives and scope of service operation (SO 1.1.1, 1.1.2)

Purpose

To coordinate and carry out the activities and processes required to deliver and manage services at agreed levels to business users and customers. Service operation is also responsible for the ongoing management of the technology that is used to deliver and support services.

Objectives

- Maintain business satisfaction and confidence in IT through effective and efficient delivery and support of agreed IT services
- Minimize the impact of service outages on day-to-day business activities
- Ensure that access to agreed IT services is only provided to those authorized to receive those services

Scope

- **The services themselves** – activities that form part of a service are included in service operation, whether it is performed by the service provider, an external supplier or the user or customer of that service
- **Service management processes** – the ongoing management and execution of the many service management processes that are performed in service operation
- **Technology** – the management of the infrastructure used to deliver services
- **People** – regardless of what services, processes and technology are managed, they are all about people. It is people who drive the demand for the organization's services and products and it is people who decide how this will be done.

ITILFND02-02-9 Account for the purpose, objectives and scope of service operation
(SO 1.1.1, 1.1.2)

Service Operation provides best practice for managing services in supported environments, guidance on achieving effectiveness and efficiency in service delivery and support to ensure value for customers, users and service providers. It covers managing the availability of services, controlling demand, optimizing capacity utilization, scheduling of operations, avoiding or resolving service incidents and managing problems, new models and architectures such as shared services, utility computing, web services and mobile commerce to support service operation.

Service Operations processes are:
1. Event management
2. Incident management
3. Request fulfillment
4. Problem management
5. Access management

Service Operations functions are:
1. Service desk
2. Technical management
3. IT operations management
4. Application management

ITILFND02-02-10 Briefly explain what value service operation provides to the business (SO 1.1.4)

The value service operation provides the business

Selecting and adopting the best practice as recommended in the Service Operation publication will assist organizations in delivering significant benefits. Adopting and implementing standard and consistent approaches for service operation will:

☑ Reduce unplanned labor and costs for both the business and IT through optimized handling of service outages and identification of their root causes

☑ Reduce the duration and frequency of service outages which will allow the business to take full advantage of the value created by the services they are receiving

☑ Provide operational results and data that can be used by other ITIL processes to improve services continually and provide justification for investing in ongoing service improvement activities and supporting technologies

☑ Meet the goals and objectives of the organization's security policy by ensuring that IT services will be accessed only by those authorized to use them

☑ Provide quick and effective access to standard services which business staff can use to improve their productivity or the quality of business services and products

☑ Provide a basis for automated operations, thus increasing efficiencies and allowing expensive human resources to be used for more innovative work

ITILFND02-02-10 Briefly explain what value service operation provides to the business (SO 1.1.4)

Operations is where "the rubber meets the road", where value is ultimately seen and realized for the customer.

Steps taken (or not taken) in strategy, design, and transition will deeply affect the value equation for services in operation. Properly done, good strategy, design and transition will help ensure costs are kept down for operation of the service, that availability, performance, security, continuity and customer satisfaction are what they should be.

So... having a look at these value statements, and considering your service operation processes, how does your organization stack up? What is working well, and what does it look like in your organization when it does? What is missing or inadequate, and what does it look like in your organization as a result?

ITILFND02-02-11 Account for the main purpose, objectives and scope of CSI (CSI 1.1.1, 1.1.2)

Purpose:
To align IT services with changing business needs by identifying and implementing improvements to IT services that support business processes

Objectives
- Review, analyze, prioritize and make recommendations on improvement opportunities in each lifecycle stage: service strategy, service design, service transition, service operation and CSI itself
- Review and analyze service level achievement
- Identify and implement specific activities to improve IT service quality and improve the efficiency and effectiveness of the enabling processes
- Improve service delivery cost effectiveness, maintain customer satisfaction
- Ensure applicable quality management methods are used to support continual improvement activities
- Ensure that processes have clearly defined objectives and measurements that lead to actionable improvements
- Understand what to measure, why it is being measured and what the successful outcome should be

Scope Provides guidance in four main areas:
1. The overall health of ITSM as a discipline
2. The continual alignment of the service portfolio with the current and future business needs
3. The maturity and capability of the organization, management, processes and people utilized by the services
4. Continual improvement of all aspects of the IT service and the service assets that support them

ITILFND02-02-11 Account for the main purpose, objectives and scope of CSI (CSI 1.1.1, 1.1.2)

Continual Service Improvement provides guidance on creating and maintaining value for customers through better service strategy, design, transition and operation, combining principles, practices and methods from quality management, change management and capability improvement. It describes best practice for achieving incremental and large-scale service quality improvements, operational efficiency and business continuity, and for ensuring the service portfolio continues to be aligned to business needs, and guidance for linking improvement efforts and outcomes with service strategy, design, transition and operation, and a closed loop feedback system based on Plan-Do-Check-Act (PDCA)

Other topics include
- Service measurement
- Demonstrating value with metrics
- Developing baselines
- Maturity assessments

CSI processes are:
1. The seven-step improvement process

ITILFND02-02-12 Briefly explain what value CSI provides to the business (CSI 1.1.4)

The value CSI provides to the business

Selecting and adopting the best practice as recommended in the CSI publication will assist organizations in delivering significant benefits. It will help readers to set up CSI and the process that supports it, and to make effective use of the process to facilitate the effective improvement of service quality.

Adopting and implementing standard and consistent approaches for CSI will:
- ☑ Lead to gradual and continual improvement in service quality, where justified
- ☑ Ensure IT services remain continuously aligned to business requirements
- ☑ Result in gradual improvements in cost effectiveness through a reduction in costs and/or the capability to handle more work at the same cost
- ☑ Use monitoring and reporting to identify opportunities for improvement in all lifecycle stages and in all processes
- ☑ Identify opportunities for improvements in organizational structures, resourcing capabilities, partners, technology, staff skills and training, and communications

ITILFND02-02-12 Briefly explain what value CSI provides to the business (CSI 1.1.4)

Estimates and assumptions are necessarily made in service strategy, design, and transition. When "the rubber meets the road" and services are transitioned into operation, after a period you will have actual versus estimated data.

Also, over time, people will change, processes will change, technology and suppliers will change, as will business objectives, so it is appropriate that continually, in this sea of data and change, the IT service provider looks for opportunities to improve services.

Efforts expended on CSI should produce value and benefits as outlined in the preceding page – lower costs, better match to business needs, and the like.

So... having a look at these value statements, and considering your continual service improvement processes, how does your organization stack up? What is working well, and what does it look like in your organization when it does? What is missing or inadequate, and what does it look like in your organization as a result?

CHAPTER 3
ITILFND03 GENERIC CONCEPTS AND DEFINITION

The purpose of this unit is to help you to define some of the key terminology and explain the key concepts of service management. The syllabus recommends that this unit is covered as part of the content in the other units. At the end of this unit, you should be able to define and explain the following key concepts:

03-1.   Utility and warranty (SS 2.1.6)

03-2.   Assets, resources and capabilities (SS 2.2.1)

03-3.   Service portfolio (SS 4.2.4.1, Fig. 4.14)

03-4.   Service catalogue (both two- and three-view types) (SD 4.2.4.5, Fig. 4.4, Fig. 4.5)

03-5.   Governance (SS 2.3.1)

03-6.   Business case (SS 3.6.1.1)

03-7.   Risk management (SS 5.6.5.1, 5.6.5.2)

03-8.   Service provider (SS 2.1.4)

03-10. Supplier (SS 2.1.5)

03-11. Service level agreement (SLA) (SD 4.3.4)

03-12. Operational level agreement (OLA) (SD 4.3.4)

03-13. Underpinning contract (SD 4.8.4.2)

03-14. Service design package (SD Appendix A)

03-15. Availability (SD 4.4.4.3)

03-16. Service knowledge management system (SKMS) (ST 4.7.4.3)

03-17. Configuration item (CI) (ST 4.3.4.2)

03-18. Configuration management system (ST 4.3.4.3)

03-19. Definitive media library (DML) (ST 4.3.4.4)

03-20. Change (ST 4.2.4.4)

03-21. Change types (standard, emergency and normal) (ST 4.2.4.3, 4.2.4.7, 4.2.5.11)

03-24. Event (SO 4.1 1st para)

03-25. Alert (Glossary)

03-26. Incident (SO 4.2 1st para)

03-27. Impact, urgency and priority (SO 4.2.5.4)

03-28. Service request (SO 4.3 1st para)

03-29. Problem (SO 4.4 1st para)

03-30. Workaround (SO 4.4.5.6)

03-31. Known error (SO 4.4.5.7)

03-32. Known error database (KEDB) (SO 4.4.7.2)

03-33. The role of communication in service operation (SO 3.6)

03-35. Release policy (ST 4.1.4.2)

03-36. Types of services (SS 3.2.2.4, Tab 3.5)

03-37. Change proposals (ST 4.2.4.6)

03-38. CSI register (CSI 3.4)

03-39. Outcomes (SS 2.1.1)

03-40. Patterns of business activity (SS 4.4.5.2)

03-41. Customers and users (SS 2.1.5)

03-42. The Deming Cycle (plan, do, check, act) (CSI 3.8, Fig. 2.8)

ITILFND03-03-1 Define and explain utility and warranty (SS 2.1.6.)

Utility and warranty

Utility and warranty are the two element of a service's business value from the customer's perspective; the value of a service is only delivered when both are designed and delivered.

Utility	Warranty
Functionality offered by product / service to meet a particular need What the service does Fitness for purpose Removes constraints on the performance	Assurance that a product / service will meet its agreed requirements How it is delivered Fitness for use Increases the potential to perform

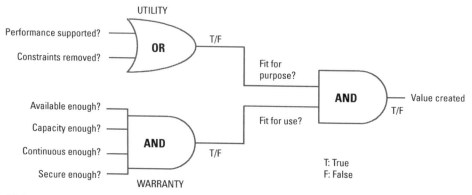

SS Figure 2.2: Services are designed, built and delivered with both utility and warranty

Utility is the functionality offered by a product or service to meet a particular need. It is 'what the service does', and can be used to determine whether a service is able to meet its required outcomes, or is 'fit for purpose'. Utility refers to those aspects of a service that contribute to tasks associated with achieving outcomes. Utility is therefore any attribute of a service that removes, or reduces the effect of, constraints on the performance of a task.

Warranty is an assurance that a product or service will meet its agreed requirements. This may be a formal agreement such as a service level agreement or contract, or a marketing message or brand image. Warranty refers to the ability of a service to be available when needed, to provide the required capacity, and to provide the required reliability in terms of continuity and security. Warranty can be summarized as 'how the service is delivered', and can be used to determine whether a service is 'fit for use'. For example, any aspect of the service that increases the availability or speed of the service would be considered warranty. Warranty can therefore represent any attribute of a service that increases the potential of the business to be able to perform a task. Warranty refers to any means by which utility is made available to the users.

ITILFND03-03-1 Define and explain utility and warranty (SS 2.1.6.)

For example, a service that enables a business unit to process orders should allow sales people to access customer details, stock availability, shipping information etc. Any aspect of the service that improves the ability of sales people to improve the performance of the task of processing sales orders would be considered utility.

Can you recall an example of something which you bought but proved worthless because it did not provide the needed utility or warranty?

Utility is what the service does, and warranty is the extent to which it does it (how well it can be expected to perform or work).

Let us say you go to the home store and buy a dehumidifier. Here are some examples of utility and warranty:
- Does it take water out of the air? (All models do (or should!); this is a dehumidifier's primary utility)
- How much water can I expect it to take out of the air per day? (Some models take out as many as 65 pints per day, and others do not; this is an example of warranty)
- Where will it work? (Some models work in unheated basements, others do not; example of warranty)
- What will it cost to run? (Some models are Energy Star compliant and cheap to run, others are not; an example of warranty)
- What sort of noise can I expect? (Some models are noisy; an example of warranty)
- Will the water drain off automatically or will I need to change a condensation bucket? (Some models have a gravity drain, others have a pump that will pump the water up to elevations higher than the condensation bucket; an example of warranty)

For any service or product to have utility it must either support performance or remove constraints. So for example, I might buy one mobile phone service over another if it allows me to tether to my computer for Internet access, removing the constraint of needing a hardwired or wireless access point connection.

If you look at the diagram on the left hand page, you will see that the warranty components are precisely matched to the key provisions of a service level agreement:
1) Availability provisions – when will the service be available
2) Capacity (performance) provisions – transaction turnaround times, etc.
3) IT service continuity provisions – what happens in the case of a business interruption, when will the service be restored
4) Security provisions – how will we protect the confidentially, integrity and availability of the service's information assets?

ITILFND03-03-2 Define and explain assets, resources and capabilities (SS 2.2.1)

Assets, resources and capabilities

Asset Any resource or capability
Resources and Capabilities Two types of asset used by both service providers and customers
Customer asset Any resource or capability used by a customer to achieve a business outcome
Service asset Any resource or capability used by a service provider to deliver services to a customer

Capabilities	Resources
Management	Financial capital
Organization	Infrastructure
Processes	Applications
Knowledge	Information
People (experience, skills and relationships)	People (number of employees)

SS Figure 2.4: Examples of capabilities and resources

© Crown copyright 2011. Reproduced under license from the Cabinet Office.

The service relationship between service providers and their customers revolves around the use of assets – both those of the service provider and those of the customer. Each relationship involves an interaction between the assets of each party.

Many customers use the service they receive from a service provider to build and deliver services or products of their own and then deliver them on to their own customers. In these cases, what the service provider considers to be the customer asset would be considered to be a service asset by their customer.

Without customer assets, there is no basis for defining the value of a service. The performance of customer assets is therefore a primary concern for service management.

ITILFND03-03-2 Define and explain assets, resources and capabilities (SS 2.2.1)

A good way to think of resources is as 'factors of production', the basic materials that go into producing services. Getting back to the omelet analogy, they are the ingredients and tools, things like eggs and whisks and stoves and bowls. To make an omelet, you need know-how, a step-wise process, and a way of organizing assets (like how things are laid out in our kitchen and fridge) that make for efficiency and effectiveness (a great-tasting omelet).

This distinction is important, as there must be a balance between what you invest in resources versus capabilities. Said another way, you can't get it done by investing in one or the other (a great kitchen with great ingredients with a bad cook gets you a bad omelet; a great cook with rotten eggs gets you a bad omelet); you have to strike a balance. There is a certain tipping point or "entry level ticket" investment required in both types of assets to succeed – it doesn't have to be 'gold-plated' investment, for sure, but it has to be there.

As an example, one of the authors and his wife play the card game bridge. You simply cannot play bridge without cards of some sort – this is a basic resource, followed by a card table and chairs etc. (some would say snacks as well J). These are examples of resources needed for bridge playing. Likewise, you cannot play bridge if you do not understand at least the basics of bidding and playing tricks. These are examples of capabilities.

Some mnemonics to help you remember:
Resources: Finicky, I Approve if Perfect
Capabilities: Man Overboard, Please Keep Probing!

ITILFND03-03-3 Define and explain the service portfolio (SS 4.2.4.1, Figure 4.14)

The service portfolio

Service Portfolio
The complete set of services managed by a service provider; used to manage the entire lifecycle of all services, and includes three categories: service pipeline (proposed or in development), service catalogue (live or available for deployment), and retired services.

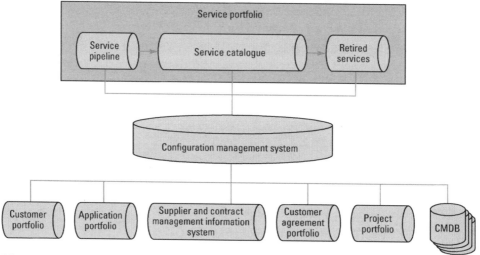

SS Figure 4.14 illustrates the components of the service portfolio.

The service portfolio represents the commitments and investments made by a service provider across all customers and market spaces, including contractual commitments and new service development and ongoing service improvement plans initiated by CSI. The portfolio also includes third-party services, an integral part of service offerings to customers. Some third-party services are visible to the customers while others are not.

The service portfolio is the complete set of services that is managed by a service provider and identifies those services in a conceptual stage, namely all services the organization would provide if it had unlimited resources, capabilities and funding. This documentation exercise facilitates understanding of the opportunity costs of the existing portfolio and better fiscal discipline. If a service provider understands what it cannot do, then it is better able to assess if it should continue as is or re-allocate resources and capabilities.

The service portfolio represents all the resources presently engaged or being released in various stages of the service lifecycle. Each stage requires resources for completion of projects, initiatives and contracts. This is a very important governance aspect of service portfolio management (SPM). Entry, progress and exit are approved only with approved funding and a financial plan for recovering costs or showing profit as necessary. The service portfolio should have the right mix of services in the pipeline and catalogue to secure the financial viability of the service provider, since the service catalogue is the only part of the portfolio that lists services that recover costs or earn profits.

ITILFND03-03-3 Define and explain the service portfolio (SS 4.2.4.1, Figure 4.14)

We have scarce resources and time. Given this, where should we invest our efforts? What services should we introduce? Retire? Change? What criteria should we use to decide? Let us be clear on this and manage the full lifecycle of services as a portfolio – this is what the service portfolio is about.

As business needs and available technologies evolve, IT strategies, and therefore the portfolio of services required to achieve the position indicated by those strategies, need to change.

Basically what we are doing here is applying the generic principles of portfolio management (as applied to financial portfolios of stocks, bonds and other investments, and more similarly, to portfolios of projects, as in project portfolio management) to services.

The other part of this idea is making sure you have ready access to the basic information required to effectively and efficiently run a services business – who are your customers, what agreements do you have with them, and what are the associated service level commitments and provider and customer responsibilities? Who are your suppliers and where are the contracts you have with them and what are their terms and conditions? What applications do you have? What projects do you have in the pipe, and what is their status-schedule, resources, costs? What is the configuration of your services, including all components, and how they relate to one another, for reference in all phases of service management, for example, troubleshooting incidents and planning changes?

All of this information is in the stores and systems shown at the bottom of SS Figure 4.14. The CMS is how all of it is accessed, and is intended to provide a 'single pane of glass' view into all of this information, underpinning the service portfolio-that is, what you have planned, in operation, and what you have retired.

ITILFND03-03-4 Define and explain the service catalogue (two and three-view types) (SD 4.2.4.5, Figure 4.4, Figure 4.5)

Service catalogue structure

Service catalogue

A database or structured document with information on all live IT services, including those available for deployment. It is part of the service portfolio and contains information about two types of IT service: customer-facing services that are visible to the business; and supporting services required by the service provider to deliver customer-facing services.

SS Figure 4.4 shows a service catalogue with two views:

1. **Business/customer service catalogue view** –contains details of all IT services delivered to the customers (customer-facing services), with relationships to business units and processes that rely on the IT services. This is the customer view of the service catalogue. In other words, this is the service catalogue for the business to see and use.
2. **Technical/supporting service catalogue view** –contains details of all the supporting IT services, together

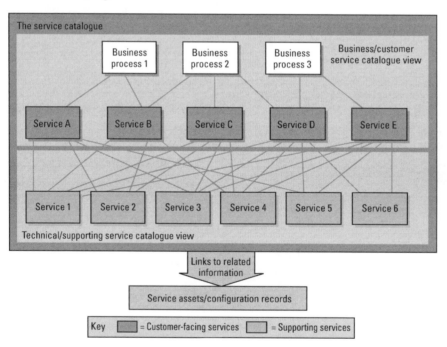

SD Figure 4.4: Two-view service catalogue

SS Figure 4.5 shows a service catalogue with three views:

1. **Wholesale customer view** – this contains details of all the IT services delivered to wholesale customers (customer-facing services), together with relationships to the customers they support.
2. **Retail customer view** – this contains details of all the IT services delivered to retail customers (customer-facing services), together with relationships to the customers they support.
3. **Supporting services view** – this contains details of all the supporting IT services, together with relationships to the customer-facing services they underpin and the components, CIs and other supporting services necessary to support the provision of the service to the customers.

The customer-facing service catalogue view facilitates the development of a much more proactive or even pre-emptive service level management (SLM) process and supports close business alignment with clearly defined relationships between services and SLAs. The supporting service catalogue view is extremely beneficial when constructing the relationship between services, SLAs, operational level agreements (OLAs) and other underpinning agreements and components, as it will identify the technology required to support a service and the support group(s) that support the components. The combination of all views is invaluable for quickly assessing the impact of incidents and changes on the business.

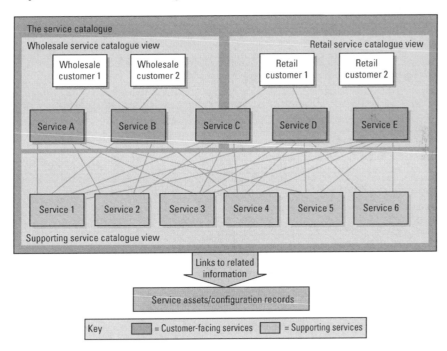

SD Figure 4.5 Three-view service catalogue

ITILFND03-03-5 Define and explain governance (SS 2.3.1)

Governance

Governance
Governance ensures policies and strategy are actually implemented, and that required processes are correctly followed; includes defining roles and responsibilities, measuring and reporting, and taking actions to resolve any issues identified.

Corporate Governance

- "*Corporate* Governance is about promoting corporate fairness, transparency, and accountability" (Emphasis added)
  - *J. Wolfensohn, President, World Bank (Financial Times, June 21, 1999)*
- Example: Sarbanes-Oxley Act (SOX) of 2002
  - ♦ Demands corporate fairness, mandates complete transparency of transactions, and holds executives accountable for any material deficiencies

Governance is the single overarching area that ties IT and the business together, and services are one way of ensuring that the organization is able to execute that governance. Governance is what defines the common directions, policies and rules that both the business and IT use to conduct business.

Many ITSM strategies fail because they try to build a structure or processes according to how they would like the organization to work instead of working within the existing governance structures.

Governance works to apply a consistently managed approach at all levels of the organization – first by ensuring a clear strategy is set, then by defining the policies whereby the strategy will be achieved. The policies also define boundaries, or what the organization may not do as part of its operations.

Governance must be able to evaluate, direct and monitor the strategy, policies and plans.
The international standard for corporate governance of IT is ISO/IEC 38500.

ITILFND03-03-5 Define and explain governance (SS 2.3.1)

You can think of governance as being like a gyroscope, used in rockets and spacecraft to keep them on track (more accurately, they keep them from going off track). Governance is a steering mechanism for accountability, to help ensure we do what we say we are going to do, that we will "walk the talk".

In the end, key stakeholders like board members, shareholders, and auditors want to know that you have documented what you are doing, that you are doing it, that you can show evidence that you are doing it, and that what you are doing is in accordance with all applicable regulatory requirements. Think about it – this end cannot be reached on its own accord – there must be a strategy to support the journey.

Think about the work in your organization. List a couple of activities. Next to them, add a column and answer the question, "performance is effective when…"; this is the performance standard for the activity. Now, add a third column, "governance mechanisms". For each, list at least one thing that helps keep the activity on track to reached the required level of performance. These are governance mechanisms.

ITILFND03-03-6 Define and explain business case (SS 3.6.1.1)

Business case

Business case
Justification for a significant item of expenditure. Includes information about costs, benefits, options, issues, risks and possible problems.

A business case is a decision support and planning tool that projects the likely consequences of a business action; its consequences can take on qualitative and quantitative dimensions.

Sample business case structure
    Introduction – business objectives addressed
    Methods and assumptions – boundaries of the business case
    Business impacts – financial, non-financial results anticipated
    Risks and contingencies – probability that alternative results will emerge
    Recommendations – specific actions recommended

The structure of a business case varies from organization to organization. What they all have in common is a detailed analysis of business impact or benefits. Business impact is in turn linked to business objectives, which are the reasons for considering a service management initiative in the first place. Some examples:

- The business objectives for commercial provider organizations are usually the objectives of the business itself, including financial and organizational performance.
- The business objectives of an internal service provider should be linked to the business objectives of the business unit to which the service is being provided, and the overall corporate objectives.
- The business objectives for not-for-profit organizations are usually the objectives for the constituents, population or membership served as well as financial and organizational performance.

It is important to note that a single business impact can affect multiple business objectives, and that multiple business impacts can affect a single business objective.

ITILFND03-03-6 Define and explain business case (SS 3.6.1.1)

We use the following mnemonic for remembering the parts of a business case:
"In McKinleyville, Beavers Ravaged Redwoods".

Where initiatives have potential or proven significant risk or cost to the business – for example, major changes to a service, or the proposed introduction or retirement of a service – and where multiple alternatives exist for meeting the desired outcome, a business case must be made.

Your organization may use a different structure and sequence and call the sections something different, but in general, a business case must include:
1) Some sort of short introduction or executive summary (Introduction)
2) Background on the scope and methods applied to the business case, along with the assumptions that bound it (Methods and Assumptions)
3) An analysis of the positive and negative aspects of moving on the business case (as well as the opportunity cost of not moving forward) (Business Impacts)
4) An analysis of the potential risks (again, ideally both associated with moving forward and not moving forward) along with contingencies to pursue if those risks accrue (Risks and Contingencies)
5) An finally, as a basis for a go / no go decision on the initiative, given the nature of the solution, impacts, risks, and alternatives, we must suggest a preferred path forward (Recommendations)

What format do business cases take in your organization? Is there a standard format followed? How does it differ from what is suggested in ITIL? How is it the same?

ITILFND03-03-7 Define and explain risk management (SS 5.6.5.1, 5.6.5.2)

Risk
A possible Event that could cause harm or loss, or affect the ability to achieve objectives; can also be defined as uncertainty of outcome, and can be used in the context of measuring the probability of positive outcomes and negative outcomes.

Risk management
The process responsible for identifying, assessing and controlling risks; also at times used to refer to the second part of the overall process after risks have been identified and assessed, as in "risk assessment and management."

Depending on the scope and complexity of the service management implementation strategy, the team may need a separate plan to deal with the identified risks. This plan will become part of any overall project plan that is part of executing the strategy and reviewed at regular control points. Some projects will assign an individual to monitor and manage the risks associated with the project.

It is the project manager's responsibility to ensure risks are identified and measures are put in place to mitigate them. Usually the project team will jointly identify and document the risks, including the potential impacts and – if known – the probability of the risk occurring.

Identifying the risks – involves naming the risk. When first identifying the risk it is not necessary to try to explain or quantify the risk, but just to get as many ideas as possible about what might threaten the success of a project or strategy. Each identified or suspected risk should be documented together with its potential consequences.

Analysing the risks – quantifying the impact and probability of the risk. The impact is the effect on a strategy or project (and its customers) should the risk become reality. Most risk management approaches use both qualitative and quantitative descriptions of these areas.

Managing risks – once risks have been assessed and documented, together with their action plans, the risk management plan must be reviewed regularly to ensure appropriate actions have been taken and are working as expected. Any of the risks may change status throughout the project. These changes must be monitored and built into the normal project control mechanisms – e.g. every project meeting should include a review of the risk management plan and the assessment of any new risks.

Risk management is a repetitive activity and it is likely that the entire process will be repeated several times.

ITILFND03-03-7 Define and explain risk management (SS 5.6.5.1, 5.6.5.2)

A risk is a possibility of an uncertain outcome – if the event is 100% assured to happen, it is not a risk, it is a certainty.

As with all things and IT, resources, time and attention are scarce, so you must take care to allocate them carefully to the identification, assessment and control of risks.

Identify – Analyze – Manage. These are the three steps to risk management.

Remember I-A-M, as in "I Am".

Risk management cannot be 'tacked on' to doing service management somehow in the last minute of the month. It has to be built into the fabric of 'how we do things around here'; in every change discussion – what are the risks? When discussing go / no go on projects – what are the risks? It is not that a culture of fear should be engendered ("Gee, I had better not get out of bed in the morning, there is a risk I might be struck by a satellite falling out of the sky". On the contrary, a positive perception is needed for the well-intended, purposeful, useful shared practice of surfacing and handling risks. In other words the way we do things around risk management should not follow the adage, "the nail that sticks up must be hammered back down".

It has to be every IT professional's responsibility, for good reason. An example may help illustrate.

When one of the authors started in IT in the mid 1980s, he worked in mainframe technical services and reported to a manager who was extremely bright, with only one platform and two operating systems (MVS and VM) to support. Given this situation, the manager really could survey the situation, identify and communicate all the risks, and give the team its marching orders. Fast forward to today, where this manager has a number of staff coding XML, and he can just about spell XML, there is no way he can surface and manage all the risks.

This is a silly example, but it does describe the situation we find ourselves in more and more - that is, because of the level of complexity and change in IT, no one person can see all the risks and coordinate contingencies and mitigations. All in IT must do it, for their patch.

And it is important that they have a shared way of doing this, that is mutually understood and used – 'how we do things around here". This engenders acceptance of risk management as a norm, and working in concert, all of which add should support the efficient and effective handling of risk.

THREE main types of service providers: internal, shared, external

Service provider
An organization supplying services to one or more internal customers or external customers.
'Service provider' is often used as an abbreviation for 'IT service provider'.

While most aspects of service management apply equally to all types of service provider, other aspects such as customers, contracts, competition, market spaces, revenue and strategy take on different meanings depending on the specific type. The three types are:

- **Type I: internal service provider** – an internal service provider that is embedded within a business unit. There may be several Type I service providers within an organization.
- **Type II: shared services unit** – an internal service provider that provides shared IT services to more than one business unit
- **Type III: external service provider** – a service provider that provides IT services to external customers

Based on Cabinet Office Crown Copyright Material

ITSM concepts are often described in the context of only one of these types and as if only one type of IT service provider exists or is used by a given organization. In reality most organizations have a combination of IT service providers. In a single organization it is possible that some IT units are dedicated to a single business unit, others provide shared services, and yet others have been outsourced or depend on external service providers.

Many IT organizations who traditionally provide services to internal customers find that they are dealing directly with external users because of the online services that they provide.

ITILFND03-03-8 Define and explain service provider (SS 2.1.4)

Larger organizations typically have a mix of Type I (internal), Type II (shared), and Type III (external) service organizations. For example, a pharmaceutical family of companies may have IT service providers associated with each company that provide company-specific services; a shared services organization is set up to provide services that are not unique, to leverage economies of scales. Where outsourcing makes sense, external providers are employed. The idea is to arrive at the ideal blend of the three types of providers for the optimal cost and quality for IT services.

In your organization, what are the different services and the type of service provider for each service? Which type do you see as most important for your organization?

Some organizations go through cycles of centralization and decentralization, insourcing and outsourcing. Is this the case for your organization? Are there instances where one or the other was highly beneficial or problematic? Can you think of some reasons why?

ITILFND03-03-10 Define and explain supplier (SS 2.1.5)

Service management stakeholders: Supplier, Customer, User

Stakeholder
A person with an interest in an organization, project, IT service, etc. Stakeholders may be interested in the activities, targets, resources or deliverables. Stakeholders may include customers, partners, employees, shareholders, owners etc.

Customers	Users	Suppliers
Those who buy goods or services Person or group who defines and agrees the service level targets May be internal or external Also sometimes used informally to mean user – for example, 'This is a customer-focused organization'	Those who use the service on a day-to-day basis Distinct from customers, as some customers do not use the IT service directly	Third parties responsible for supplying goods or services that are required to deliver IT services Examples of suppliers include commodity hardware and software vendors, network and telecom providers, and outsourcing organizations

Stakeholders have an interest in an organization, project or service etc. and may be interested in the activities, targets, resources or deliverables from service management. Examples include organizations, service providers, customers, consumers, users, partners, employees, shareholders, owners and suppliers. The term 'organization' is used to define a company, legal entity or other institution. It is also used to refer to any entity that has people, resources and budgets – for example, a project or business.

Within the service provider organization there are many different stakeholders including the functions, groups and teams that deliver the services. There are also many stakeholders external to the service provider organization.

ITILFND03-03-10 Define and explain supplier (SS 2.1.5)

Suppliers in ITIL terms always sit outside of the business and IT service provider. In other words, they are not part of the same corporate entity, but from a separate corporate entity.

Unidentified stakeholders are a key risk to a service provider, so it is important to be aware of who your stakeholders are, especially customers, suppliers and users. Just as important is understanding what their stake is – what does "good" look like, from each of their perspectives?

Supplier are a good example when it comes to talking about unidentified stakeholders because they are often overlooked. Do you know who your suppliers are? Can you list them? Can you locate their contracts? Do you know what their contract terms are? Do you know how they are performing relative to the contract terms? Do you know what mechanisms are in place to surface and manage their performance?

ITILFND03-03-11 Define and explain service level agreement (SLA) (SD 4.3.4)

Service Level Agreement (SLA)
An agreement between an IT service provider and a customer. The SLA describes the IT service, documents service level targets, and specifies the responsibilities of the IT service provider and the customer. A single SLA may cover multiple IT services or multiple customers.

- Developed to match the business needs and expectations
- Provides the basis for managing the relationship between the service provider and the customer
- Should not be used as a way of holding one side or the other to ransom – emphasis must be on agreement
- Will typically define the warranty a service is to deliver and describe the utility of the service

SLM is the name given to the process of ensuring that the required and cost-justifiable service quality is maintained and gradually improved by planning, coordinating, drafting, agreeing, monitoring and reporting of SLAs, and the ongoing review of service achievements. SLM is not only concerned with ensuring that current services and SLAs are managed, but it is also involved in ensuring that new service level requirements are captured and that new or changed services and SLAs are developed to match the business needs and expectations. SLAs provide the basis for managing the relationship between the service provider and the customer, and SLM provides that central point of focus for a group of customers, business units or lines of business.

An SLA is a written agreement between an IT service provider and the IT customer(s), defining the key service targets and responsibilities of both parties. The emphasis must be on agreement, and SLAs should not be used as a way of holding one side or the other to ransom. A true partnership should be developed between the IT service provider and the customer, so that a mutually beneficial agreement is reached – otherwise the SLA could quickly fall into disrepute and a 'blame culture' could develop that would prevent any true service quality improvements from taking place. An SLA will typically define the warranty a service is to deliver and describe the utility of the service.

ITILFND03-03-11 Define and explain service level agreement (SLA) (SD 4.3.4)

An SLA is one of the central mechanisms, if not the central mechanism, for making service management happen. It is the bridge between the IT service provider and customer, specifying their agreement about what will be provided (utility), to what level of service (warranty, and typically Availability, Capacity (performance), Continuity, and Security provisions), along with provider and customer responsibilities and roles for provision and use of the service, respectively.

This last point is critical; many IT professionals think mostly in terms of their responsibilities in service provision, but without a customer being clear on and taking ownership of their responsibilities, things will not work.

It is all about getting expectations right. For example, I may commit to painting your house and estimate the amount of time required, but I will specify for example, that your responsibilities are to move furniture out of the way, cover furniture etc. so that I can move quickly and do the job specified. If you don't want to meet your responsibilities, then we have to renegotiate the scope and cost of the job.

Take for example the situation of change management. This cannot be only the IT service provider's responsibility. The customer has to have 'skin in the game' as well. In the course of the year, what do you expect them to do? For example, will they initiate change requests and filter spurious requests before they hit change management? Will they participate in the Change Advisory Board (CAB) for major or significant relevant changes?

The whole idea with SLM is to identify your customer (the person or group who pays the bills for the service) and make sure you have a written agreement with them that has been discussed and agreed that specifies what the service will do (utility) and to what level (warranty). The reason it needs to be explicit is because the service provider has to make sure the service, as designed, can consistently deliver the value the customer is looking for.

What SLAs do you have in place in your organization? What are the terms? Do they specify provisions for availability, capacity, continuity and security? What about customer and IT service provider roles and responsibilities?

ITILFND03-03-12 Define and explain operational level agreement (OLA) (SD 4.3.4)

Operational Level Agreement (OLA)

An agreement between an IT service provider and another part of the same organization. It supports the IT service provider's delivery of IT services to customers and defines the goods or services to be provided and the responsibilities of both parties.

For example, there could be an operational level agreement between:

- The IT service provider and a procurement department to obtain hardware in agreed times
- The service desk and a support group to provide incident resolution in agreed times

An OLA is an agreement between an IT service provider and another part of the same organization that assists with the provision of services – for instance, a facilities department that maintains the air conditioning, or network support team that supports the network service. An OLA should contain targets that underpin those within an SLA to ensure that targets will not be breached by failure of the supporting activity.

SLM is responsible for ensuring that all targets and measures agreed with the business in SLAs are supported by appropriate OLAs with internal support units and underpinning contracts with external partners and suppliers. In the case of the latter, this is the contribution that SLM makes to supplier management, which has primary responsibility for the relationship between the IT service provider and its suppliers.

ITILFND03-03-12 Define and explain operational level agreement (OLA) (SD 4.3.4)

You cannot be effective in IT service delivery and support if you can't count on the other groups in IT to do their part. That is where an OLA comes in.

Say for example part of your SLA between the IT organization and customer states that you will fix all hard drive crashes within 8 hours. First you might have an underpinning contract (UC - more on that in the next topic) or UC with a supplier to be onsite with a new hard drive and swap it out for the bad unit within 2 hours of notification by the Service Desk. Then you might have an OLA between the Service Desk and Deskside Support that specifies that Deskside Support will lay down the approved corporate image (OS, applications) on the hard drive within 2 hours of the hard drive being replaced. You might then have an OLA that states that the Data Protection group restores the user's data from the last backup within 2 hours of the hard drive being re-imaged.

So in total you have 2 + 2 + 2 = 6 hours + 2 hours of 'wiggle room' to ensure you can consistently hit the 8 hours specified in the SLA.

The idea here is that the IT service provider should not commit to an SLA with the customer that they cannot consistently hit. A related principle is that no group within IT should be beholden to meeting an SLA then not be able to meet it consistently because there is no agreement between that group and other groups on which that group depends which supports such a commitment – that would be a recipe for best effort at best and disaster at worst, not the certain, regular meeting of commitments that is in the best interest of both the customer and the IT service provider.

What OLAs do you have in place in your organization? How are they working for you? What happens in your organization when OLAs are missing or inadequate? What happens when they are as they should be?

ITILFND03-03-13 Define and explain underpinning contract (SD 4.8.4.2)

Underpinning contract
A contract between an IT service provider and a third party. The third party provides goods or services that support delivery of an IT service to a customer. The underpinning contract defines targets and responsibilities that are required to meet agreed service level targets in one or more service level agreements

The contents of a basic underpinning contract or service agreement are:
- **Basic terms and conditions** – the term (duration) of the contract, the parties, locations, scope, definitions and commercial basis.
- **Service description and scope** – the functionality of the services being provided and its extent, along with constraints on the service delivery, such as performance, availability, capacity, technical interface and security. Service functionality may be explicitly defined, or in the case of well-established services, included by reference to other established documents, such as the service portfolio and the service catalogue.
- **Service standards** – the service measures and the minimum levels that constitute acceptable performance and quality – for example, IT may have a performance requirement to respond to a request for a new desktop system in 24 hours, with acceptable service deemed to have occurred where this performance requirement is met in 95% of cases. Service levels must be realistic, measurable and aligned to the organization's business priorities and underpin the agreed targets within SLRs and SLAs.
- **Workload ranges** – the volume ranges within which service standards apply, or for which particular pricing regimes apply.
- **Management information** – the data that must be reported by the supplier on operational performance – take care to ensure that management information is focused on the most important or headline reporting measures on which the relationship will be assessed. KPIs related to supplier CSFs and balanced scorecards may form the core of reported performance data.
- **Responsibilities and dependencies** – description of the obligations of the organization (in supporting the supplier in the service delivery efforts) and of the supplier (in its provision of the service), including communication, contacts and escalation.

An extended service agreement may also contain:
- Service debit and credit regime (incentives and penalties)
- Additional performance criteria

ITILFND03-03-13 Define and explain underpinning contract (SD 4.8.4.2)

The relationship between SLAs, OLAs, and UCs was explained in the previous section. The key thing to understand for all of them is the parties involved:

Performer	Agreement / Contract	Customer
IT Service Provider	SLA	The Customer
Internal IT Group	OLA	Other Internal IT Group
IT Service Provider	UC	External supplier / vendor

The key thing to understand about a UC is that it is in fact a legal contract between two separate corporate entities, a contract where if the terms are not met lawsuit and court battle might ensue. The same cannot be said of SLAs and OLAs – they are between internal customers and an internal provider.

What UCs do you have in place, between what IT groups and what suppliers? Do you know the terms? Are suppliers meeting those terms? What is the impact on the organization when they meet (and do not meet) those terms?

A vital first step in service management is identifying all of these parties, the associated agreements, and their terms and conditions. This knowledge (in addition to identifying un-represented or under-represented parties and missing or inadequate agreements) is the foundation for managing the agreement dimension of service management.

ITILFND03-03-14 Define and explain service design package (SDP) (SD Appendix A)

Service design package (SDP)
Document(s) defining all aspects of an IT service and its requirements through each stage of its lifecycle. A service design package is produced for each new IT service, major change or IT service retirement.

Service Design Package Contents

The SDP specifies all aspects of the service and its lifecycle requirements

Requirements
- Business requirements
- Service applicability
- Service contacts

☑ Design of the "service solutions"
☑ Design of Service Management "systems and tools"
☑ Design of the "technology architectures" and "management architectures" and tools
☑ Design of the "processes" needed
☑ Design of "measurement systems", methods, metrics

Service design
- Service functional requirements
- Service level requirements
- Service and operational management requirements
- Service design and topology

Organizational readiness assessment
- Organizational readiness assessment

When should a Service Design Package (SDP) be produced?
☑ During the design stage for each new service
☑ When a major change to a service is to be done
☑ When a service is removed
☑ When the SDP itself has to be changed

Service lifecycle plan
- Service program
- Service transition plan
- Service operational acceptance plan
- Service acceptance criteria

ITILFND03-03-14 Define and explain service design package (SD Appendix A)

To remember the parts of a service design package, think, 'LORD' –
Service **L**ifecycle Plan
Organizational Readiness Assessment
Requirements
Service **D**esign

The SDP is a central concept in service management and should be studied. The specifications shown on the opposite page are sufficient to pass the Foundation examination, but if you have access to the ITIL core publications, you should study the sample found in Appendix A of Service Design.

One of the key messages here is that Service Design is a bigger concept – and larger scope of work – than just application development or infrastructure engineering. Yes, all have requirements specification, but here is an important difference (and important to recall for the examination): it is called *service* design, so it is first and foremost about designing and delivering artifacts that support a service through its lifecycle. This is a bigger set of work and deliverables than just application development and infrastructure engineering. Artifacts specific to *service* management being developed and delivered, for example *service* functional requirements, *service* level requirements, SLAs / OLAs, UCs, etc. And since we are talking about designing to support the service through its life, we include design elements for lifecycle phases, e.g., an organization readiness assessment ("Is the organization ready to accept this service? What must be done to get it ready?"

Also importantly (for the examination as well), while it is called *service* design, it is NOT just about designing services. It is also about designing all the associated mechanisms that support a service through its lifecycle. So, it is about *process* design; it is about *service portfolio design*, and *measurement systems and metrics design*.

If you think about this in terms of running a services business, this all makes sense. If I start a landscaping business, I cannot just design the services – trimming, grass cutting, weeding and so forth. I must also design the customer contract and invoice forms, the datasheets that cover the benefits and costs of the services, and why you should use us for them – all of these systems and tools and processes must be developed and delivered for me to run my services business, however rudimentary.

ITILFND03-03-15 Define and explain availability (SD 4.4.4.3)

Availability, reliability, maintainability, serviceability

Availability
The ability of a service, component or CI to perform its agreed function when required; often measured and reported as a percentage; only include down time in the calculation when it occurs within the agreed service time (AST), but also record and report total down time.

Reliability
A measure of how long a service, component or CI can perform its agreed function without interruption; service reliability can be improved by increasing individual component reliability or by increasing resilience of the service to individual component failure (e.g., increasing component redundancy by using load-balancing techniques); often measured and reported as the mean time between service incidents (MTBSI) or mean time between failures (MTBF).

Maintainability
Measure of how quickly and effectively a service, component or CI can be restored to normal working after failure; measured and reported as mean time to restore service (MTRS).

Serviceability
Ability of a third-party supplier to meet the terms of its contract that includes agreed levels of availability, reliability and/or maintainability for a supporting service or component.

Measuring Availability, Reliability, and Maintainability

$$\text{vailability (\%)} = \frac{\text{Agreed service time (AST)} - \text{downtime}}{\text{AST}} \times 100$$

$$\text{Reliability (MTBSI in hours)} = \frac{\text{Availability time in hours}}{\text{Number of breaks}}$$

$$\text{Reliability (MTBF in hours)} = \frac{\text{Availability time in hours} - \text{Total downtime in hours}}{\text{Number of breaks}}$$

$$\text{Maintainability (MTRS in hours)} = \frac{\text{Total downtime in hours}}{\text{Number of service breaks}}$$

Use MTRS to avoid ambiguity with the more common mean time to repair (MTTR) which in some definitions includes only repair, but in others includes recovery time. The down time in MTRS covers all factors that make the service, component or CI unavailable include time to record, respond, resolve, physically repair or replace, and recover.

Vital business function (VBF)
Part of a business process that is critical to the success of the business; an important consideration of business continuity management, IT service continuity management and availability management.

Availability terms, related measurements, inter-relationships

SD Figure 4.8: Availability terms and measurements

© Crown copyright 2011. Reproduced under license from the Cabinet Office.

Although the key SLA service target is availability, if customers want reliability and maintainability targets in the SLA. they should cover end-to-end service reliability and maintainability; in OLAs and UCs they should cover component and supporting service targets and often include availability targets for components or supporting services.

Certain VBFs may need special designs in service design plans, incorporating:

- **High availability** A characteristic of the IT service that minimizes or masks the effects of IT component failure to the users of a service.
- **Fault tolerance** The ability of an IT service, component or CI to continue to operate correctly after failure of a component part.
- **Continuous operation** An approach or design to eliminate planned downtime of an IT service. Note that individual components or CIs may be down even though the IT service remains available.
- **Continuous availability** Approach or design to achieve 100% availability. A continuously available IT service has no planned or unplanned downtime.

ITILFND03-03-16 Define and explain service knowledge management system (SKMS) (ST 4.7.4.3)

Service Knowledge Management System (SKMS)

Service Knowledge Management System (SKMS)
A set of tools and databases that is used to manage knowledge, information and data. The SKMS includes the Configuration Management System (CMS), as well as other databases and information systems. The SKMS includes tools for collecting, storing, managing, updating, analyzing and presenting all the knowledge, information and data that an IT service provider will need to manage the full lifecycle of IT services.

The SKMS will contain many different types of data, information and knowledge. Examples of items that should be stored in an SKMS include:
- The service portfolio
- The configuration management system (CMS)
- The definitive media library (DML)
- Service level agreements (SLAs), contracts, operation level agreements (OLAs)

Specifically within IT service management, knowledge management will be focused within the service knowledge management system (SKMS), which is concerned, as its name implies, with knowledge. Underpinning this knowledge will be a considerable quantity of data, which will also be held in the SKMS. One very important part of the SKMS is the configuration management system (CMS). The CMS describes the attributes and relationships of configuration items, many of which are themselves knowledge, information or data assets stored in the SKMS.

Other examples of items that should be stored in an SKMS include:
- The information security policy
- The supplier and contract management information system (SCMIS), including suppliers' and partners' requirements, abilities and expectations
- Budgets, cost models, business plans, CSI register, service improvement plans
- The capacity plan and capacity management information system (CMIS)
- The availability plan and availability management information system (AMIS)
- Service continuity invocation procedure
- Service reports
- A discussion forum where practitioners can ask questions, answer each other's questions, and search for previous questions and answers
- An indexed and searchable repository of project plans from previous projects
- A known error database provided by a vendor which lists common issues in their product and how to resolve them
- Skills register, and typical and anticipated user skill levels
- Diagnostic scripts
- A managed set of web-based training courses
- Weather reports, needed to support business and IT decision-making
- Customer/user personal information, for example to support a blind user who needs to have specific support from the service desk

Configuration records, pointing to and describing configuration items, are stored in the CMDB in the CMS within the SKMS. The CMDB feeds through the CMS into the SKMS.

ITILFND03-03-16 Define and explain service knowledge management system (SKMS)
(ST 4.7.4.3)

To run a services business well – and make no mistake, with IT service management, you are running IT as a services business – you must have timely insight into key information for decision and action. You must know:

- What services you have planned; what current services you offer, and what services you have retired (the three parts of the service portfolio)
- You must have a tool to access information about all the items in your configuration and how they relate to one another (the CMS)
- You must have a 'single source of truth', a definitive place where you store your original OEM software, the definitive versions of in-house developed software, and licensing information, a source that you draw on when you build things out for production so you don't shoot yourself and others in the foot (the DML)
- You must know, for each service, the 'agreement stack' and ensure it adds up to support consistent service delivery and support as agreed with customers (SLAs, OLAs, and UCs)
- You must have ready access to secure, version-controlled definitive copies of all key documents as listed on the 'other examples' list on the facing page.

The general idea with the SKMS is it is the all-encompassing container for all knowledge about services, including specifications, historical information, etc. It includes not just the data and information itself, but also the tools to access, present, search, traverse, secure, and control that information.

For examination purposes, the key thing to remember is that the SKMS includes just about everything else.

What sort of information does your organization keep track of, and how does it compare to the list on the left? Is the information up to date and readily accessible? If so or if not, what is happening in the organization because of it?

Configuration Items (CIs), CI categories

Service Knowledge Management System (SKMS)
A set of tools and databases that is used to manage knowledge, information and data. The SKMS includes the Configuration Management System (CMS), as well as other databases and information systems. The SKMS includes tools for collecting, storing, managing, updating, analyzing and presenting all the knowledge, information and data that an IT service provider will need to manage the full lifecycle of IT services.

There will be a variety of CIs; the following categories may help to identify them:

CI Categories	Description
Service Lifecycle CIs	Services, how delivered, expected benefits, costs, and when realized
Service CIs	Service capability assets / service resource assets
Organization CIs	Documentation (e.g., business strategy, policies)
Internal CIs	From individual projects, tangible and intangible assets
External CIs	External customer requirements and agreements
Interface CIs	To deliver end-to-end service

CIs may vary widely in complexity, size and type, ranging from an entire service or system including all hardware, software, documentation and support staff to a single software module or a minor hardware component. CIs may be grouped and managed together: e.g. a set of components may be grouped into a release. CIs should be selected using established selection criteria, grouped, classified and identified in such a way that they are manageable and traceable throughout the service lifecycle. The following are example categories of CIs:

- **Service lifecycle CIs** such as a business case give a picture of the service provider's services, how they will be delivered, what benefits are expected, at what cost and when they will be realized.
- **Service CIs**: include *capability assets*: management, organization, processes, knowledge, people and *resource* assets: financial capital, systems, applications, information, data, infrastructure and facilities, financial capital, people, and service model / package, release package, acceptance criteria
- **Organization CIs** – some documentation will define the characteristics of a CI whereas other documentation will be a CI in its own right and need to be controlled.
- **Internal CIs** comprising those delivered by individual projects, including tangible (data center) and intangible assets.
- **External CIs** such as external customer requirements and agreements, releases from suppliers or sub-contractors and external services.
- **Interface CIs** that are required to deliver the end-to-end service across a service provider interface (SPI), for example an escalation document that specifies how incidents will be transferred between two service providers.

ITILFND03-03-17 Define and explain configuration item (CI) (ST 4.3.4.2)

It is important to note that CIs include not just hardware and software components (which is what might typically come to mind in terms of items in your infrastructure), but also things like:

- Entire **IT services** (this makes sense as there is a recursive relationship among CIs – just as an entire airplane is a part, and its wing is a part, with sub-assemblies that are parts, and so on, so to an IT services is made up of components and sub-components, each of which is a CI)
- **Buildings** – yes, facilities are CIs
- **People** – this one throws many IT professionals for a loop, and is important to remember for examination purposes – think about it – don't you want to know about the people related to a service, and how they relate (what their role is)? When introducing a service, or when changing a service, how will you fully assess impact if you don't know this? Can you see that if you don't know this you might make a change and miss an implication with negative results? (For example, if you swap out the database for a new technology and don't consider support, and it is a highly available system with no support staff trained on that technology available on weekends, you've got yourself a problem).
- **Documentation** – as with the example above, key documentation like architecture diagrams and troubleshooting guides must be packaged with the design or else you will have problems downstream with service support and delivery; when a change is made, it is vital that if the change affects these documents then that change is reflected in the documents – how will you ensure this is done if these documents are not managed as CIs and related to the system, so that when reviewing the impact of the change, their update can be included?

As for categories of CIs, in practice it is useful to tag related CIs into groups that make sense for management and reporting purposes. For example, you may ask questions like, "how many distribution servers do we have deployed in ASIAPAC region that look like such and such?" when considering the impact of a change. Grouping / associating CIs to categories helps you get to this information quickly.

Useful categories of CIs include:

- Service lifecycle CIs – all the documents use to manage the CI through its lifecycle
- External CIs – it is important to have visibility into CIs your services depend on, even and especially if they are external to your organization
- Interface CIs – cross-organization and provider boundaries and handoffs are where service support and delivery can often break down so it may be useful to call out and manage these CIs as this type

ITILFND03-03-18 Define and explain configuration management system (ST 4.3.4.3)

Configuration Management System (CMS)
A set of tools, data and information that is used to support service asset and configuration management

- Holds all the information about CIs within the designated scope
- Used for a wide range of purposes, e.g. asset data held in the CMS may be made available to external fixed asset management systems to perform financial reporting outside service asset and configuration management
- Maintains the relationships between all service components and may also include records for related incidents, problems, known errors, changes and releases
- May include data from configuration records stored in several physical CMDBs, which come together at the information integration layer to form an integrated CMDB

To manage large and complex IT services and infrastructures, service asset and configuration management requires the use of a supporting system known as the configuration management system (CMS).

The CMS holds all information about CIs within the designated scope. Some of these items will have related specifications or files that contain the contents of the item, and these should be stored in the SKMS. For example, a service CI will include the details such as supplier, cost, purchase date and renewal date for licenses and maintenance contracts; related documentation such as SLAs and underpinning contracts will be in the SKMS.

Changes to every configuration item must be authorized by change management and all updates must include updates to the relevant configuration records. In some organizations, authority to modify CIs within the SKMS is assigned to configuration librarians, who are also responsible for modifying the configuration records in the CMS. In other organizations there is a separation of duties to ensure that no one person can update both the asset in the SKMS and the corresponding configuration record in the CMS.

The CMS maintains the relationships between all service components and may also include records for related incidents, problems, known errors, changes and releases. The CMS may also link to corporate data about employees, suppliers, locations and business units, customers and users; alternatively, the CMS may hold copies of this information, depending on the capabilities of the tools in use.

At the data level, the CMS may include data from configuration records stored in several physical CMDBs, which come together at the information integration layer to form an integrated CMDB. The integrated CMDB may also incorporate information from external data sources such as an HR or financial database. Since this data is normally owned by other business units, agreements will be needed about what data is to be made available and how it will be accessed and maintained. This arrangement should be formally documented in an OLA. The CMS will provide access to (versus duplicate) external data wherever possible.

ITILFND03-03-18 Define and explain configuration management system (ST 4.3.4.3)

It is necessary but not sufficient to support service management to have data about CIs and how they relate to one another so that you can plan and manage, assess the impact of changes, and the extent of incidents and problems. You must have easy access to that information.

The CMS therefore covers storage, retrieval, presentation, and reporting. There are some key areas where automation to support service management is necessary, and this is one of them.

Note that the CMS draws on one or more physical configuration management databases (CMDBs); this is often the case and a federated CMDB model is often the choice. There are many reasons for this, not the least of which is assigning ownership of the data locally where the details and context are understood and the integrity of data is of primary importance.

What sort of tool(s) do you have in place that function as a CMS? What sort of CMDBs, can you locate these in your organization? How accurate is the information they provide? How easy is it to access? Think of some instances where the data provided has made a critical difference – positive and negative – in a decision and action taken around changes and problems.

For examination purposes remember that the CMS is contained in the SKMS and is the tool that accesses the CMDB, and not the same as the CMDB.

ITILFND03-03-19 Define and explain definitive media library (DML) (ST 4.3.4.4)

Definitive Media Library (DML)
One or more locations in which the definitive and authorized versions of all software
configuration items are securely stored. The definitive media library may also contain associated
configuration items such as licenses and documentation. It is a single logical storage area even
if there are multiple locations. The definitive media library is controlled by service asset and
configuration management and is recorded in the configuration management system.

- May consist of one or more software libraries or file-storage areas, separate from development, test or live file store areas
- Contains the master copies of all controlled software in an organization
- Should include definitive copies of purchased software (along with license documents or information), as well as software developed on site
- Master copies of controlled documentation for a system are also stored in the DML in electronic form

The exact configuration of the DML is defined during the planning activities. The definition includes:
- Medium, physical location, hardware and software to be used, if kept online – some service asset and configuration management support tools incorporate document or software libraries, which can be regarded as a logical part of a DML
- Naming conventions for file-store areas and physical media
- Environments supported, e.g. test and live environments
- Security arrangements for submitting changes and issuing documentation and software, plus backup and recovery procedures
- The scope of the DML, e.g. source code, object code from controlled builds and associated documentation
- Archive and retention periods
- Capacity plans for the DML and procedures for monitoring growth in size
- Audit procedures
- Procedures to ensure that the DML is protected from erroneous or unauthorized change (e.g. entry and exit criteria for items)
- Procedures to ensure that the DML is backed up and that the contents are available for use in service continuity plans as appropriate

Electronic assets in the DML are held within the SKMS, and every item in the DML is a CI.

ITILFND03-03-19 Define and explain definitive media library (DML) (ST 4.3.4.4)

There are a couple of concepts in ITIL that are by themselves worth the price of the effort required to absorb and apply the material. The DML is one of them. Think about all the issues in organizations caused by drawing from an unsanctioned, incorrect, out of date source when building out capability in production; hours wasted troubleshooting 'ghosty' issues; things like 2500 salespersons laptops being loaded with a prerelease version of the operating system (unfortunately a real example) because the CD used was the one under the pizza box in the build room L.

What is wonderful is that a relatively simply shared commitment about 'how we do things around here' and a simple, almost Luddite concept and mechanism can help snap this vicious cycle and turn it into a virtuous one. And that concept is the DML.

Quite simply, with the DML we agree that we are going to load all the definitive versions (read: versions that are approved for use – important! More than one version can be definitive at one time, for example, when you are straddling one or more approved versions of an OS) our original OEM software and associated licensing information and documentation, and all our in-house developed software, our "golden bits" – and we further agree that when we build out capability for production we will draw from this known good source so that we avoid shooting ourselves and others in the foot.

The authors cannot begin to tell you how powerful and effective this one simple idea is in organizations. It takes some commitment and hygiene, but the results (and associated turndown of trouble and strife) are well worth it.

For examination purposes, it is important to remember that the DML contains not just software but licensing information and system documentation; that the DML (like just about everything else) is contained in the SKMS; that the DML is a physical store that can be made electronic (if you consider that the origins of this idea date back to the days of the tape library and tape librarians, with a physical fireproof media vault in the data center, subject to the organization's records retention policies, this makes sense).

ITILFND03-03-20 Define and explain change (ST 4.2.4.4)

Request for Change (RFC)
A formal proposal for a change to be made. It includes details of the proposed change, and may be recorded on paper or electronically. The term RFC is often misused to mean a change record, or the change itself.

Change
The addition, modification or removal of anything that could have an effect on IT services. The scope should include changes to all architectures, processes, tools, metrics and documentation, as well as changes to IT services and other configuration items.

Change Record
A record containing the details of a change. Each change record documents the lifecycle of a single change. A change record is created for every request for change that is received, even those that are subsequently rejected.

The terms 'change', 'change record' and 'RFC' are often used inconsistently, leading to confusion.

- **Change** – the addition, modification or removal of anything that could have an effect on IT services. The scope should include changes to all architectures, processes, tools, metrics and documentation, as well as changes to IT services and other configuration items.
- **RFC** – a request for change – a formal proposal for a change to be made. It includes details of the proposed change, and may be recorded on paper or electronically. The term 'RFC' is often misused to mean a change record, or the change itself.
- **Change record** – a record containing the details of a change. Each change record documents the lifecycle of a single change. A change record is created for every request for change that is received, even those that are subsequently rejected. Change records should reference the configuration items that are affected by the change. Change records may be stored in the configuration management system or elsewhere in the service knowledge management system.

RFCs are only used to submit requests; they are not used to communicate the decisions of change management or to document the details of the change. A change record contains all the required information about a change, including information from the RFC, and is used to manage the lifecycle of that change.

ITILFND03-03-20 Define and explain change (ST 4.2.4.4)

An RFC is a form or screen filled out to formally propose that a change be made. It includes (or should include) all details necessary to make a go / no-go decision on the change – who, what, where, when, why, how, and how much.

ITIL distinguished between the RFC, Change Record, and the Change itself. The Change Record may draw on information originally included in the RFC, but is distinct, and used throughout the lifecycle of the Change. The change itself is of course distinct from what is recorded about it in the RFC and Change Record, although obviously related – this should be obvious but is worth stating. For example, the change itself (let us say flattening and rebuilding a server) is related but distinct from the form or screen (RFC) request for change and the Change Record recording details of the change.

Does your organization and the tools you use to manage change distinguish between the change itself, an RFC, and change record as ITIL does? Where do your language used and tools vary from this? Can you think of an issue this has caused?

Change request TYPES: Standard, emergency, normal

Change type	Description
Standard	A pre-authorized change that is low risk, relatively common and follows a procedure or work instruction – for example, a password reset or provision of standard equipment to a new employee. Requests for change are not required to implement a standard change, and they are logged and tracked using a different mechanism, such as a service request. Examples include: • An upgrade of a PC to use specific standard, pre-budgeted software • Provision of standard equipment and services to a new employee • Desktop move for a single user • Low-impact, routine application change to handle seasonal variation
Emergency	A change that must be introduced as soon as possible – for example, to resolve a major incident or implement a security patch. The change management process will normally have a specific procedure for handling emergency changes. See also emergency change advisory board. Emergency changes are sometimes required and should be designed carefully and tested as much as possible before use, or the impact of the emergency change may be greater than the original incident. Details of emergency changes may be documented retrospectively. The number of emergency changes proposed should be kept to an absolute minimum, as they are more disruptive and prone to failure.
Normal	Any service change that is not a standard change or an emergency change. There are three types of normal changes: Minor change – authorized by change management staff directly Significant change – requires advice from change advisory board (CAB) Major change – requires change proposal, business management approval

A change request is a formal communication seeking an alteration to one or more configuration items. This could take several forms, e.g. a 'request for change' document, service desk call or project initiation document. Different types of change require different types of requests. For example, a major change may require a change proposal, which is usually created by the service portfolio management process. An organization needs to ensure appropriate procedures and forms are available to cover anticipated requests.

Changes are often categorized as major, significant and minor, depending on the level of cost and risk involved, and on the scope and relationship to other changes. This categorization may be used to identify an appropriate change authority. As much use as possible should be made of devolved authorization, both through the standard change procedure and through the authorization of minor changes by change management staff.

ITILFND03-03-21 Define and explain change types (standard, emergency and normal) (ST 4.2.4.3, 4.2.4.7, 4.2.5.11)

It is vitally important to distinguish between and correctly classify change requests as standard, emergency or normal change request types. The reason is simple: you don't have an army of people and unlimited time to assess each change – each assessment is time-bound, like a mariner's decision to change course – so you want to put the least amount of (and correct) "eyeballs" on the change request that is necessary to make a good go / no-go decision.

Standard changes are a key throttling mechanism to reduce the number of eyeballs required for a change to be approved. Standard changes are pre-approved by policy – the idea here is, "go ahead and make the change, it is pre-approved, the Change Authority doesn't have to be called on to approve this, he or she just wants to make sure there is a record of it". For clarity: the Change Manager is often the Change Authority, but it doesn't have to be -- for example within normal or minor changes the Change Authority might well be the Operations Manager.

Emergency changes follow a fast track and require intense scrutiny after the fact (post-implementation review) to ensure this fast-track mechanism isn't abused. Why did this require an emergency change? How could it have been prevented? How do we prevent it in the future? Emergency changes of course require "eyeballs' on the change, and are normally reviewed and approved (or kicked back) by the emergency change advisory board (ECAB) which is a subset of the CAB, typically made up of the Change and Problem Managers.

Normal changes require "eyeballs" on them as well, different and increasing levels based on the nature of the change.

For **normal, minor changes**, the Change Authority can either approve or reject himself or herself. For example, adding memory to a non-vital server may be a minor change. The general spirit here is, "this is minor – go ahead and knock yourself out".

For **normal, significant changes**, the Change Authority doesn't have enough information to make a good decision around the change, so he/she needs advice, and turns to the change advisory board (CAB) for advice. For example if a new SAN technology is being proposed for a system upgrade, the Change Authority will want to make sure the vendor, with their Technical Services / Infrastructure Engineering teams, is at the table at the CAB meeting to advise him/her on the change so he or she can make a good decision.

For **normal, major changes**, those with major implications for the business, significant risk, allocation of resources or disbursement of funds, the Change Authority must call on the business (executive management) to consider and approve or reject the change.

So you see that by classify change request types, we are attempting to get only the number and type of "eyeballs" on the change necessary to make a good decision to go or not go on the change.

ITILFND03-03-24, 25, 26 Define and explain event (SO 4.1 1st paragraph), 3-25 alert (glossary), 3-26 incident (SO 4.2 1st paragraph)

Events, Alerts, and Incidents

Event

A change of state that has significance for the management of an IT service or other configuration item. The term is also used to mean an alert or notification created by any IT service, configuration item or monitoring tool. Events typically require IT operations personnel to take actions, and often lead to incidents being logged.

Alert

A notification that a threshold has been reached, something has changed, or a failure has occurred. Alerts are often created and managed by system management tools and are managed by the event management process.

Incident

An unplanned interruption to an IT service or reduction in the quality of an IT service. Failure of a configuration item that has not yet affected service is also an incident – for example, failure of one disk from a mirror set.

Events

Events are typically recognized through notifications created by an IT service, CI or monitoring tool. Effective service operation is dependent on knowing the status of the infrastructure and detecting any deviation from normal or expected operation. This is provided by good monitoring and control systems, which are based on two types of tools:

- **Active monitoring tools** – poll key CIs to determine their status and availability. Any exceptions will generate an alert that needs to be communicated to the appropriate tool or team for action.
- **Passive monitoring tools** – detect and correlate operational alerts or communications generated by CIs

Alerts

Notifications that a threshold has been reached, something has changed, or a failure has occurred. Alerts are often created and managed by system management tools and are managed by the event management process.

Incidents

An incident is an unplanned interruption to an IT service or reduction in quality of an IT service or a failure of a CI that has not yet impacted an IT service.

Relationship between Events, Alerts, and Incidents

- All Alerts are Events but not all Events trigger an Alert
- All Incidents are Events but all Events are not Incidents

ITILFND03-03-24, 25, 26 Define and explain event (SO 4.1 1st paragraph), 3-25 alert (glossary), 3-26 incident (SO 4.2 1st paragraph)

An event is something that has happened that is of management significance; it could be informational, "I've cut a log file, just want you to know", a warning, "utilization on that circuit is approaching the threshold you set of 20%, you probably want to know that", or an exception, "e.g., danger Will Robinson, critical server down".

An alert is a notification of an event. So you see not all events require or spawn alerts (I do not want to be paged for an informational, you'll clog up the system – just tell me about exceptions).

Similarly, only some events spawn incidents; from the examples above, you can be sure critical server down exceptions will be auto-ticketed into incident records, and in some cases warnings may result in the same (so that action can be tracked and taken to preempt performance or availability issues).

You will likely have a test question on the exam that is designed to ensure you can distinguish between events, alerts, and incidents, so make sure you understand the distinction.

Some of the language used in the ITIL books around this could be clearer:
• All Alerts are Events but not all Events trigger an Alert
• All Incidents are Events but all Events are not Incidents

Further guidance will help understanding. In the example given we suggest that another way to consider this is that all Alerts are triggered by Events but not all Events trigger an Alert" and "All Incidents are triggered by Events but not all Events (e.g. informational) trigger Incidents".

ITILFND03-03-27 Define and explain impact, urgency and priority (SO 4.2.5.4)

Impact	A measure of the effect of incident, problem, or change on business processes • How service levels will be affected
Urgency	A measure of how long it will be until an incident, problem or change has a significant impact on the business
Priority	A category used to identify the relative importance of an incident, problem or change. Priority is based on impact and urgency, and is used to identify required times for actions to be taken. • For example, the service level agreement may state that Priority 2 incidents must be resolved within 12 hours

Incident prioritization can normally be determined by taking into account both the urgency of the incident (how quickly the business needs a resolution) and the level of business impact it is causing. An indication of impact is often (but not always) the number of users being affected. In some cases, the loss of service to a single user can have a major business impact – it all depends upon who is trying to do what – so numbers alone are not enough to evaluate overall priority! Other factors that can contribute to impact levels are:

- Risk to life or limb
- The number of services affected – may be multiple services
- The level of financial losses
- Effect on business reputation
- Regulatory or legislative breaches

SO Table 4.1 gives an effective way of calculating the elements and deriving overall priority.

SO Table 4.1: Simple priority coding system

Urgency	Impact			
		High	Medium	Low
	High	1	2	3
	Medium	2	3	4
	Low	3	4	5
Priority code	**Description**	**Target resolution time**		
1	Critical	1 hour		
2	High	8 hours		
3	Medium	24 hours		
4	Low	48 hours		
5	Planning	Planned		

Clear guidance – produced during service level negotiations – should be provided for all support staff to enable them to determine the correct urgency, impact and priority.

An incident's priority may be dynamic – if circumstances change, or if an incident is not resolved within SLA target times, then the priority must be altered to reflect the new situation. Changes to priority that might occur in the management of an incident should be recorded in the incident record to provide an audit trail of why the priority was changed.

ITILFND03-03-27 Define and explain impact, urgency and priority (SO 4.2.5.4)

Prioritization in some organizations is a black art, with no real algorithm in shared common use; this typically leads to incidents, problems and changes being pursued in an order and with resources assigned that are out of step with the true priority of the issue.

ITIL attempts to clarify the components of priority, in an effort to make the components of the calculation clearer and better.

For examination purposes, it is important to remember that **Urgency** follows a time vector only (when do you need it?). **Impact** is generally the number of nodes or users affected (how widespread is this?) but can also be deep impact based on the nature of the scenario, system and user(s) even if it is just one or a few users or nodes involved. **Priority** is the highest order idea, and contains impact, urgency, and all other factors such as technical severity.

ITILFND03-03-28 Define and explain service request (SO 4.3 1st paragraph)

Service Request
A formal request from a user for something to be provided – for example, a request for information or advice; to reset a password; or to install a workstation for a new user. Service requests are managed by the request fulfillment process, usually in conjunction with the service desk. Service requests may be linked to a request for change as part of fulfilling the request.

Examples of service requests include:
- Request to change a password
- Request to install a new software application on a particular workstation
- Request to relocate some items of desktop equipment

The term 'service request' is used as a generic description for many different types of demands that are placed upon the IT organization by the users. Many of these are typically requests for small changes that are low risk, frequently performed, low cost etc. (e.g. a request to change a password, a request to install an additional software application onto a particular workstation, a request to relocate some items of desktop equipment) or may be just a request for information.

Their scale and frequent, low-risk nature means that they are better handled by a separate process, rather than being allowed to congest and obstruct the normal incident and change management processes. Effective request fulfillment has a very important role in maintaining end user satisfaction with the services they are receiving and can directly impact how well IT is perceived throughout the business.

ITILFND03-03-28 Define and explain service request (SO 4.3.1ST paragraph)

ITIL distinguishes among the following scenarios:
- Something is broken, I can't work (an Incident)
- Something needs to be introduced or changed that is of management significance / constitutes a material change in your configuration specification (a Change)
- Someone needs something that falls within the normal operation of a system, e.g., can you add me to that print queue or reset my password (a Service Request) or I am requesting something that does involve a change (in which case there is a Service Request that is linked to an RFC as part of fulfilling the request)

The general need is for things to get fixed and for requests to be handled, but at the same time, that we have a record of any changes that are made that cause material changes to CI specifications (either net new equipment or material changes to existing equipment). And the changes must be tracked in the change system, to ensure visibility. Here are some scenarios to consider:
- A user calls with a broken hard drive; an incident is logged and the hard drive is swapped out like-for-like – same size, model, etc.; there is no need for an RFC to be raised and linked because there is no material change to the CI specification
- A user calls with a broken printer and the printer cannot be fixed and cannot be swapped out like-for-like as the model is no longer available; the user is given a new printer after an RFC is raised and linked to the incident ticket; this ensures traceability of 'what changed?'

Service requests are more like work orders ("please do this for me") than incident tickets. Although some organizations track these in their incident or change systems because of system limitations, service requests are distinct in that they are sometimes handled by different teams with different workflows than incidents, and need to be reported on and managed separately from incidents and changes.

Does your organization distinguish between incidents, changes and service requests? Is linking a service request or incident that requires a material change to CIs a common practice in your organization? If not, can you recall issues that have occurred as a result?

ITILFND03-03-29 Define and explain problem (SO 4.4 1st paragraph)

Problem
A cause of one or more incidents. The cause is not usually known at the time a problem record is created, and the problem management process is responsible for further investigation.

- The lifecycle of all problems is managed by Problem Management
- Prioritized in the same way and for the same reasons as incidents
  - Frequency + impact of related incidents also taken into account

The severity of a problem can be determined by answering the following questions:
Can the system be recovered, or does it need to be replaced?
- How much will it cost?
- How many people, and what skills, will be needed to fix the problem?
- How long will it take to fix the problem?
- How extensive is the problem (e.g. how many CIs are affected)?

ITILFND03-03-29 Define and explain problem (SO 4.4.1ST paragraph)

Getting clear on the distinction between a problem and an incident is very important. A problem is the root cause of one or more incidents. Let us say on a Monday morning we start experiencing users calling because their drive mappings have dropped off (they have mapped a drive, e.g., to a team shared file store, and that mapping is no longer there).

The service desk will log each incident and workaround by helping each user remap their drive. But they keep dropping off. At the end of the day we have 854 instances of drive mappings dropping off. We have a problem.

Something (the problem) is causing all of these drive mappings to drop off. If our ticketing system allows for it, we create a problem record and link all of the instances of the drive mapping dropping off incidents to it; we store workaround information linked to the problem ticket for easy reference. The service desk continues to fix incidents that come in, but we still have a problem to solve.

Someone needs to figure out when the problem started, where the problem is located, and to identify a solution. In this case a team led by the problem manager, and including the service desk manager and some network engineers, works to locate the root cause.

First they try to isolate the problem to a specific new kind of network card to see if that is the issue by correlating the incidents to the users machines; it turns out there is no correlation.

Then they look at what changed over the weekend; it turns out a change was made to the microcode on some routers. After some investigation it is determined that this is causing the issue; after further investigation it is determined that a patch is needed from the manufacturer to fix the problem; an RFC is raised; a Change is approved and scheduled; the change is applied; the problem goes away; the incidents stop occurring.

Some things to remember for testing purposes: very important – an incident and a problem are not the same thing, a problem is the root cause of one or more incidents; secondly, an incident doesn't 'become' a problem; a problem always stands separate from but related to the incidents it causes.

ITILFND03-03-30 Define and explain workaround (SO 4.4.5.6)

Problem
A cause of one or more incidents. The cause is not usually known at the time a problem record is created, and the problem management process is responsible for further investigation.

- Temporary way of overcoming the difficulties
- Workarounds for problems documented in known error records
- Problem record remains open until solution is found

Example: a manual amendment may be made to a corrupted input file to allow a program to complete its run successfully and allow a billing process to complete satisfactorily

In some cases it may be possible to find a workaround to the incidents caused by the problem – a temporary way of overcoming the difficulties. It is important that work on a permanent resolution continues where this is justified – in this example the reason for the file becoming corrupted in the first place must be found and corrected to prevent this happening again.

When a workaround is found, it is therefore important that the problem record remains open and details of the workaround are documented within the problem record.

In some cases there may be multiple workarounds associated with a problem. As problem investigation and diagnosis activities carry on, there may be a series of improvements that do not resolve the problem, but lead to a progressive improvement in the quality of the workarounds available. These may impact on the prioritization of the problem as successive workaround solutions may reduce the impact of future related incidents, either by reducing their likelihood or improving the speed of their resolution.

ITILFND03-03-30 Define and explain workaround (SO 4.4.5.6)

A workaround does not fix a problem; it literally 'works around' it. In the example in the previous topic, showing users how to remap their mapped drives when they drop off doesn't solve the root cause of the problem, it just 'works around' – this is an example of a workaround.

Another example: a user is running late for her meeting and needs to print out slides in color for the executives at the meeting; the color laser in the printer kiosk on her floor is down; she calls the service desk, and the analysts shows her how to route her print stream to the print kiosk on the next floor up; the analyst has 'worked around' the issue; an trouble ticket still needs to be cut and a work order made for the printer to be fixed, but in the meantime, the issue has been worked around. The analyst can use that same workaround for other users on that floor until the printer at their kiosk is fixed.

For testing purposes it is important to remember that workarounds for problems are stored in known error records (a problem is an unknown error and has its own record; as information accumulates about the problem towards and through resolution, it is stored in a linked known error record).

In general, you should be able to identify a verbatim definition of an incident, service request, problem, known error, and workaround, and distinguish between them.

ITILFND03-03-31 Define and explain known error (SO 4.4.5.7)

Known error
A problem that has a documented root cause and a workaround. Known errors are created and managed throughout their lifecycle by problem management. Known errors may also be identified by development or suppliers.

- The known error record should identify the problem record it relates to and document the status of actions being taken to resolve the problem, its root cause and workaround
- All known error records should be stored in the Known Error Database (KEDB)

As soon as the diagnosis is complete, and particularly where a workaround has been found (even though it may not yet be a permanent resolution), a known error record must be raised and placed in the KEDB so that if further incidents or problems arise, they can be identified and the service restored more quickly. In some cases it may be advantageous to raise a known error record even earlier in the overall process, even though the diagnosis may not be complete or a workaround found. This might be used for information purposes or to identify a root cause or workaround that appears to address the problem but hasn't been fully confirmed. Therefore, it is inadvisable to set a concrete procedural point for exactly when a known error record must be raised. It should be done as soon as it becomes useful to do so!

ITILFND03-03-31 Define and explain known error (SO 4.4.5.7)

Some IT professionals take issue with ITIL's definition of a known error; they state that there are instances where a root cause can be found but there literally is no workaround for it. For examination purposes, it is important to take the ITIL view: a known error is, "a problem that had a documented root cause **and** a workaround" (emphasis added).

The whole idea with recording known errors in records is to make sure information on the problem and in particular workarounds can be disseminated quickly and completely through the organization to minimize the impact of the problem as long as it is active, and to provide a record for comparison and possible use if similar problems occur again in the future.

For testing purposes, remember that a problem is an unknown error, and a known error is well known – the root cause is known. You must be able to distinguish between the two and know which is applicable given a scenario.

ITILFND03-03-32 Define and explain known error database (KEDB) (SO 4.4.7.2)

Known Error Database (KEDB)
A database containing all known error records. This database is created by problem management
and used by incident and problem management. The known error database may be part of
the configuration management system, or may be stored elsewhere in the service knowledge
management system.

- The purpose of a KEDB is to allow storage of previous knowledge of incidents and problems – and how they were overcome – to allow quicker diagnosis and resolution if they recur
- The KEDB should be used during the incident and problem diagnosis phases to try to speed up the resolution process – and new records should be added as quickly as possible when a new problem has been identified and diagnosed
- The KEDB is part of the CMS and may be part of a larger SKMS

The known error record should hold exact details of the fault and symptoms that occurred, together with precise details of any workaround or resolution action that can be taken to restore the service and/or resolve the problem. An incident count will also be useful to determine the frequency with which incidents are likely to recur and influence priorities, etc.

A business case for a permanent resolution for some problems may not exist. For example, if a problem does not cause serious disruption and a workaround exists and/or the cost of resolving the problem far outweighs the benefits of a permanent resolution, then a decision may be taken to tolerate the problem. However, it will still be desirable to diagnose and implement a workaround as quickly as possible, which is where the KEDB can help.

It is essential that any data put into the database can be quickly and accurately retrieved. The problem manager should be fully trained and familiar with the search methods/algorithms used by the selected database and should carefully ensure that when new records are added the relevant search key criteria are correctly included.

Care should be taken to avoid duplication of records (i.e. the same problem described in two or more ways as separate records). To avoid this, the problem manager should be the only person able to enter a new record. Other support groups should be encouraged to propose new records, but these should be vetted by the problem manager before entry to the KEDB. In large organizations where a single KEDB is used (recommended) with problem management staff in multiple locations, a procedure must be agreed to ensure duplication of KEDB records cannot occur, e.g., by designating one person as central KEDB manager.

All support staff should be fully trained and conversant with the value that the KEDB can offer and the way it should be used. They should be able readily to retrieve and use data.

ITILFND03-03-32 Define and explain known error database (KEDB) (SO 4.4.7.2)

Where do we store known errors? Why, in the known error database (KEDB) of course. And what is the KEDB contained within? Why, the SKMS of course (while it may be a bit of an exaggeration to state that just about everything is contained in the SKMS, for testing purposes, it does not hurt to think this way).

Why track known errors in their own database? Well, it is analogous to a bug tracking database for an application prior to production (in fact, at transfer to production, all known errors with an application currently in the development bug tracking database should be transferred to the live application KEDB): you want to have a clear idea of what known errors exist, one place to go for workarounds, to speed dissemination of information and diagnosis.

What does your organization do relative to this practice? Do you distinguish between problems and known errors (and for that matter, incidents?)? If so, how does this help? If not, what is the impact on the organization?

ITILFND03-03-33 Define and explain the role of communication in service operation (SO 3.6)

the Role of Communication in Service Operation

- Good communication is needed with other IT teams and departments, with users and internal customers, and between the service operation teams and departments
- Issues can often be prevented or mitigated with appropriate communication
- All communication must have an intended purpose or a resultant action
- Do not communicate information unless there is a clear audience
- That audience should have been actively involved in determining the need for that communication and what they will do with the information
- There should be review of ongoing communications on a periodic basis to validate that they are still required by the audience

Communication is primary and the means of communication must ensure that they serve this goal. It is possible to use any means of communication as long as all stakeholders understand how and when the communication will take place and indicate their need to continue to use it. Types of Communication Typical in Service Operation include:

Routine operational communication	Communication between shifts	Performance reporting
Communication in projects	Communication related to changes	Communication related to exceptions
Communication related to emergencies	Training on new or customized processes and service designs	Communication of strategy, design and transition to service operation

There is no definitive medium for communication, nor is there a fixed location or frequency. In some organizations communication has to take place in meetings. Other organizations prefer to use email or the communication inherent in their service management tools.

There should therefore be a policy around communication within each team or department and for each process. Although this should be formal, the policy should not be cumbersome or complex. For example, a manager might require that all communications regarding changes must be sent by email. As long as this is specified in the department's SOPs, there is no need to create a separate policy for it.

ITILFND03-03-33 Define and explain the role of communication in service operation
(SO 3.6)

It is likely that exam questions will be in list format for this question, for example, which of the following is a list of typical communications in service operation? You will have to pick the real examples out from the false ones, and that includes picking out the verbatim, real answers from non-verbatim, plausible ones.

One key tip for handling list questions is to start from the back of the lists and compare values; typically the more plausible answers are at the front of the list; in this way you can use the process of elimination faster to get through the question.

Take the time to examine the diagram on the facing page; if you have spent any amount of time in service operation, you should see these are indeed the 'usual suspects' of communication in service operation: routine communications, shift turnover, reporting, communications related to projects, changes, and exceptions (critical events worthy of management attention), emergencies; training and communication related to service transition, and communications relative to strategy and design.

Meetings are part of communication in service operation; the factors for successful meetings are no different than in other parts of the business, but worth noting: having and communicating (in advance!) a clear agenda, ensuring meeting rules and procedures like 'parking lots' are understood and observed, that minutes are taken where appropriate, and that various techniques are used to encourage the level and kind of participation required to meet the meeting objectives. Typical meetings in service operations include operations meetings, departmental, group or team meetings, and customer meetings.

To remember the typical types of communication in service operation, remember Ms. Aretha Franklin and R- R-E-S-P-E-C-T-S
    Routine
    Reporting
    Exceptions
    Shift
    Projects
    Emergencies
    Changes
    Training
    Strategy / Design / Transition

ITILFND03-03-35 Define and explain release policy (ST 4.1.4.2)

Policy
Formally documented management expectations and intentions; used to direct decisions and ensure consistent, appropriate development and implementation of processes, standards, roles, activities, IT infrastructure etc.

A release policy must be defined for one or more services and include:
- Unique identification, numbering and naming conventions for different types of release together with a description
- Roles, responsibilities at each release and deployment process stage
- Requirement to only use software assets from the DML
- Expected frequency for each type of release
- Approach for accepting and grouping changes into a release
- Mechanism to automate the build, installation and release distribution processes to improve re-use, repeatability and efficiency
- How the release's configuration baseline is captured / verified against the actual release, e.g. hardware, software, documentation, knowledge
- Exit and entry criteria and authority for acceptance of the release into each service transition stage and into the controlled test, training, disaster recovery and other supported environments
- Criteria and authorization to exit early life support and handover to the service operation functions

A release that consists of many different types of service assets may involve many people, often from different organizations. Define typical responsibilities for release handover and acceptance and modify as required for specific transitions. Define key roles and responsibilities at handover points to ensure everyone understands their role and level of authority and those of others in the release and deployment management process.

The policy should define types of releases; a typical example:

Major releases	Large areas of new functionality, some of which may eliminate temporary fixes to problems. A major upgrade or release usually supersedes all preceding minor upgrades, releases and emergency fixes.
Minor releases	Small enhancements and fixes, some of which may already have been issued as emergency fixes. A minor upgrade or release usually supersedes all preceding emergency fixes.
Emergency releases	Corrections to a small number of known errors, or sometimes an enhancement to meet a high-priority business requirement.

All releases should have a unique identifier that can be used by service asset and configuration management and the documentation standards. The types of release should be defined, as this helps to set customer and stakeholder expectations about the planned releases. A release policy may specify, for example, that only strict 'emergency fixes' will be issued between formally planned releases of enhancements and non-urgent corrections.

The following example is an extract from a service release policy for a retail organization:

ST Table 4.2: Extract from a service release policy for a retail organization

Service	Release definition*	Naming/numbering	Frequency/ occurrence	Release window
Store service	Type A Type B or C Emergency	SS_x SS_1.x or SS_1.1.x SS_1.1.1.x	Annual (Feb) Quarterly As required	Wednesday 01.00–04.00 hours Not holiday weekends Not 1 September to 31 January
E-store web service	Type A Type B or C Emergency	ESWnnn_x ESWnnn_1.x ESWnnn_1.1.x	6 months Monthly As required	01.00–02.00 hours Not holiday weekends Not 1 October to 10 January
E-store delivery service	Type A Type B Type C Emergency	ESDnnn_x ESDSnnn_1.x ESDnnn_1.1.x ESDnnn_1.1.1.x	6 months Quarterly Monthly As required	01.00–02.00 hours Highest level of authorization required during holiday weekends
*Release definitions				
Type A Type B Type C Emergency	Something that impacts the whole system/service. A release that will impact part of the system, e.g. single sub-system or sub-service. Correction to a single function. A change required to restore or continue service to ensure that the service level agreement (SLA) is maintained.			

Naming/numbering conventions: Characters
- before the underscore (for example SS, ESWnnn, ESDnnn) identify the service
- after the underscore (for example x, 1.x, 1.1.x) identify the specific release
- to the right of decimal points represent successively minor releases

ITILFND03-03-36 Define and explain types of services (SS 3.2.2.4, Table 3.5)

Examples of Core, Enabling, and Enhancing Services

SS Table 3.5: Examples of core, enabling and enhancing services

Example	Core service	Enabling service	Enhancing service
IT services (office automation)	Word processing	Download and installation of updates	Document publication to professional printer for high-quality brochure
IT services (benefits tracking)	Employees of a company can monitor the status of their benefits (such as health insurance and retirement accounts)	A portal that provides a user-friendly front-end access to the benefits tracking service	Customers can create and manage a fitness or weight-loss program. Customers who show progress in their program are awarded a discount on their premiums.

© Crown copyright 2011. Reproduced under license from the Cabinet Office.

All services, internal or external, can be further classified in terms of how they relate to one another and their customers. Services can be classified as core, enabling or enhancing.

Core services of a bank, for example, could be providing financial capital to small and medium enterprises. Value is created for the bank's customers only when the bank can provide financial capital in a timely manner.

Enabling services could include aid offered by loan officers in assessing working capital needs and collateral; the application-processing service; flexible disbursement of loan funds; a bank account into which the borrower can electronically transfer funds. As basic factors, enabling services only give the provider an opportunity to serve the customer. Enabling services are necessary for customers to use the core services satisfactorily. Customers generally take such services for granted, and do not expect to be additionally charged for the value of such services. Examples of commonly offered enabling services are service desks, payment, registration and directory services.

Enhancing services provide the 'excitement factor'; examples are more difficult to provide, particularly because they tend to drift over time to be subsumed into core or enabling services since what is exciting today becomes expected if it is always delivered. An example is the provision of a broadband internet service in a hotel room – a differentiator a few years ago is now a basic and expected.

ITILFND03-03-36 Define and explain types of services (SS 3.2.2.4, Table 3.5)

Your mobile phone service provides a great example of core, enabling, and enhancing services, including how certain sub-services shift from being one to the other over time.

Core services of course include being able to place calls. Text messaging used to be considered an enhancing service (a 'deal sweetener') but is now typically considered a core service.

Enabling services include all of the sub-services you don't see or care about that support the core services (for example, maintenance of the wireless network) but also things like the fact that the carrier will provide a website with a FAQ page and ability to manage your account, and service desk services.

As of this publication, you could consider video calling, family mapping, and other features as enhancing services, but as pointed out in the examples, some of these may become part of the fabric of how we work and live and gain promotion to core services over time.

Think about your organization:
- Do you present yourself to your customers as a set of services?
- Do you parse out what is core (seen by the customer, something they recognize and pay for) versus enabling?
- Do you distinguish between core and enhancing services?
- Can you think of examples of enhancing services in your organizations that went on to be promoted to core as they became more vital to users?

ITILFND03-03-37 Define and explain change proposals (ST 4.2.4.6)

Change Proposal

A document that includes a high level description of a potential service introduction or significant change, along with a corresponding business case and an expected implementation schedule. Change proposals are normally created by the service portfolio management process and are passed to change management for authorization.

A change proposal should include:

- A high-level description of the new, changed or retired service, including business outcomes supported, and utility and warranty to be provided
- A full business case including risks, issues and alternatives, as well as budget and financial expectations
- An outline schedule for design and implementation of the change

Major changes that involve significant cost, risk or organizational impact will usually be initiated through the service portfolio management process. Before the new or changed service is chartered it is important that the change is reviewed for its potential impact on other services, on shared resources, and on the change schedule.

Change proposals are submitted to change management before chartering new or changed services in order to ensure that potential conflicts for resources or other issues are identified. Authorization of the change proposal does not authorize implementation of the change but simply allows the service to be chartered so that service design activity can begin.

Change management reviews the change proposal and the current change schedule, identifies any potential conflicts or issues and responds to the change proposal by either authorizing it or documenting the issues that need to be resolved. When the change proposal is authorized, the change schedule is updated to include outline implementation dates for the proposed change.

After the new or changed service is chartered, RFCs will be used in the normal way to request authorization for specific changes. These RFCs will be associated with the change proposal so that change management has a view of the overall strategic intent and can prioritize and review these RFCs appropriately.

ITILFND03-03-37 Define and explain change proposals (ST 4.2.4.6)

Changes come from a variety of sources, and one of them is the service portfolio process. The output of the SPM process is a change proposal that advocates the introduction, change, or retirement of a service. It is of course vital that the business case, rationale, and supporting evidence for the change are provided to change management, or the risk is run that the change will be rejected.

You should be clear, therefore, that not all changes require a change proposal. It is for changes much "bigger than a breadbox", changes that are **major**, that require business management review and approval, not just change management (minor) or CAB advice (significant). It is for changes that require the due diligence of a business case and all pertinent details needed to make a good decision as to whether to proceed with or reject the change. As you can see from the description on the opposite page, the "when" of the change – the change schedule – is a key factor in the decision.

How does what your organization practices and what level of documentation is required compare to that which is outlined on the opposite page for change proposals? What is happening in your organization, both good and bad, as a result?

ITILFND03-03-38 Define and explain CSI register (CSI 3.4)

Opportunity no.	Date raised	Size (small, medium, large)	Timescale (short, medium, long)	Description	Priority (urgent, 1, 2, 3)	KPI metric	Justification	Raised by	To be actioned by	Date required by
1	01/04/2011	Small	Short	A number of failures have occurred when implementing updated or new applications. This has been caused by the testing procedure in release and deployment using out-of-date test data. The requirement is to update tne test data in repository test 4371	Urgent	n% reduction in failures	Significant reduction in failures after transition and resulting business Impact	A. Other	J. Doe	14/4/2011
2	01/05/2011	Medium	Long	Event management: the number of alerts from the ABC 479 module of the payroll suite is still excessive causing unnecessary analysis time. Additional filtering required	2	n% reduction in spurious events	Will help reduce the amount of analysis time and avoid potential oversight of significant events	N. More	J. Smith	01/07/2011
3	01/06/2011	Medium	Long	Training Issue: Service desk staff would benefit from additional training in the use of the human resources (HR) Joiners and leavers application	3	n% improvement in relevant staff trained in the HR joiners and leavers application	All queries to the service desk on this application currently have to be escalated to the application management team. With some basic training a number of these could be dealt with by first line support	B. Floor	F. Less	01/09/2011
4	01/07/2011	Large	Medium	Change management process: having multiple authorization channels has caused issues with some users because of uncoordinated changes	3	Alignment to single channel	Redesign of the change management process will reduce confusion and impact to stakeholders	J. Jones	B. Car	10/10/2011

CSI Appendix B shows a simple example of a CSI register. Evaluate your own requirements and amend the register to suit their own purposes. A CXSI register is a database or structured document used to record and manage improvement opportunities throughout their lifecycle. The CSI register...

- Contains important information for the overall service provider and should be held and regarded as part of the service knowledge management system (SKMS)
- Introduces a structure and visibility to CSI so that all initiatives are captured and recorded, and benefits realized
  - Benefits will be measured to show that they have given the desired results
- Provides a coordinated, consistent view of potentially many improvement activities
  - It is important to define the interface from the CSI register of initiatives with strategic initiatives and with processes such as problem management, capacity management and change management

ITILFND03-03-38 Define and explain CSI register (CSI 3.4)

The CSI register is a really simple idea: let us apply project portfolio management principles to the set of planned and active improvement initiatives we have; let us record them in one place, know when they will or have started and will be complete; let us have a brief description of what the project is, juxtaposed against other projects so we can make sense of it and understand it in context; let us have a method for arriving at priority and assigning it to initiatives, and identify up front the KPIs that will tell us whether or not the initiative is tracking; let us record the justification for the initiative so that later we can compare against actual progress and results and manage accordingly; let us identify who raised the initiative in the first place and when, and who is responsible fir driving it to successful completion.

These are all reasonable things to do. The idea here is to make sure there is an active, working record of all service improvement initiatives in one place, to support effective and efficient management and communication regarding the initiatives, their progress and results, and to support go / no-go decisions in the first place, and later, decisions to add to, drop, or modify initiatives.

Think about your organization: do you track improvement initiatives centrally and separately, or is this tracking dispersed around the organization or mixed in with other projects that are not about service improvement per se? What positive benefits are you seeing if you are tracking service improvements separately and centrally? What is happening in your organization if this is not how you are doing things?

ITILFND03-03-39 Define and explain outcomes (SS 2.1.1)

Outcome
The result of carrying out an activity, following a process, or delivering an IT service; used to refer to intended results as well as to actual results.

- An outcome-based definition of service moves IT organizations beyond business–IT alignment towards business–IT integration
- Customer outcomes become the ultimate concern of business relationship managers instead of the gathering of requirements, which is necessary but not sufficient
  - Requirements are generated for internal coordination and control only after customer outcomes are well understood
- Customers seek outcomes but do not wish to have accountability or ownership of all the associated costs and risks

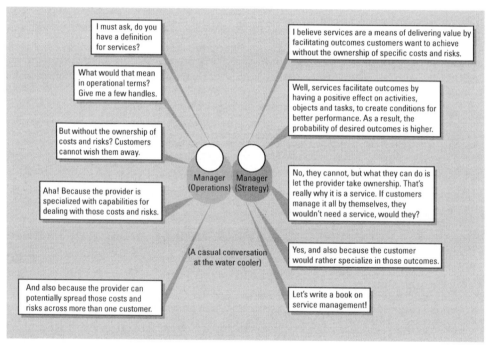

SS Figure 2.1: Conversation about the definition and meaning of services

© Crown copyright 2011. Reproduced under license from the Cabinet Office.

ITILFND03-03-39 Define and explain outcomes (SS 2.1.1)

At the risk of oversimplification, it can be said that there are two basic approaches to managing things:
1) Focus on activities – making sure activities are identified and get done
2) Focus on outcomes – making sure objectives are met

The first approach, focusing on activities, is especially relevant and necessary for new staff and new practices – if we have no data or experience with outcomes in this area, better to focus on activities. So for example, you will see in business that new salespeople are often given activity goals – make so many calls per day, for example – rather than outcome goals, for example, sell $100,000 worth of product per month.

Having said this, over-focus and misapplication of focus on activity can lead to activity for activity's sake, and a lack of focus on and achieving the ultimate objectives that are the organization's key outcomes. That is why outcome-based management is in the end considered by many to be superior – the focus is on the ultimate focus – the outcome. The danger here of course is over-focus on the 'ultimate' goal may lead to a lack of focus and tie in on a day-to-day basis on the activities that will get you there.

The general idea is to shoot for the right balance between knowing and acting on the outcomes you are aiming for and the activities that will get you there.

Overall, if forced to choose between an organization full of professionals who are outcome focused – who 'get it' – the outcomes you are shooting for, and get on with it – pursue activities that realize those outcomes, and a set of professionals whose focus is 'the task', the authors would choose the former. This is because in the end, the customer will judge you on outcomes, not tasks.

An example is change management. The outcome is, "minimize the business disruption of change, and know what changed". Regardless of the activities you are engaging in, if you achieve this objective, you are succeeding at change management; this is the standard by which you should hold yourself, that you should hold others to, that they should hold you to, and that ultimately the customer will hold all of you to when it comes to change management. The standard is NOT, "well, I know the change failed but I submitted my RFC on time with all the fields filled out as indicated in the procedure" – this is an activity goal. While it is true that activities are required to meet outcomes, the correct outcome trumps the activity every time.

One important feature of outcome-based management is that it provides greater flexibility in achieving objectives, because the focus is on the ends, not the means. Said another way, an organization overly focused on activities may lose track of the right outcomes. For example, they are building the world's best buggy whips, when no one wants buggy whips any longer, or, in an IT example, providing the world's best dialup access when everyone has gone Internet.

ITILFND03-03-40 Define and explain patterns of business activity (SS 4.4.5.2)

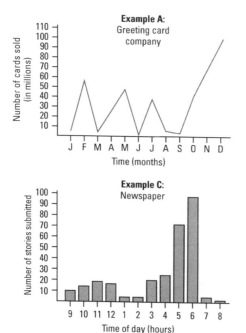

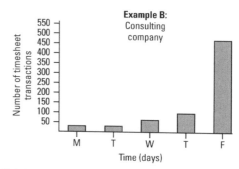

Each chart shows patterns of business activity (PBA). Each activity relies on IT services and each places a demand on the IT service provider's assets.

Example A – annual PBA: Greeting cards need to be designed, manufactured and distributed for each major holiday. The fluctuation in sales will result in a fluctuation in demand for IT services.

Example B – weekly PBA: Consultants need access to a timesheet system to track their activities so that customers can be billed. Most consultants wait until the end of the week to complete their timesheets. Some consultants record their activities daily.

Example C – daily PBA: Journalists have to meet the deadline of 6pm to submit their stories for publication. After the deadline, only high-impact corrections are made. The later in the day, the more critical the IT services become, and also the more utilized. Most journalists use the lunch hour to interview people for stories.

SS Figure 4.40: Examples of patterns of business activity

© Crown copyright 2011. Reproduced under license from the Cabinet Office.

The PBA profile should include the following:
- Classification – this indicates the type of PBA, and could refer to where it originates (user or automated), the type and impact of outcomes supported, and the type of workload supported
- Attributes – such as frequency, volume, location and duration
- Requirements – such as performance, security, availability, privacy, latency or tolerance for delays
- Service asset requirements – design teams will draft a utilization profile for each PBA in terms of what resources it uses, when and how much of each resource

ITILFND03-03-40 Define and explain patterns of business activity (SS 4.4.5.2)

Pattern of Business Activity (PBA)

A workload profile of one or more business activities. Patterns of business activity are used to help the IT service provider understand and plan for different levels of business activity.

Are patterns of business activity material to IT professi onals? You bet they are. Think about the business you support: aren't there certain times that specific services and applications are more critical than others? That demand is much higher or lower than at other times? Wouldn't it make sense, in fact, isn't it imperative that IT understands this rhythm of the business and shapes and tunes itself to it?

For example, some candy manufactures make the largest share of their profits right around Halloween, Easter, and Christmas – shouldn't IT shift its resources to accommodate this seasonality?

Department stores often have big, one-day, once-a-year sales – shouldn't IT know when they are and stage resources accordingly?

Certain financial application features may go lightly used and have low impact on the business 99% of the time, but then become mission critical at month, quarter, and year-end financial close – shouldn't IT know about it?

The answer to these questions is, "of course". And identifying and managing capacity to meet the demands of patterns of business of activity is a key activity in a customer and service focused IT provider.

While this may seem like "extra work", consider that, given scarce resources, being able to shape your capacity to meet better understood, actual demand is more efficient than not; that shaping capacity to meet demand is in the end less work than dealing with the issues of over and under capacity, or being on your back foot because of a lack of understanding of what is happening in the business, when, and what the consequences are for IT in terms of requirements for its baseline capacity and capability, and for peaks and valley, and how those peaks and valleys will be met.

Does your organization track patterns of business activities? Does it use the methods and language suggested here in ITIL?

ITILFND03-03-41 Define and explain customers and users (SS 2.1.5)

Stakeholder

A person with an interest in an organization, project, IT service etc.; may be interested in the activities, targets, resources or deliverables; may include customers, partners, employees, shareholders, owners etc.

Customers	Users	Suppliers
• Those who buy goods or services • Person or group who defines and agrees the service level targets • May be internal or external • Also sometimes used informally to mean user – for example, 'This is a customer-focused organization'	• Those who use the service on a day-to-day basis • Distinct from customers, as some customers do not use the IT service directly	• Third parties responsible for supplying goods or services that are required to deliver IT services • Examples of suppliers include commodity hardware and software vendors, network and telecom providers, and outsourcing organizations

Examples of stakeholders include organizations, service providers, customers, consumers, users, partners, employees, shareholders, owners and suppliers. The term 'organization' is used to define a company, legal entity or other institution. It is also used to refer to any entity that has people, resources and budgets – for example, a project or business.

Within the service provider there are many different stakeholders including the functions, groups and teams that deliver the services. There are also many stakeholders external to the service provider organization, as shown above: customers, users, and suppliers.

Customers who work in the same organization as the IT service provider and those who work for other organizations are distinguished as follows:
- **Internal customers.** These are customers who work for the same business as the IT service provider. For example, the marketing department is an internal customer of the IT organization because it uses IT services. The head of marketing and the chief information officer both report to the chief executive officer. If IT charges for its services, the money paid is an internal transaction in the organization's accounting system, not real revenue.
- **External customers.** These are customers who work for a different business from the IT service provider. External customers typically purchase services from the service provider by means of a legally binding contract or agreement.

ITILFND03-03-41 Define and explain customers and users (SS 2.1.5)

While there are many kinds of stakeholders associated with an IT service provider, the key distinction that ITIL makes is between **customers** and **users**. It is essential that you understand this central distinction.

Customers pay for services; users use services. It is as simple as that. Why make this distinction?

ITIL does not make distinctions for distinctions' sake. Wherever you see a distinction being made, it is because there are implications for managing IT services. Said another way, if you don't make the distinction, you are bound to not be managing something that is important.

The distinction between customers and users is a primary example of this in ITIL. Many organizations have really good, systematic processes and ownership assigned for keeping users happy – but what about customers? Some IT organizations the authors have worked with were unable to pinpoint even after lengthy discussions who their customers were, who actually paid the bills for the services they provided. Obviously these organizations did not have roles and processes in place to keep customers happy. This was and is not a minor oversight.

Similarly, the authors have seen organizations with very systematic management of "pay the bills" customer satisfaction, with little or no focus on user satisfaction (this typically comes home to roost when the administrative staff assigned to executive start complaining loudly about IT).

The obvious solution is to apportion scarce resources appropriately to the roles and systematic processes to ensure both customer and user satisfaction. It is not a small point to understand that this starts with acknowledging that these stakeholder roles exist and are different in the first place.

Does your organization distinguish between customers and users? What roles are in place to support their ongoing satisfaction? What systematic procedures are in place for the same? Where these roles and systems are missing or inadequate in your organization, what happens? What happens when such roles and systems are in place?

ITILFND03-03-42 Define and explain the Deming Cycle (plan, do, check, act) (CSI 3.8, Figure 2.8)

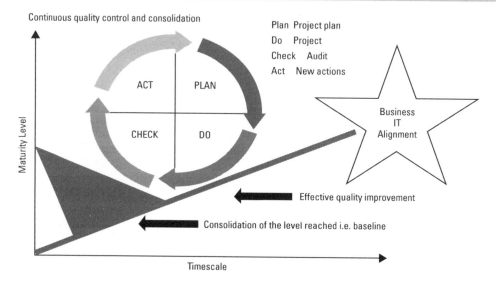

W. Edwards Deming proposed the Deming Cycle for quality improvement which is very applicable in CSI. The four stages of the cycle are Plan, Do, Check and Act, followed by a consolidation phase to prevent rolling backwards. PDCA sets a clear pattern for CSI efforts:

- **Plan** – *establish goals for improvement*
- **Do** – *develop and implement a project to close the gap*
- **Check** – *compare the implemented environment to the measures of success established in the Plan phase*
- **Act** – *determine if further work is required to close remaining gaps, allocation of resources necessary to support another round of improvement*

The goal in using the Deming Cycle is steady, ongoing improvement. It is a fundamental tenet of Continual Service Improvement. The Deming Cycle is critical at two points in CSI:
1) CSI implementation
2) CSI's application to services, service management processes.

At implementation, all four stages of the Deming Cycle are used. With ongoing improvement, CSI draws on the Check and Act stages to monitor, measure, review and implement initiatives. The cycle is underpinned by a process-led approach to management where defined processes are in place, the activities are measured for compliance to expected values and outputs are audited to validate and improve the process. The PDCA cycle is a fundamental part of many quality standards including ISO/IEC 20000.

ITILFND03-03-42 Define and explain the Deming Cycle (plan, do, check, act)
(CSI 3.8, Figure 2.8)

Plan – Do – Check – Act, the phases of the Deming Cycle – you must remember these
for the examination. You can expect a question that will list a set of phases with some
distractors in there – Plan, Do, Consolidate, Activate, and the like – and you will need
to distinguish the correct list from the incorrect ones.

The Deming Cycle is simple and that is one of its strengths. While you can always add
or refine phases to any process, it is hard to argue the logic of PDCA:
1. First you Plan – what is your goal for improvement
2. Then you Do – you take action
3. Then you Check your results
4. Then you Act, meaning, you adjust course based on the results you check and take
   further action

Remember P-D-C-A.
   Plan
   Don't
   Count on
   Absolution

CHAPTER 4
ITILFND04 KEY PRINCIPLES AND MODELS (90M)

The purpose of this unit is to help you to comprehend and account for the key principles and models of service management and to balance some of the opposing forces within service management. The recommended study period for this unit is minimum 1 hour and 30 minutes.

Characteristics of Value

Defined by customers	The ultimate decision about whether that service is valuable or not rests with the customer
Affordable mix of features	The customers will select the service or product that represents the best mix of features at the price they are willing to pay
Achievement of objectives	Many services are not designed to produce revenue, but to meet some other organizational objective, e.g., social responsibility programs, or human resource management
Changes over time and circumstance	As each customer changes to meet the challenges of their environment, so do their service needs and values

The value of a service can be considered to be the level to which that service meets a customer's expectations. It is often measured by how much the customer is willing to pay for the service, rather than the cost of the service or any other attribute of the service itself.

Understanding IT value requires three pieces of information

Services contribute value to an organization only when their value is perceived to be higher than their cost, so understanding the value of IT requires three pieces of information:

What service(s) did IT provide?	If IT is only perceived as managing a set of servers, networks and PCs it will be very difficult for the customer to understand how these contributed to value. In order for a customer to calculate the value of a service, they must be able to discern a specific, discrete service and link it directly to specific business activities and outcomes.
What did the service(s) achieve?	The customer will identify what they were able to do with the service, and just how important that was to them and their organization.
How much did the service(s) cost?	When a customer compares the cost or price of a service with what the service enabled them to achieve, they will be able to judge how valuable the service actually was. If IT is unable to determine the cost of the service, it will be very difficult for them to claim that they delivered value, and very difficult for the customer to perceive IT as 'valuable'.

Creating value

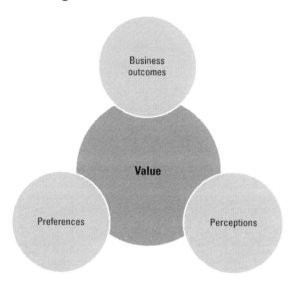

SS Figure 3.6: Components of value

© Crown copyright 2011. Reproduced under license from the Cabinet Office.

There is more to value than just the function of the service and its cost; value is defined in three areas:
1. Business outcomes achieved,
2. The customer's preferences
3. The customer's perception of what was delivered.

Calculating the value of a service can be straightforward financially. Where outcomes are not financial it is harder to quantify although it may be possible to qualify it. Value is defined not only in terms of the customer's business outcomes; it is also highly dependent on customer's perceptions and preferences which affect how they see the value of one service or provider over another.

Understanding customer perception of value

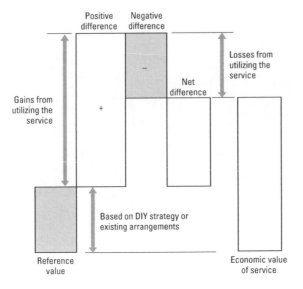

SS Figure 3.7: How customers perceive value

A service provider cannot decide the value of a service but can influence how the value is perceived by the customer. The figure illustrates how customers perceive value (after Nagle and Holden, 2002). The starting point for customer perception is the reference value. The positive difference of the service is based on the perceived added benefits provided by the service provider; the negative difference is the perception of what is lost by investing in the service. The net difference is the perception the customer has of how much better (or worse) the service is than the reference value after discounting the negative difference. The economic value is the total value the customer perceives the service to deliver: reference value + net difference as measured by the customer.

ITILFND04-04-3 Understand the importance of people, processes, products and partners for service management (SD 3.1.5, Figure 3.3)

Comprehensive and Integrated Service Design

IT systems and services must be designed, planned, implemented and managed appropriately for the overall business to provide IT services that:
- Are business- and customer-oriented, focused and driven
- Are cost-effective
- Meet the customer's security requirements
- Are flexible and adaptable, yet fit for purpose at the point of delivery
- Can absorb an ever-increasing demand in volume and speed of change
- Meet increasing business demands for continuous operation
- Are managed and operated to an acceptable level of risk
- Are responsive, with appropriate availability and capacity matched to business needs

People, Processes, Products, and Partners (the Four P's) of Implementing ITIL Service Management as a Practice

Many designs, plans and projects fail from lack of preparation and management; ITSM implementation requires preparing and planning the effective and efficient use of the four Ps: the people, the processes, the products (services, technology and tools) and partners (suppliers, manufacturers and vendors), as illustrated in SD Figure 3.3.

SD Figure 3.3: The four P's

© Crown copyright 2011. Reproduced under license from the Cabinet Office.

service design Actions to ensure solutions meet Business Needs
- Add the new service solution to the service portfolio from the concept phase; update the portfolio to reflect current status through incremental or iterative development
- During initial service/system analysis understand the service's go-live *SLRs*
- See if SLRs can be met with current resources, capabilities; if organizational policies require it, build results of modeling activities into capacity plan
- If new infrastructure or extended support is required for the service financial management for IT services will need to be involved to set the budget
- Conduct an initial business impact and risk analysis well before implementation as input to IT service continuity strategy, availability, capacity, and security design
- The service desk will need to be made aware of new services well in advance of live operation to prepare and train service desk staff and potentially IT customer staff.
- The technical management, application management and IT operations management functions (see ITIL Service Operation) also need to be made aware of new services to allow them to plan for effective operational support of the services.
- Service transition can start planning implementation and build the change schedule
- Supplier management must be involved if the new service requires procurement

ITILFND04-04-3 Explain the importance of people, processes, products and partners for service management (SD 3.1.5, Figure 3.3)

The "4 Ps" of service management are a key concept you must recall for the examination and are also vital for properly applying the concepts of service management.

The old service management mantra in ITIL V1 and V2 was "People, Process, and Technology"; this has been replaced by "People, Products, Partners, and Processes"; 'Partners' is a key addition in the ITIL 2007 edition, recognizing the fact that in the age of agility and outsourcing, where service design a make or buy decision, not just about deciding on creating something, that the design of supplier relationships and management structures is key, and that design itself includes choice of suppliers for all or part of the components of the service design.

The other three Ps – people, products, and processes – are simply renamed from the old PPT of people, process, and technology. The general idea here is that you have a clear understanding of the true scope of service management.

It was a big idea back in the days of ITIL V1 and V2 that IT was better run as a service – so while products (technology) are absolutely vital, they are only one of the 'four legs of the stool' of service management. You must also include the people dimension through the lifecycle – strategy, design, transition, operation, and continual improvement - and the processes that underpin service delivery and support. And of course, partners, as mentioned above.

This is not a small point. Attention to all four dimensions of scope is required for effective service management. The whole idea here is that your plans and designs and transitions and operations and improvements must consider all four scope components to the right level of detail to be effective. You cannot skip planning for organizational readiness and just install new technology, for example, unless you want to fail. Likewise you cannot skip addressing key process questions, like how you are going to manage change, or you will fail. All dimensions must be considered to succeed.

Think about your organization and its strategies / plans, designs, transitions, operations, and improvement efforts – does the scope of these commonly include all four Ps? What happens in your organization when they do? What happens in your organization when one of the Ps is either missing from or inadequate in the scope? Can you think of examples?

Five Major Aspects of Holistic Service Design

A holistic approach should be adopted for all service design aspects and areas to ensure consistency and integration within all activities and processes across the entire IT technology, providing end-to-end business-related functionality and quality. It is important that a holistic, results-driven approach to all aspects of design is adopted, and that when changing or amending any of the individual elements of design all other aspects are considered. When designing and developing a new application, this should not be done in isolation, but should also consider the impact on the overall service, the management information systems and tools (e.g. service portfolio and service catalogue), the architectures, the technology, the service management processes, and the necessary measurements and metrics. This will ensure not only that the functional elements are addressed by the design, but also that all of the management and operational requirements are addressed as a fundamental part of the design and are not added as an afterthought.

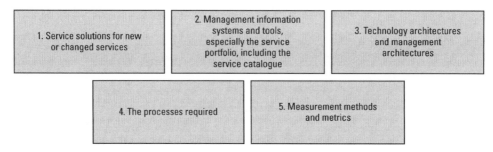

This holistic approach and the five aspects of design identified above are important parts of the service provider's overall service management system. This approach should also be used when the change to the service is its retirement. Unless the retirement of a service or any aspect of a service is carefully planned, the retirement could cause unexpected negative effects on the customer or business which might otherwise have been avoided.

Not every change within an IT service will require the instigation of the same level of service design activity. It can be argued that every change, no matter how small, needs to be designed, but the scale of the activity necessary to ensure success will vary greatly from one change type to another. Every organization must define what categories of change require what level of design activity and ensure that everyone within the organization is clear on these requirements. In other words, all changes should be assessed for their service design requirements to determine the correct service design activities to undertake in each circumstance. This should be part of the change management process impact assessment described within *ITIL Service Transition*.

ITILFND04-04-4 Explain the five major aspects of service design (SD 3.1.1) 1) service solutions for new or changed services, 2) management information systems and tools, 3) technology architectures and management architectures, 4) the processes required, 5) measurement methods and metrics

You can see from the opposite page that *service* design is a bit of a misnomer. Yes, the scope of service design includes services – adding them, changing them. But it also includes the design of things that are not services per se, but underpin services and service management:

- The design of the *service portfolio*
- *Technology and management architecture* design
- The design of *processes*
- The design of *measurement methods and metrics*

As you can see, the last four things mentioned above are not services; it is important to remember is that they are in-scope for service design (hence the misnomer) and taken together with service design, they are called the five major aspects of service design in ITIL.

Give some thought to these aspects. Think about your organization. Are all of these aspects included in the scope of what your organization does in design? Does your organization do a good job of scaling the level of effort and scrutiny required in each area based on the nature of the change? What is working well and what is not?

ITILFND04-04-9 Explain the continual service improvement approach
(CSI 3.1, CSI 3.1.1, Figure 3.1)

The Continual Service Improvement Approach

Service improvement must focus on increasing the efficiency, maximizing the
effectiveness and optimizing the cost of services and underlying ITSM processes. The
only way to do this is to ensure improvement opportunities are identified throughout
the entire service lifecycle.

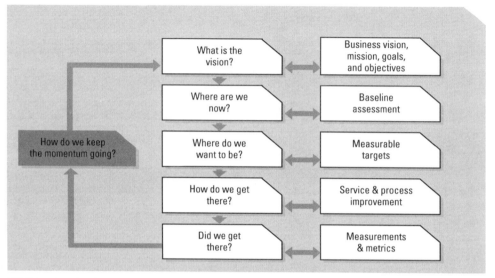

CSI Figure 3.1: Continual service improvement approach

© Crown copyright 2011. Reproduced under license from the Cabinet Office.

CSI Figure 3.1 shows an overall approach to continual service improvement (CSI)
and illustrates a continual cycle of improvement. This approach can be summarized
as follows:

1. Embrace the vision by understanding the high-level business objectives. The vision
   should align the business and IT strategies.
2. Assess the current situation to obtain an accurate, unbiased snapshot of where the
   organization is right now. This baseline assessment is an analysis of the current
   position in terms of the business, organization, people, process and technology.
3. Understand and agree on the priorities for improvement based on a deeper
   development of the principles defined in the vision. The full vision may be years
   away but this step provides specific goals and a manageable timeframe.
4. Detail the CSI plan to achieve higher quality service provision by implementing or
   improving ITSM processes.
5. Verify that measurements and metrics exist and milestones were achieved, process
   compliance is high, and business objectives and priorities are met by the service
   level.
6. Finally, the approach should ensure that the momentum for quality improvement is
   maintained by assuring that changes become embedded in the organization.

ITILFND04-04-9 Explain the continual service improvement approach
(CSI 3.1, CSI 3.1.1, Figure 3.1)

It is vital when improving to start with the overall vision of the future that is desired. The actual improvement effort may only deliver on a piece of the vision, but it is a necessary stop to think through this context and tie back the improvement effort to the big bets of the organization and its desired future state.

An important next step is getting a baseline for where you are now. In the rush to improve, some skip this step, but it is problematic to do so. There are two primary reasons 1) without a baseline for where you are, you don't really have a good sense for how severe the problem or attractive the opportunity is that you're trying to pursue, and 2) during the initiative, you will lose momentum if you can't show progress against something as tangible as possible, and at the end of the initiative, you won't get to do the next one if you cannot show as tangible as possible results; these are the functions of a baseline.

As mentioned earlier, the vision is a large concept, an overall desired future state; aiming for that with one improvement initiative is like trying to swallow a watermelon whole. You have to take one bite at a time to get the whole thing down, and that is what answering "where do we want to be?" accomplishes.

We need a plan and action to get from where we are to where we want to be, and a way of knowing we have arrived; this is accomplished by measurement and metrics against the baseline.

And along the path we need a way to keep the momentum going. Without attention to this step, improvement efforts tend to peter out (for example, when a key driver for the project takes a new position). It is important also demarcate the end of one improvement, call it done, and celebrate before moving on; elsewise to those involved it may feel like the 101st year of the 100 years war.

Examine the figure on the left. Does this represent the steps included in how your organization does things? Is there anything that is missing or inadequate? What happens as a result? Is there anything you do particularly well? What is the impact on the business as a result?

Remember the six steps:
Vision? Where Now? Where want to be? How? Did we get there (Arrive)? Momentum?
VW WHAM

ITILFND04-04-10 Understand the role of measurement for continual service improvement and explain how CSFs and KPIs relate (CSI 5.5.1), Baselines (CSI 3.9.1), and types of metrics (technology, process, service) (CSI 5.5)

Role of measurement for CSI – relationship between CSFs, KPIs

Critical Success Factor (CSF)
Something that must happen if an IT service, process, plan, project or other activity is to succeed; used to measure achievement of each CSF, e.g., a CSF of "protect IT services when making Changes" may be measured by KPIs, "percentage reduction of unsuccessful Changes," "percentage reduction in Changes causing Incidents," etc.

Key Performance Indicator (KPI)
A metric that is used to help manage an IT service, process, plan, project or other activity. KPIs are used to measure the achievement of critical success factors. Many metrics may be measured, but only the most important of these are defined as KPIs and used to actively manage and report on the process, IT service or activity.

Sample CSFs and KPIs for the seven-step improvement process
  CSF All improvement opportunities identified; **KPI** % reduced defects, e.g., 3% reduction in failed changes; 10% in security breaches
  CSF The cost of providing services is reduced; **KPI** % decrease in overall cost of service provision, e.g., 2.5% reduction in the average cost of an incident; 5% reduction in the cost of processing a particular type of transaction
  CSF The required business outcomes from IT services are achieved; **KPI** A 3% increase in customer satisfaction with the service desk; 2% increase in customer satisfaction with the warranty offered by the payroll service.

Relationship between CSFs and KPIs – How many CSFs and KPIs?
At any given time:
○ Define *no more than two to five KPIs per CSF*
○ Associate *no more than two to five CSFs* with a service or process
○ In the early stages of a CSI initiative:
○ Define, monitor and report on only *two to three KPIs for each CSF*
  ○ As the maturity of a service and service management processes increase, additional KPIs can be added
  ○ Based on what is important to the business and IT management, the KPIs may change over a period of time
  ○ As service management processes are implemented, this will often change the KPIs of other processes

As service management processes are implemented, KPIs will change. For example increasing first-contact resolution is a common KPI for incident management. This is a good choice to begin with, but will change when you implement problem management.

Two basic kinds of KPIs, qualitative and quantitative

Qualitative KPIs example
CSF: Improving IT service quality
KPI: 10% better customer
satisfaction on handling incidents in
next six months
Metrics:
o Original customer satisfaction
   score for handling incidents
o Ending customer satisfaction
   score for handling incidents
Measurements:
o Incident survey score
o Number of survey scores

Quantitative KPIs example
CSF: Reducing IT costs
KPI: 10% cost reduction, printer incidents
Metrics:
o Original cost of handling incidents
o Final cost of handling incidents
o Cost of the improvement effort
Measurements:
o Time on the incident by first-level
   operative and their average salary
o Time on incident by second-level; average
   salary
o Time on problem management activities
   by 2nd-level
o Time on training first-level on the
   workaround
o Cost of 3rd-party vendor service call
o Time and material, 3rd-party vendor

Is the KPI fit for use? Key questions

o What does the KPI really tell us about goal achievement? If we fail to meet the target set for a KPI, does that mean we fail to achieve some of our goals? And if we succeed, does this mean we will achieve our goals?
o How easy is it to interpret the KPI? Does it help decide a course of action?
o When do we need the information? How often? How fast must we get it?
o To what extent is the KPI stable and accurate? Sensitive to uncontrollable external influences? Effort needed for non-marginal improvement?
o How easy is it to change the KPI itself? How easy is it to adapt the measurement system to changing circumstances or changes in our goals for IT service provision?
o To what extent can the KPI be measured now? Under which conditions can measurement continue, and which impede measurement? Which conditions make results meaningless?
o Who owns this KPI? Who is responsible for collecting and analysing the data? Accountable for improvements based on the data?

Role of measurement for CSI – WHY ESTABLISH Baselines?

o As markers or starting points for later comparison is an important beginning point for highlighting improvement
o At each level: strategic goals and objectives, tactical process maturity, and operational metrics and KPIs
o As an initial data point to see if a service or process needs improvement

Three Types of Metrics to Collect to Support CSI Activies

1. **Technology metrics** –often associated with component and application-based metrics
2. **Process metrics** –captured in the form of CSFs, KPIs and activity metrics for the service management processes. These metrics can help determine the overall health of a process. Four key questions that KPIs can help answer are around quality, performance, value and compliance of following the process. CSI would use these metrics as input in identifying improvement opportunities for each process.
3. **Service metrics** – these metrics are the results of the end-to-end service. Component metrics are used to compute the service metrics.

CHAPTER 5
ITILFND05
PROCESSES (645M)

The purpose of this unit is to help you understand how the service management processes contribute to the ITIL service lifecycle, to explain the purpose, objectives, scope, basic concepts, activities and interfaces for four of the core processes, and to state the purpose, objectives and scope for eighteen of the remaining processes. The list of activities to be included from each Process is the minimum required and should not be taken as an exhaustive list.

ITILFND05-05-21 State the purpose, objectives and scope for service portfolio management (SS 4.2.1, 4.2.2), including the service portfolio (SS 4.2.4.1, Figure 4.14)

Service Portfolio Management
The process responsible for managing the service portfolio. Service portfolio management ensures that the service provider has the right mix of services to meet required business outcomes at an appropriate level of investment. Service portfolio management considers services in terms of the business value that they provide.

Service Portfolio
The complete set of services that is managed by a service provider; used to manage the entire lifecycle of all services, and includes three categories: service pipeline (proposed or in development), service catalogue (live or available for deployment), and retired services.

Service Portfolio Management Process - Purpose

The purpose of service portfolio management is to ensure the service provider has the right mix of services to balance the investment in IT with the ability to meet business outcomes.

Service Portfolio Management Process - Objectives

- Provide a process and mechanisms to enable an organization to investigate and decide on the services to offer, based on an analysis of the potential return and acceptable level of risk
- Maintain the definitive portfolio of services provided, articulating the business needs each service meets and business outcomes it supports
- Provide a mechanism for the organization to evaluate how services enable them to achieve their strategy and respond to changes in internal or external environments
- Control services offered, under what conditions and at what level of investment
- Track investment in services throughout their lifecycle, enabling the organization to evaluate its strategy and its ability to execute it
- Analyze which services are no longer viable and when to retire them

Service Portfolio Management Process - scope

- All services a service provider plans to deliver, those currently delivered and those that have been withdrawn from service
  - The primary concern of service portfolio management is whether the service provider is able to generate value from the services
  - Service portfolio management will therefore track investments in services and compare them to the desired business outcomes
- Service portfolio management evaluates the value of services throughout their lifecycles, and must be able to compare what newer services have offered over the retired services they have replaced

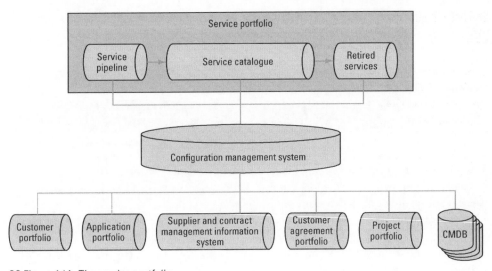

SS Figure 4.14: The service portfolio

© Crown copyright 2011. Reproduced under license from the Cabinet Office.

SS Figure 4.14 illustrates the components of the service portfolio.

The service portfolio represents the commitments and investments made by a service provider across all customers and market spaces. It represents present contractual commitments, new service development and ongoing service improvement plans initiated by CSI. The portfolio also includes third-party services, which are an integral part of service offerings to customers. Some third-party services are visible to the customers (e.g. desktop repairs) while others are not (e.g. wide area networking services).

In other words, the service portfolio is the complete set of services that is managed by a service provider. The service portfolio also identifies those services in a conceptual stage, namely all services the organization would provide if it had unlimited resources, capabilities and funding. This documentation exercise facilitates understanding of the opportunity costs of the existing portfolio and better fiscal discipline. If a service provider understands what it cannot do, then it is better able to assess if it should keep doing what it is doing or re-allocate its resources and capabilities.

The service portfolio represents all the resources presently engaged or being released in various stages of the service lifecycle. Each stage requires resources for completion of projects, initiatives and contracts. This is a very important governance aspect of service portfolio management (SPM). Entry, progress and exit are approved only with approved funding and a financial plan for recovering costs or showing profit as necessary. The service portfolio should have the right mix of services in the pipeline and catalogue to secure the financial viability of the service provider, since the service catalogue is the only part of the portfolio that lists services that recover costs or earn profits.

ITILFND05-05-22 State the purpose, objectives and scope for financial management for IT services (SS 4.3.1, 4.3.2), including business case (SS 3.6.1.1)

Financial Management for IT Services
The process responsible for managing an IT service provider's budgeting, accounting and charging requirements. It is also the process that is used to quantify the value that IT services contribute to the business.

Financial Management for IT Services Process – Purpose
- Secure the appropriate level of funding to design, develop and deliver services that meet the strategy of the organization
- Act as a gatekeeper that ensures that the service provider does not commit to services that they are not able to provide
- Identify the balance between the cost and quality of service and maintain the balance of supply and demand between the service provider and their customers

Financial Management for IT Services Process – Objectives
- Defining and maintaining a framework to identify, manage and communicate the cost of providing services
- Evaluating financial impact of new or changed strategies
- Securing funding to manage the provision of services
- Facilitating good stewardship of service and customer assets to ensure the organization meets its objectives together with service asset and configuration management and knowledge management.
- Balancing the relationship between expenses and income according to the organization's financial policies
- Managing and reporting expenditure on service provision on behalf of the organization's stakeholders
- Executing financial policies and practices in the provision of services
- Accounting for money spent on service creation, delivery and support
- Forecasting financial requirements to meet service commitments to customers and compliance with regulatory and legislative requirements
- Defining a framework to recover service provision from customers where appropriate

Financial Management for IT Services Process – scope

Budgeting	The process of predicting and controlling the income and expenditure of money within the organization Consists of a periodic negotiation cycle to set budgets (usually annual) and the monthly monitoring of the current budgets
Accounting	Process that enables the IT organization to account fully for the way its money is spent (particularly to identify costs by customer, by service and by activity) Usually involves accounting systems, ledgers, charts of accounts, journals; should be overseen by someone accountancy-trained
Charging	Process required to bill customers for services supplied to them Requires sound IT accounting practices and systems

Financial management is typically well established and understood in an organization. Professional accountants manage dedicated finance departments, which set financial policies, budgeting procedures, financial reporting standards, accounting practices and revenue generation or cost recovery rules.

In an IT context, financial management is often a separate function either reporting to the CIO or the CFO, but with some form of functional reporting between the two areas. Regardless of where the function is actually situated in the organization, financial management for IT services is a specialized area that requires an understanding of the world of finance and business as well as the world of technology.

A common misunderstanding is that all accountants are the same – without understanding that there are different specializations in accounting. Specifically, financial management for IT services requires accountants with a good understanding of cost accounting – a discipline often found in manufacturing environments. It is important that the correct skills are specified when hiring a person to manage IT finances.

IT financial policies and practices must be consistent with the rest of the organization. This is a requirement of most financial management legislation, regulations and best practice, but also facilitates better communication and reporting between IT and other business units.

In internal service providers financial management plays a translational role between corporate financial systems and service management. The result of a service-oriented accounting function is that far greater detail and understanding is achieved on service provision and consumption, and data generation feeding directly into the planning process.

ITILFND05-05-22 State the purpose, objectives and scope for financial management for IT services (SS 4.3.1, 4.3.2), including business case (SS 3.6.1.1)

Business Case

Business case
Justification for a significant item of expenditure. Includes information about costs, benefits, options, issues, risks and possible problems.

- A decision support and planning tool that projects the likely consequences of a business action
- The consequences can take on qualitative and quantitative dimensions
- Sample business case structure
  1. Introduction – business objectives addressed
  2. Methods and assumptions – boundaries of the business case
  3. Business impacts – financial, non-financial results anticipated
  4. Risks and contingencies – probability that alternative results will emerge
  5. Recommendations – specific actions recommended

A business case is a decision support and planning tool that projects the likely consequences of a business action. The consequences can take on qualitative and quantitative dimensions. A financial analysis, for example, is frequently central to a good business case.

The structure of a business case varies from organization to organization. What they all have in common is a detailed analysis of business impact or benefits. Business impact is in turn linked to business objectives. For example, the business objectives of:

- A commercial provider organizations are usually the objectives of the business itself, including financial and organizational performance.
- An internal service provider should be linked to business objectives of the business unit to which the service is being provided, and the overall corporate objectives.
- Not-for-profit organizations are usually objectives for the constituents, population or membership served as well as financial and organizational performance.

While most of a business case argument relies on cost analysis, there is much more to a service management initiative than financials. A non-financial business impact can be identified by how the achievement of one or more business objectives is affected. For example, an organization changes its sales order service to track individual customer transactions, and report on purchasing trends for each customer. The financial impact for the business is not immediately obvious, but becomes clearer once the non-financial impacts are defined. These include the ability to engage in targeted (and more effective) marketing, better anticipation of stock levels (resulting in lower cost of procurement and storage) and higher customer loyalty.

ITILFND05-05-22 State the purpose, objectives and scope for financial management for IT services (SS 4.3.1, 4.3.2), including business case (SS 3.6.1.1)

We use the following mnemonic for remembering the parts of a business case: "In McKinleyville, Beavers Ravaged Redwoods".

Where initiatives have potential or proven significant risk or cost to the business – for example, major changes to a service, or the proposed introduction or retirement of a service – and where multiple alternatives exist for meeting the desired outcome, a business case must be made.

Your organization may use a different structure and sequence and call the sections something different, but in general, a business case must include:
1) Some sort of short introduction or executive summary (Introduction)
2) Background on the scope and methods applied to the business case, along with the assumptions that bound it (Methods and Assumptions)
3) An analysis of the positive and negative aspects of moving on the business case (as well as the opportunity cost of not moving forward) (Business Impacts)
4) An analysis of the potential risks (again, ideally both associated with moving forward and not moving forward) along with contingencies to pursue should those risks accrue (Risks and Contingencies)
5) And finally, as a basis for a go / no go decision on the initiative, given the nature of the solution, impacts, risks, and alternatives, we must suggest a preferred path forward (Recommendations)

What format do business cases take in your organization? Is there a standard format followed? How does it differ from what is suggested in ITIL? How is it the same?

ITILFND05-05-23 State the purpose, objectives and scope for business relationship management (SS 4.5.1, 4.5.2, Table 4.10)

Business Relationship Management (BRM)
The process responsible for maintaining a positive relationship with customers; BRM identifies customer needs and ensures that the service provider is able to meet these needs with an appropriate catalogue of services. This process has strong links with service level management.

Business Relationship Management Process – Purpose
- Establish and maintain a business relationship between the service provider and the customer based on understanding the customer and its business needs
- Identify customer needs and ensure that the service provider is able to meet these needs as business needs change over time and between circumstances

Business Relationship Management Process – Objectives
- Ensure the service provider understands the customer's perspective of service, and is therefore able to prioritize its services and service assets appropriately
- Ensure high levels of customer satisfaction, indicating the service provider is meeting the customer's requirements
- Establish and maintain a constructive relationship between the service provider and the customer based on understanding the customer and their business drivers
- Identify changes to the customer environment that could impact the type, level or utilization of services provided
- Identify technology trends that may impact type, level or utilization of services
- Establish / articulate business requirements for new or changes to services
- Ensure that the service provider is meeting the business needs of the customer
- Work with customers to ensure services / service levels are able to deliver value
- Mediate if there are conflicting requirements for services from different business units
- Establish formal complaints and escalation processes for the customer

Business Relationship Management Process – Scope
BRM focuses on understanding how services meet customer requirements. To achieve this, the process must focus on understanding and communicating:
- Business outcomes that the customer wants to achieve
- Services currently offered to the customer, and how they are used by the customer
- How services are currently offered including who is responsible for them, agreed levels of service, quality of services delivered and any changes that are anticipated
- Technology trends that could impact current services and the customer, and how
- Levels of customer satisfaction; action plans in place to deal with the causes
- How to optimize services for the future
- How the service provider is represented to the customer

ITILFND05-05-23 State the purpose, objectives and scope for business relationship management (SS 4.5.1, 4.5.2, Tab 4.10)

We know that service level management focuses on the service and what underpins it, and reaches up and out to the business; the primary objective of service level management is to understand the service required, along with service levels, and to make sure that all the things that are required to support those service levels are in place.

A related role is business relationship management. The difference in focus is right there in the name: service level management manages service levels; business relationship management manages the relationship with the business.

Said another way, a business relationship manager sits up in bed at night and can't sleep because the relationship with the business is out of kilter, and the service level manager does the same when a proposed or existing service does not have everything it needs to consistently meet required utility and warranty.

As you can imagine, part of the business relationship management role is to educate the customer on the features of IT services and their benefits in general and specifically for the customer. The importance of this education role cannot be overstated. The business relationship management function's primary role is to act as a translator for the business, to translate the value of a proposed or current service or change or problem resolution or opportunity found in a technology trend for the customer. This requires keen business communication skills, understanding of the business and IT at a management level, and comprehension of not just current technology trends but what they might mean for the business.

You can expect a tight tie here with service portfolio management, working with BRM and the customer to sort which services to introduce, change, and retire.

As with all ITIL processes, BRM exists and is called out because it represents something of management significance. It is not enough to have the specification, quality, or delivery; expectations must be systematically set and perceptions must be systematically managed; understanding of the other and other-centered communication must be practiced. This is the job of business relationship management as it relates to customers.

ITILFND05-05-31 Explain the purpose, objectives, scope, basic concepts, process activities and interfaces for service level management (SLM) (SD 4.3.1.4.3.2, 4.3.6.4), including service-based SLA (SD 4.3.5.1), multi-level SLAs (SD 4.3.5.1, Figure 4.7), service level requirements (SLRs) (SD 4.3.5.2), SLA monitoring (SLAM) chart (SD 4.3.5.5, CSI Figure 4.4) service review (SD 4.3.5.6), service improvement plan (SIP) (SD 4.3.6.3), the relationship between SLM and BRM (SD 4.3.2.1)

Service Level Management (SLM)

Process responsible for negotiating achievable SLAs and ensuring they are met; responsible for ensuring all IT service management processes, OLAs and underpinning contracts are appropriate for the agreed service level targets; monitors and reports on service levels, holds regular service reviews with customers, identifies required improvements.

Service Level Management Process – Purpose

o Ensure all current / planned services are delivered to agreed achievable targets
  o Accomplished through a constant cycle of negotiating, agreeing, monitoring, reporting on and reviewing IT service targets and achievements, and through instigation of actions to correct or improve the level of service delivered

Service Level Management Process – Objectives

o Define, document, agree, monitor, measure, report and review the level of IT services provided; instigate corrective measures whenever appropriate
o Provide and improve a relationship / communication with the business and customers in conjunction with business relationship management
o Ensure specific and measurable targets are developed for all IT services
o Monitor and improve customer satisfaction with quality of service delivered
o Ensure IT and customers have a clear expectation of service levels to be delivered
o Ensure that even when all agreed targets met, the levels of service delivered are subject to proactive, cost-effective continual improvement

Service Level Management Process – Scope

o Development of relationships with the business
o Negotiation and agreement of current requirements and targets, documentation and management of SLAs for all operational services, future requirements and targets; documentation and management of SLRs for all proposed new or changed services
o Development and management of OLAs aligned with SLA targets
o Review of all underpinning supplier contracts and agreements with Supplier Management to ensure targets are aligned with SLA targets
o Proactive prevention of service failures, reduction of service risks and improvement in service quality, in conjunction with all other processes
o Reporting, management of all services, SLA breach / weakness review
o Instigation and coordination of SIPs for management, planning and implementation of all service and process improvements

Service Level Management Process – Key Activities

1. Determine, document, and agree on requirements for new services SLRs, make SLAs
2. Monitor service performance against SLAs, report out
3. Conduct service review and instigate improvements within an overall SIP
4. Assist with Business Service Catalogue, maintain templates
5. Develop contacts and relationships, record and manage complaints and compliments
6. Collate, measure, and improve customer satisfaction
7. Review and revise SLAs, service scope, and UCs

Service Level Management Process – critical interfaces

o **Business relationship management** –ensures that the service provider has a full understanding of the needs and priorities of the business and that customers are appropriately involved/represented in the work of service level management

o **Service catalogue management** –provides accurate information about services and their interfaces and dependencies to support determining the SLA framework, identifying customers/business units that need to be engaged by SLM and to assist SLM in communicating with customers regarding services provided

o **Incident management** –provides critical data to SLM to demonstrate performance against many SLA targets, operates with the fulfillment of SLA targets as a CSF. SLM negotiates support-related targets such as target restoration times, and then fulfillment of targets is embedded in the operation of the incident management process

o **Supplier management** –works collaboratively with SLM to define, negotiate, document and agree terms of service with suppliers to support the achievement of commitments made by the service provider in SLAs. Supplier management also manages the performance of suppliers and contracts against these terms of service to ensure related SLA targets are met

o **Availability, capacity, IT service continuity and information security management** –contribute to SLM by helping to define service level targets that relate to their area of responsibility and to validate that targets are realistic. Once targets are agreed, day-to-day operation of each process ensures targets are met

o **Financial management for IT services** –works with SLM to validate the predicted cost of delivering the service levels required by the customer to inform their decision-making process and to ensure that actual costs are compared to predicted costs as part of overall management of the cost effectiveness of service

o **Design coordination** – during service design, is responsible for ensuring overall service design activities are completed successfully. SLM plays a critical role in this through the development of agreed SLRs and the associated service targets which the new or changed service must be designed to achieve

Service Level Agreements (SLAs)

Service Level Agreement (SLA)

An agreement between an IT service provider and a customer. An SLA describes the IT service, documents service level targets, and specifies the responsibilities of the IT service provider and customer. A single SLA may cover multiple IT services or multiple customers.

Also, SLAs:
- Are used to formalize service-based relationships, internally and externally
- Normally vary considerably in the detail covered
- Are not to be used for external relationships unless part of an underlying contract
- May not be legally enforceable but instead 'represents the goodwill and faith of the parties signing it' (for stand-alone SLAs)

Service Level Agreement (SLA) Structures – Service-Based, Customer-Based, and Multi-Level SLAs Example 3-layer structure

1. Service-Based
   - Covers SLM issues for a specific service, for all Customers of that service
   - One for each service in the SLA
2. Customer-Based
   - Agreement with an individual Customer group, covering all services they use
3. Multi-Level
   - Multi-level SLA, for example, a three-layer structure:
     - Corporate Level: all generic issues for all
     - Customer Level: all issues for a particular customer
     - Service Level: all issues to a specific service

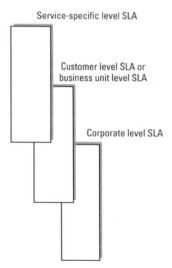

Service-specific level SLA

Customer level SLA or business unit level SLA

Corporate level SLA

SD Figure 4.7: Multi-level SLAs

Determining, documenting and agreeing requirements for new services and producing SLRs

Service Level Requirement (SLR)

A customer requirement for an aspect of an IT service. SLRs are based on business objectives and used to negotiate agreed service level targets.

Service Level Target

A commitment documented in an SLA based on service level requirements, needed to ensure that the IT service is able to meet business objectives. They should be SMART, and are usually based on key performance indicators.

SLRs relate primarily to the warranty of the service:
o What levels of service are required by the customer to be able to receive the value of the utility of the service?
o How available does the service need to be? How secure?
o How quickly must it be restored if it should fail?

This is one of the earliest activities in service design. Once the service catalogue has been produced and the SLA structure has been agreed, the first SLRs must be drafted. While many organizations have to give initial priority to introducing SLAs for existing services, it is also important to establish procedures for agreeing service level requirements for new services being developed or procured. The SLRs should be an integral part of the overall service design criteria which also include the functional or 'utility' specifications. SLRs should, from the very start, form part of the testing/ trialing criteria as the service progresses through the stages of design and development or procurement.

Involve customers from the outset, but rather than approaching customers with a 'blank page', it may be better to produce an outline SLR draft with potential performance targets and management and operational requirements, as a starting point for more detailed and in-depth discussion. Be careful, though, not to go too far and appear to be presenting the customer with a 'fait accompli' as this may unnecessarily limit open and productive dialogue. In order to ensure a focus on required business outcomes, it is important to maintain clarity in the difference between the SLR and the specific service level target(s) associated with the achievement of the SLR. For example, an SLR relating to performance might be expressed by the customer as 'fast enough to support the anticipated volume of orders to be placed during peak activity periods without failures or delays', while the service level target negotiated to support this requirement will define specific, measurable response times and the conditions under which the target will be deemed to have been breached.

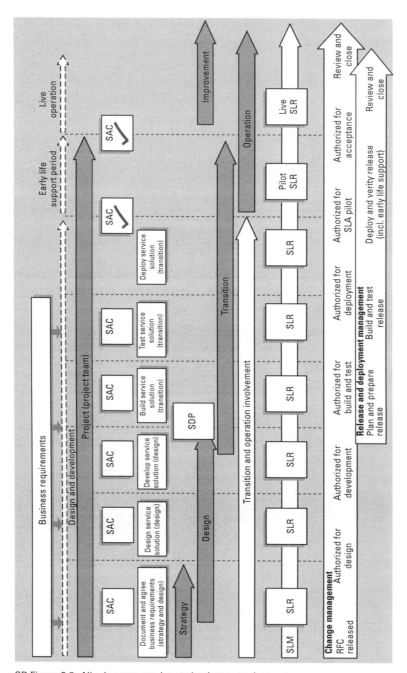

SD Figure 3.8: Aligning new services to business requirements

Determining high-level, business objective-oriented SLRs typically begins in service strategy when defining information for the decision to charter and fund the service. SPM and BRM involvement in determining warranty is heavy. Once the service charter is set, SLM continues to vet any added SLRs and refines SLRs to a detailed measurable level needed for service design.

Producing service reports

o Immediately after the SLA is agreed and accepted, monitoring must be instigated, and service achievement reports must be produced
  o Operational reports must be produced frequently
  o Exception reports should be produced whenever an SLA has been broken
o What must be defined and agreed with customers:
  o SLA reporting mechanisms, intervals and reports
  o Frequency and format of service review meetings
o Periodic reports must be produced and circulated to customers and appropriate IT managers in advance of service level reviews and include
  o Details of performance against all SLA targets
  o Trends
  o Specific actions being undertaken to improve service quality

Service Level Agreement Monitoring (SLAM) Charts

o Used to monitor and report achievements against Service Level Targets
o Color coded to show whether each agreed Service Level Target has been met, missed, or nearly missed during each of the previous 12 months

Month / Target	1	2	3	4	5	6	7	8	9	10	11	12
SLA1												
SLA2												
SLA3												
SLA4												
SLA5												
SLA6												
SLA7												
SLA8												
SLA9												
SLA10												

Based on Cabinet Office Crown Copyright Material CSI Figure 4.4: Service level achievement chart

A useful technique is to include a SLA monitoring (SLAM) chart at the front of a service report to give an 'at-a-glance' overview of how achievements have measured up against targets. These are most effective if color coded (red, amber, green, and sometimes referred to as RAG charts as a result).

Conduct Service Reviews, Instigate Improvement within an Overall SIP

o Hold regular, periodic (monthly or at least quarterly) review meetings with customers to review prior period service achievement and preview coming period issues
o Place actions from such meetings on the customer and provider as appropriate to improve weak areas where targets are not being met
  o Minute all actions, and review progress at the next meeting to ensure actions are being followed up and properly implemented
o Focus particular attention on each breach of service level to determine the exact cause and what can be done to prevent any recurrence
  o If the service level was (or has become) unachievable, review, renegotiate, and agree different service targets
  o If the service break was due to a failure of a third-party or internal support group, review the underpinning agreement or OLA

Service Improve Plan (SIP)

Service Improvement Plan (SIP)
A formal plan to implement improvements to a process or IT service

o Initiated when service quality has degraded with a goal of restoring it
o Formal project undertaken by a provider to identify and make measurable improvements in a specified work area or process
o Shows customers steps to be taken to improve service in the next SLA revision
o Focus may include user training, system testing, documentation

The SLM process often generates a good starting point for a Service Improvement Plan (SIP) – and the service review process may drive this. A SIP, one of the outputs of SLM, is an overall program or plan of prioritized improvement actions, encompassing appropriate services and processes, together with associated impacts and risks.

Business Relationship Management and SLM

o While the SLM process exists to ensure that agreed achievable levels of service are provided to the customer and users, the business relationship management process is focused on a more strategic perspective
o BRM takes as its mission the identification of customer needs and ensuring that the service provider is able to meet the customers' needs
  o Focuses on the overall relationship service provider / customer relationship, working to determine which services the provider will deliver

ITILFND05-05-31 Explain the purpose, objectives, scope, basic concepts, process activities and interfaces for service level management (SLM) (SD 4.3.1.4.3.2, 4.3.6.4), including service-based SLA (SD 4.3.5.1), multi-level SLAs (SD 4.3.5.1, Figure 4.7), service level requirements (SLRs) (SD 4.3.5.2), SLA monitoring (SLAM) chart (SD 4.3.5.5, CSI Figure 4.4) service review (SD 4.3.5.6), service improvement plan (SIP) (SD 4.3.6.3), the relationship between SLM and BRM (SD 4.3.2.1)

Service level management is concerned with ensuring *achievable* targets are agreed; during service design this means talking to the business about what they want and what it will take to deliver it consistently, including the products / technology, people, process, partners, agreements (SLAs / OLAs / UCs), sub-services, and the like. The general spirit of SLM should be, "yes we can do it, and this is what it will cost". A "fudge factor" needs to be built in to ensure service levels can be met consistently, and SLM must make absolutely certain that what is being agreed is achievable, for example, it is impossible to provide 5 9's of availability while riding on a 1 9 network.

While services are live SLM reports achievements against targets and instigates action to preempt or correct issues.

It is important to understand and distinguish between the objectives of service level management and other ITIL processes, in particular, business relationship and service catalogue management. The relationship with availability, capacity, IT service continuity, and security management should be clear, as these are primary provisions of a service level agreement (capacity often being covered under 'performance', for example, so many transactions per second, as performance is rooted in capacity).

For examination purposes, it is important to be able to identify and distinguish between service-, customer-based, and multi-level SLAs. Distinguishing between an SLA, SLR, and service level target is also important. You must be able to recall key aspects of service reporting, especially SLAM charts. Lastly, what a SIP is and SLM's role in it is important to recall.

ITILFND05-05-41 State the purpose, objectives and scope for service catalogue management (SD 4.2.1, 4.2.2)

Service Catalogue Management
The process responsible for providing and maintaining the service catalogue and for ensuring that it is available to those who are authorized to access it

Service Catalogue
Database or structured document with information on all live IT services, including those available for deployment. It is part of the service portfolio and contains information about two types of IT service: customer-facing services that are visible to the business; and supporting services required by the service provider to deliver customer-facing services.

Service Catalogue Management Process – Purpose
o Provide and maintain a single source of consistent information on all operational services and those being prepared to be run operationally
o Ensure that it is widely available to those authorized to access it

Service Catalogue Management Process – Objectives
o Manage the information contained within the service catalogue
o Ensure that the service catalogue is accurate and reflects the current details, status, interfaces and dependencies of all services that are being run, or being prepared to run, in the live environment, according to the defined policies
o Ensure the service catalogue is made available to those approved to access it in a way that supports their effective and efficient use of service catalogue information
o Ensure the service catalogue supports evolving needs of other service management processes for service catalogue information, including interfaces and dependencies

Service Catalogue Management Process – SCOPE
o Contribution to the definition of services and service packages
o Development and maintenance of service and service package descriptions appropriate for the service catalogue
o Production and maintenance of an accurate service catalogue
o Interfaces, dependencies / consistency between the catalogue and service portfolio
o Interfaces and dependencies between all services and supporting services within the service catalogue and the CMS

The service catalogue management process does NOT include:
o Detailed attention to the capturing, maintenance and use of service asset and configuration data as performed through the service asset and configuration management process (see ITIL Service Transition)
o Detailed attention to the capturing, maintenance and fulfillment of service requests as performed by request fulfillment (see ITIL Service Operation)

ITILFND05-05-41 State the purpose, objectives and scope for service catalogue management (SD 4.2.1, 4.2.2)

If you think about it, especially in a large organization, it is a big enough job just to do service level management. In smaller organizations, the process and roles associated with service catalogue management are often rolled in with that of service level management. But in a larger enterprise, it is a large job (or jobs) to just tend to the service catalogue.

The idea here is to put someone, or a group, on point to own making sure how the organization and its services are presented to customers is satisfactory. Customers should easily be able to understand services offered, options (if any), their value and cost.

Internal IT staff and suppliers should have ready access to the technical view of services.

That is why there are two views of the service catalogue: business and technical.

Think of it this way: you as a customer don't care a jot about how many cell towers your mobile phone service provider has, what technology they run, where they are positioned, how they are configured, etc. What you care about is the level of service provided: speed, coverage, and the like. This is the business view of the servicer catalogue.

Internal staff and supplier for the provider care about this technical information a great deal. How else are you going to service a cell tower if you don't know where it is, how it is configured, etc. That is the purpose of the technical view of the service catalogue.

For examination purposes, it is important to be able to recall that the service catalogue has two views: business and technical.

ITILFND05-05-42 State the purpose, objectives and scope for availability management (SD 4.4.1, 4.4.2), including service availability (SD 4.4.4.2), component availability (SD 4.4.4.2), reliability (SD 4.4.4.3), maintainability (SD 4.4.4.3), serviceability (SD 4.4.4.3), vital business functions (VBF) (SD 4.4.4.3)

Availability Management
Process responsible for ensuring IT services meet current and future availability needs of the business in a cost-effective and timely manner; defines, analyzes, plans, measures and improves all aspects of availability of IT services; ensures all IT infrastructures, processes, tools, roles etc. are appropriate for the agreed service level targets for availability.

Availability
The ability of a service, component or CI to perform its agreed function when required; often measured and reported as a percentage.

Availability Management Process – Purpose
o Ensure availability levels delivered in all IT services meet agreed availability needs and service level targets in a cost-effective and timely manner

Availability Management Process – Objectives
o Produce and maintain an appropriate and up-to-date availability plan that reflects the current and future needs of the business
o Provide advice and guidance to all other areas of the business and IT on all availability-related issues
o Ensure that service availability achievements meet all their agreed targets by managing services and resources-related availability performance
o Assist with the diagnosis and resolution of availability-related incidents and problems
o Assess the impact of all changes on the availability plan and the availability of all services and resources
o Ensure that proactive measures to improve the availability of services are implemented wherever it is cost-justifiable to do so

Availability management must ensure the agreed availability level is provided. Measurement and monitoring of IT availability is a key activity to ensure availability levels are being met consistently. Availability management should look to continually optimize and proactively improve availability of the IT infrastructure, services and the supporting organization, to provide cost-effective availability improvements with business and customer benefits.

Availability Management Process – Scope

Design, implementation, measurement, management and improvement of IT service and component availability, including two key elements, reactive and proactive activities:

Reactive activities	Proactive activities
Monitoring, measuring, analysis and management of all events, incidents and problems involving unavailability; principally performed as part of the operational roles	Proactive planning, design and improvement of availability. These activities are principally performed as part of the design and planning roles

Availability management needs to understand the service and component availability requirements from the business perspective in terms of the:
o Current business processes, their operation and requirements
o Future business plans and requirements
o Service targets and the current IT service operation and delivery
o IT infrastructure, data, applications and environment and their performance
o Business impacts and priorities in relation to the services and their usage.

The availability management process should be applied to all:
o operational services and technology, particularly those covered by SLAs
o new IT services and for existing services where SLRs or SLAs have been established
o supporting services and the partners and suppliers (both internal and external) that form the IT support organization as a precursor to the creation of formal agreements

The availability management process may also be applied to those IT services deemed to be business-critical, regardless of whether formal SLAs exist, and should consider all aspects of the IT services and components and supporting organizations that may impact availability, including training, skills, process effectiveness, procedures and tools.

The availability management process should include:
o Monitoring of all aspects of availability, reliability and maintainability of IT services and the supporting components, with appropriate events, alarms and escalation, with automated scripts for recovery
o Maintaining a set of methods, techniques and calculations for all availability measurements, metrics and reporting
o Actively participating in risk assessment and management activities
o Collecting measurements and the analysis and production of regular and ad hoc reports on service and component availability
o Knowing agreed current / future business demands for services and their availability
o Influencing service and component design to align with business availability needs
o Producing an availability plan that enables the service provider to continue to provide and improve services in line with availability targets defined in SLAs, and to plan and forecast future availability levels required, as defined in SLRs
o Maintaining a test schedule for resilience and fail-over components and mechanisms
o Assisting with the identification and resolution of any incidents and problems associated with service or component unavailability
o Proactively improving service or component availability wherever it is cost-justifiable and meets the needs of the business

Guiding principles of availability

Guiding principles that should underpin the availability management process and its focus:

o Service availability is at the core of customer satisfaction and business success: there is a direct correlation in most organizations between service availability and customer and user satisfaction, where poor service performance is defined as being unavailable

o When services fail, business, customer and user satisfaction can still be earned; the way a provider reacts in a failure has a major influence on perception and expectation

o Improving availability can only begin after understanding how the IT services support the operation of the business

o Service availability is only as good as the weakest link in the chain: it can be greatly increased by elimination of single points of failure or an unreliable or weak component

o Availability is not just a reactive process. The more proactive the process, the better service availability will be. Availability should not purely react to service and component failure. The more often events and failures are predicted, pre-empted and prevented, the higher the level of service availability

o It is cheaper to design the right level of service availability into a service from the start, rather than try and 'bolt it on' subsequently. Adding resilience into a service or component is invariably more expensive than designing it in from the start. Also, once a service gets a bad name for unreliability, it becomes very difficult to change the image. Resilience is a key consideration of ITSCM, and should be considered at the same time

Availability
Ability of an IT service or other configuration item to perform its agreed function when required. Availability is determined by reliability, maintainability, serviceability, performance and security. Availability is usually calculated as a percentage.

Availability management is completed at two inter-connected levels:

Service availability	Component availability
Involves all aspects of service availability and unavailability and the impact of component availability, or the potential impact of component unavailability on service availability	Involves all aspects of component availability and unavailability

Service availability is key to customer satisfaction and business success
o Service availability is only as good as the weakest link in the chain
o It is cheaper to design the right level of service availability into a service from the start, rather than try and 'bolt it on' subsequently

Aspects of Availability – Availability Calculation

$$\text{vailability (\%)} = \frac{\text{Agreed service time (AST)} - \text{downtime}}{\text{AST}} \times 100$$

Example:
o 24x7 uptime commitment, 6 hours downtime in a month
  ((720 hrs - 6 hrs) / 720 hrs) x 100% = 99.17%
o Total system availability = product of each component availability
  that is: availability 1 x availability 2 = total availability

Aspects of Availability – Reliability

Reliability
A measure of how long a service, component or CI can perform its agreed function without interruption. The reliability of the service can be improved by increasing the reliability of individual components or by increasing the resilience of the service to individual component failure (i.e. increasing the component redundancy, for example by using load-balancing techniques). It is often measured and reported as the mean time between service incidents (MTBSI) or mean time between failures (MTBF)

Reliability is a measure of how long a service, component or CI can perform its agreed function without interruption. The reliability of the service can be improved by increasing the reliability of individual components or by increasing the resilience of the service to individual component failure (i.e. increasing the component redundancy).

$$\text{Reliability (MTBSI in hours)} = \frac{\text{Availability time in hours}}{\text{Number of breaks}}$$

$$\text{Reliability (MTBF in hours)} = \frac{\text{Availability time in hours} - \text{Total downtime in hours}}{\text{Number of breaks}}$$

Aspects of Availability – Maintainability

> **Maintainability**
> A measure of how quickly and effectively a service, component or CI can be restored to normal working after a failure. It is measured and reported as the mean time to restore service (MTRS)

Maintainability is a measure of how quickly and effectively a service, component or CI can be restored to normal working after a failure. It is measured and reported as the mean time to restore service (MTRS) and should be calculated using the following formula:

$$\text{Maintainability (MTRS in hours)} = \frac{\text{Total downtime in hours}}{\text{Number of service breaks}}$$

MTRS downtime covers all factors that make the service, component or CI unavailable:

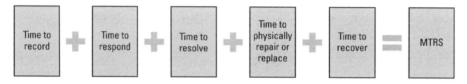

Use MTRS to avoid the ambiguity of the more common industry term mean time to repair (MTTR), which in some definitions includes only repair time, but in others includes recovery.

Aspects of Availability – Example: measuring availability, reliability and maintainability

A situation where a 24 × 7 service has run for 5,020 hours with only two breaks, one of six hours and one of 14, would give the following figures:

Availability	= (5,020–(6+14))/5,020 × 100	= 99.60%
Reliability (MTBSI)	= 5,020/2	= 2,510 hours
Reliability (MTBF)	= 5,020–(6+14)/2	= 2,500 hours
Maintainability (MTRS)	= (6+14)/2	= 10 hours

Aspects of Availability – Serviceability

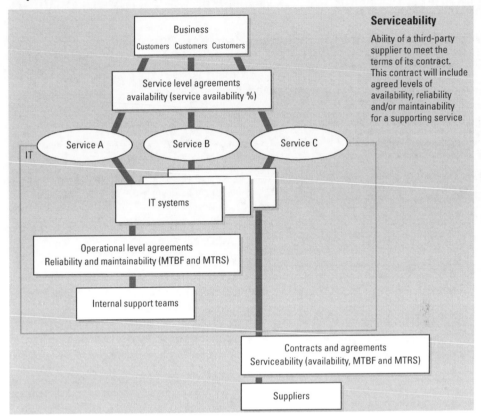

Aspects of Availability – Vital Business Function (VBF)

Vital Business Function (VBF)
Part of a business process that is critical to the success of the business. Vital business functions are an important consideration of business continuity management, IT service continuity management and availability management.

Certain VBFs may need special designs within service design plans, incorporating:
o **High availability** – a characteristic of the IT service that minimizes or masks the effects of IT component failure to the users of a service
o **Fault tolerance** – the ability of an IT service, component or CI to continue to operate correctly after failure of a component part
o **Continuous operation** – design to eliminate planned downtime of an IT service. Individual components or CIs may be down, but the IT service remains available
o **Continuous availability** – an approach or design to achieve 100% availability. A continuously available IT service has no planned or unplanned downtime

ITILFND05-05-43 State the purpose, objectives and scope for information security management (ISM) (SD 4.7.1, 4.7.2), including information security policy (SD 4.7.4.1)

Information Security Management Process – Purpose

o Align IT security with business security and ensure that the confidentiality, integrity, and availability of the organization's assets, information, data, and IT services always matches the agreed needs of the business

Information Security Management (ISM)

The process responsible for ensuring that the confidentiality, integrity and availability of an organization's assets, information, data and IT services match the agreed needs of the business. Information security management supports business security and has a wider scope than that of the IT service provider, and includes handling of paper, building access, phone calls etc. for the entire organization.

Information Security Management Process – Objectives

o Protect the interests of those relying on information, and the systems and communications that deliver information, from harm from failures of confidentiality, integrity and availability; for most organizations, the objective is met when:
  o Information is observed by or disclosed to only those who have a right to know (**confidentiality**)
  o Information is complete, accurate and protected against unauthorized modification (**integrity**)
  o Information is available and usable when required, and the systems that provide it can appropriately resist attacks and recover from or prevent failures (**availability**)
  o Transactions / information exchanges with enterprises / partners can be trusted (**authenticity and non-repudiation**)

Information Security Management Process – SCOPE

o The production, maintenance, distribution and enforcement of an information security policy and supporting security policies
o Understanding the agreed current and future security requirements of the business and the existing business security policy and plans
o Establishing a set of security controls supporting information security policy, manage risks associated with access to services, information and systems
o Documentation of all security controls, together with the operation and maintenance of the controls and their associated risks
o Management of suppliers and contracts regarding access to systems and services, in conjunction with supplier management
o Management of all security breaches, incidents and problems on all systems, services
o Proactive improvement of security controls, security risk management and reduction
o Integration of security aspects within all other ITSM processes

The ISM process must be the focal point for all IT security issues and ensure an information security policy is produced, maintained and enforced that covers use and misuse of systems and services. ISM must grasp the total IT and business security environment, including the:

o Business security policy and plans
o Current business operation and its security requirements
o Future business plans and requirements
o Legislative and regulatory requirements
o Obligations and responsibilities with regard to security contained within SLAs
o The business and IT risks and their management

Understanding this enables ISM to ensure all current and future security aspects and risks of the business are cost-effectively managed. Prioritization of confidentiality, integrity and availability must be considered in the context of business and business processes. The primary guide to defining what must be protected and the level of protection must come from the business. To be effective, security must address end-to-end business processes and cover the physical and technical aspects. Only in the context of business needs and risks can management define security. To achieve effective security governance, management must establish and maintain an information security management system (ISMS) to guide development and management of a comprehensive program supporting business needs.

Information Security Management Process – Information Security

Information Security Policy (ISP)
Policy that governs an organization's approach to information security management

The policy must cover all areas of security, be appropriate, meet business needs and include

o Overall information security policy
o Use and misuse of IT assets policy
o Access control policy
o Password control policy
o Email policy
o Internet policy
o Anti-virus policy
o Information classification policy

o Document classification policy
o Remote access policy
o Supplier access to IT service, information and components policy
o Copyright infringement policy for electronic material
o Asset disposal policy
o Records retention policy

Information security management activities should be focused on and driven by an overall information security policy and a set of underpinning specific security policies. The policy should have the full support of top executive IT management and ideally the support and commitment of top executive business management. In most cases, these policies should be widely available to all customers and users, and their compliance should be referred to in all SLRs, SLAs, OLAs, underpinning contracts and agreements. The policies should be authorized by top executive management within the business and IT, and compliance to them should be endorsed on a regular basis. All security policies should be reviewed – and, where necessary, revised – on at least an annual basis.

ITILFND05-05-44 State the purpose, objectives and scope for supplier management (SD 4.8.1, 4.8.2.), including supplier categories (SD 4.8.5.3, Figure 4.28)

Supplier Management Process – Purpose

o To obtain value for money from suppliers and provide seamless IT service quality to the business by ensuring all contracts and agreements with suppliers support business needs and that all suppliers meet contractual commitments

Supplier Management

The process responsible for getting value for money from suppliers, ensuring all supplier contracts and agreements support business needs, and all suppliers meet contractual commitments.

Supplier

A third party responsible for supplying goods or services that are required to deliver IT services; examples include commodity hardware and software vendors, network and telecommunications providers, and outsourcing organizations.

Supplier Management Process – Objectives

o Obtain value for money from suppliers and contracts
o Ensure contracts with suppliers are aligned to business needs, and support and align with agreed targets in SLRs and SLAs, in conjunction with SLM
o Manage relationships with suppliers
o Manage supplier performance
o Negotiate and agree contracts with suppliers, manage them through their lifecycle
o Maintain a supplier policy and a supporting supplier and contract management information system (SCMIS)

Supplier Management Process – Scope

o Implementation and enforcement of the supplier policy
o Maintenance of an SCMIS
o Supplier and contract categorization and risk assessment
o Supplier and contract evaluation and selection
o Development, negotiation and agreement of contracts
o Contract review, renewal and termination
o Management of suppliers and supplier performance
o Identification of improvement opportunities for inclusion in the CSI register, and the implementation of service and supplier improvement plans
o Maintenance of standard contracts, terms and conditions
o Management of contractual dispute resolution
o Management of sub-contracted suppliers

Supplier Management Process – Roles and Interfaces

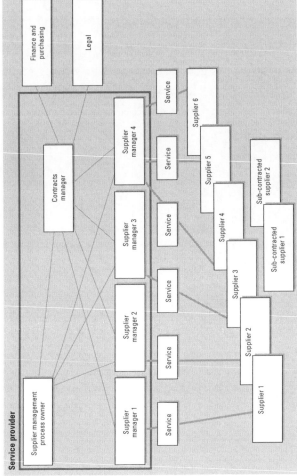

SD Figure 4.26: Supplier management – roles and interfaces

IT supplier management often has to comply with organizational or corporate standards, guidelines and requirements, particularly those of corporate legal, finance and purchasing, as illustrated in SD Figure 4.26.

In order to ensure that suppliers provide value for money and meet their service targets, the relationship between each supplier should be owned by an individual within the service provider organization. However, a single individual may own the relationship for one or many suppliers, as illustrated in SD Figure 4.26. To ensure that relationships are developed in a consistent manner and that suppliers' performance is appropriately reviewed and managed, roles need to be established for a supplier management process owner and a contracts manager. In smaller organizations, these separate roles may be combined into a single responsibility.

Supplier Management Process – Supplier categorization

Strategic – for significant 'partnering' relationships that involve senior managers sharing confidential strategic information to facilitate long-term plans

Tactical – relationships involving significant commercial activity and business interaction

Operational – for suppliers of operational products or services

Commodity – for suppliers providing low-value and/or readily available products and services

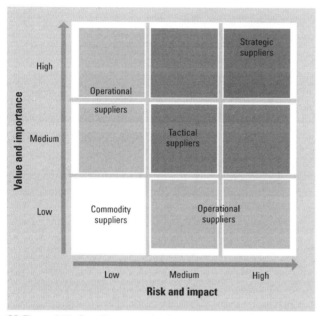

SD Figure 4.28: Supplier categorization

© Crown copyright 2011. Reproduced under license from the Cabinet Office.

The supplier management process should be adaptive and spend more time and effort managing key suppliers. Some form of categorization scheme should exist in the supplier management process to categorize suppliers and their importance to the service provider and their services to the business. One of the best ways of categorizing suppliers is to assess risk and impact of using the supplier, and value and importance of the supplier and its services to the business, as illustrated in SD Figure 4.28.

Supplier categorization – Standardized Vs. customized services

Standardized	Customized
+ The preferred approach unless a clear business advantage exists	+ May contribute to competitive advantage through differentiated service, or may be the result of operational evolution
+ Lower dependence on the supplier, supplier could be replaced easier (if necessary)	- Increased dependence on the supplier, increased risk and can result in increased cost
+ Minimal time to market when deploying new or changed business services, and in pursuing cost-reduction strategies	- For the supplier: decreased ability to achieve economies of scale through common operations, resulting in narrowed margins, and reduced capital available for future investment.

Supplier Management Process – Supplier relationships

o Having established the supplier type, the relationship must be formalized

o The term 'agreement' is used generically to refer to any formalization of a relationship between customer and supplier organizations, and may range from the informal to comprehensive legally binding contracts

o Simple, low-value relationships may be covered by a supplier's standard terms and conditions, and be managed wholly by IT

o A relationship of strategic importance to the business requires a comprehensive contract that ensures that the supplier supports evolving business needs throughout the life of the contract

o A contract needs to be managed and developed in conjunction with procurement and legal departments and business stakeholders

Supplier Management Process – The supplier and contract management information system (SCMIS)

Supplier and contract management information system (SCMIS)
A set of tools, data and information that is used to support supplier management. See also service knowledge management system.

o Contains details of the organization's suppliers, details of the products and services that they provide to the business (e.g. email service, PC supply and installation, service desk), and details of the contracts.

o Contains supplier details, a summary of each product/service (including support arrangements), information on the ordering process and contract details if applicable

o Ideally contained within the overall CMS

o In most organizations owned by the supplier management process or the procurement or purchasing department

The SCMIS is a set of tools, data and information that is used to support supplier management. The SCMIS contains details of the organization's suppliers, together with details of the products and services that they provide to the business (e.g. email service, PC supply and installation, service desk), together with details of the contracts.

The SCMIS contains supplier details, a summary of each product/service (including support arrangements), information on the ordering process and, where applicable, contract details. Ideally the SCMIS is contained in the overall CMS. In most organizations, the supplier management process or the procurement or purchasing department owns the SCMIS.

An SCMIS is beneficial because it can be used to promote preferred suppliers and to prevent purchasing of unapproved or incompatible items. By coordinating and controlling the buying activity, the organization is more likely to be able to negotiate preferential rates.

ITILFND05-05-45 State the purpose, objectives and scope for capacity management (SD 4.5.1, 4.5.2), including capacity plan (SD 4.5.6.3), business capacity management (SD 4.5.4.3), service capacity management (SD 4.5.4.3), component capacity management (SD 4.5.4.3)

Capacity Management Process - Purpose

o Ensure the capacity of IT services and IT infrastructure meets agreed capacity- and performance-related requirements in a cost-effective and timely manner

Capacity Management

The process responsible for ensuring that the capacity of IT services and the IT infrastructure is able to meet agreed capacity- and performance-related requirements in a cost-effective and timely manner. Capacity management considers all resources required to deliver an IT service, and is concerned with meeting both the current and future capacity and performance needs of the business.

Capacity

The maximum throughput a configuration item or IT service can deliver. For some types of CI, capacity may be size or volume, e.g. a disk drive.

Capacity Management Process – Objectives

o Produce and maintain an appropriate and up-to-date capacity plan, which reflects the current and future needs of the business
o Provide advice and guidance to all other areas of the business and IT on all capacity- and performance-related issues
o Ensure service performance achievements meet all of agreed targets by managing the performance and capacity of both services and resources
o Assist with the diagnosis and resolution of performance- and capacity-related incidents and problems
o Assess the impact of all changes on the capacity plan, and the performance and capacity of all services and resources
o Ensure that proactive measures to improve the performance of services are implemented wherever it is cost-justifiable to do so

Capacity management is a process that extends across the service lifecycle. A key success factor in managing capacity is ensuring it is considered during the design stage. It is for this reason that the capacity management process is included here. Capacity management is supported initially in service strategy where the decisions and analysis of business requirements and customer outcomes influence the development of patterns of business activity, lines of service (LOS) and service options. This provides the predictive and ongoing capacity indicators needed to align capacity to demand. Capacity management provides a point of focus and management for all capacity- and performance-related issues, relating to both services and resources.

Capacity Management Process – Scope

o Monitoring patterns of business activity through performance, utilization and throughput of IT services and the supporting infrastructure, environmental, data and applications components and the production of regular and ad hoc reports on service and component capacity and performance

o Undertaking tuning activities to make the most efficient use of existing IT resources

o Understanding the agreed current and future demands being made by the customer for IT resources, and producing forecasts for future requirements

o Influencing demand in conjunction with the financial management for IT services and demand management processes

o Producing a capacity plan that enables the service provider to continue to provide services of the quality defined in SLAs and that covers a sufficient planning timeframe to meet future service levels required as defined in the service portfolio and SLRs

o Assisting with the identification and resolution of any incidents and problems associated with service or component capacity or performance

o The proactive improvement of service or component performance, wherever it is cost-justifiable and meets the needs of the business

Capacity Management Process – Capacity Plan

Capacity Plan
A plan used to manage the resources required to deliver IT services. The plan contains details of current and historic usage of IT services and components, and any issues that need to be addressed (including related improvement activities). The plan also contains scenarios for different predictions of business demand and costed options to deliver the agreed service level targets.

The outputs of capacity management are used within all other parts of the process, by many other processes and by other parts of the organization. Often this information is supplied as electronic reports or displays on shared areas, or as pages on intranet servers, to ensure the most up-to-date information is always used.

Outputs of capacity management include

o Capacity plan

o Capacity management information system (CMIS)

o Service performance information and reports

o Workload analysis and reports

o Ad hoc capacity and performance reports

o Forecasts and predictive reports

o Thresholds, alerts and events

o Improvement actions

Capacity Management Process – Sub-Processes

Business Capacity Management	Translates business needs and plans into requirements for service and IT infrastructure, ensuring that the future business requirements for IT services are quantified, designed, planned and implemented in a timely fashion
Service Capacity Management	Focuses on the management, control and prediction of the end-to-end performance and capacity of the live, operational IT services usage and workloads
Component Capacity Management	Focuses on the management, control and prediction of the performance, utilization and capacity of individual IT technology components

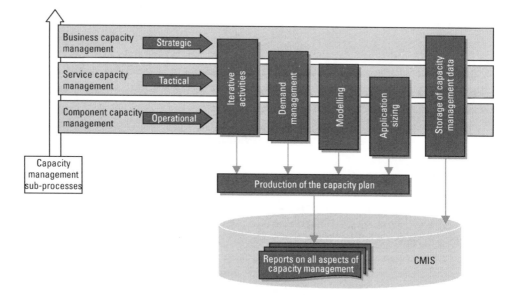

Diagram based on Cabinet Office Crown Copyright Material

There are many similar activities that are performed by each of the above sub-processes, but each sub-process has a very different focus. Business capacity management is focused on the current and future business requirements, while service capacity management is focused on the delivery of the existing services that support the business, and component capacity management is focused on the IT infrastructure that underpins service provision. The role that each of these sub-processes plays in the overall process, the production of the capacity plan and the storage of capacity-related data is illustrated in SO Figure 4.16.

ITILFND05-05-45 State the purpose, objectives and scope for capacity management
(SD 4.5.1, 4.5.2), including capacity plan (SD 4.5.6.3), business capacity management
(SD 4.5.4.3), service capacity management (SD 4.5.4.3), component capacity management
(SD 4.5.4.3)

For examination purposes, it is important to recall the three sub-processes of capacity
management and correctly select the levels of focus associated with each
1. Business capacity management
2. Service capacity management
3. Component capacity management

You may get a question that asks about what a capacity plan contains (you'll have to
pick the correct list of items); similarly, you may get a list-type question on the outputs
of capacity management, and must be able to pick the correct list of items (verbatim)
versus other lists that list plausible but incorrect items, as they are not on the list
verbatim from the ITIL publications.

It is also important to be able to recall that capacity information is stored in the CMIS.

Remember B-S-C
   Business
   Service
   Component
The three sub-processes of capacity management.

ITILFND05-05-46 State the purpose, objectives and scope for IT service continuity management (SD 4.6.1, 4.6.2), including the purpose of business impact analysis (BIA) (SD 4.6.5.2), risk assessment (SD 4.6.5.2)

IT Service Continuity Management Process - Purpose
o Support overall business continuity management (BCM) process by ensuring that, by managing risks that could seriously affect IT services, the IT service provider can always provide minimum agreed business continuity-related service levels

IT Service Continuity Management (ITSCM)
The process responsible for managing risks that could seriously affect IT services; ITSCM ensures that the IT service provider can always provide minimum agreed service levels, by reducing the risk to an acceptable level and planning for the recovery of IT services. IT service continuity management supports business continuity management.

IT Service Continuity Management Process – Objectives
o Produce and maintain a set of IT service continuity plans that support the overall business continuity plans of the organization
o Perform regular business impact analysis (BIA) to ensure continuity plans are maintained in line with changing business impacts and requirements
o Conduct regular risk assessment and management exercises to manage IT services within an agreed level of business risk in conjunction with the business, availability, and information security management processes
o Guide all other areas of the business and IT on all continuity-related issues
o Ensure that appropriate continuity mechanisms are put in place to meet or exceed the agreed business continuity targets
o Assess change impact on ITSCM plans, supporting methods, procedures
o Ensure that proactive measures to improve the availability of services are implemented wherever it is cost-justifiable to do so
o Negotiate and agree suppliers contracts for recovery capability to support all continuity plans in conjunction with the supplier management process

IT Service Continuity Management Process – Scope
o Agreement of the scope of the ITSCM process and the policies adopted
o BIA to quantify the impact loss of IT service would have on the business
o Risk assessment and management –identification and assessment of risks to identify threats to continuity / likelihood of the threats occurring
o Includes measures to manage identified threats where cost-justified
o Production of an overall ITSCM strategy integrated into BCM strategy
o Production of an ITSCM plan integrated with the overall BCM plans
o Testing of the plans
o Ongoing operation and maintenance of the plans

Business Impact Analysis (BIA) – purpose

o Quantify the impact to the business that loss of service would have; the impact could be a 'hard' impact that can be precisely identified – such as financial loss – or 'soft' impact – such as public relations, morale, safety, or loss of competitive advantage

Business Impact Analysis (BIA)

The activity in business continuity management that identifies vital business functions and their dependencies. These dependencies may include suppliers, people, other business processes, IT services etc. Business impact analysis defines the recovery requirements for IT services. These requirements include recovery time objectives, recovery point objectives and minimum service level targets for each IT service.

Business Impact Analysis (BIA) – what the BIA identifies

o The form that the damage or loss may take, e.g., lost income, additional costs, damaged reputation, loss of goodwill, loss of competitive advantage, breach of law, health and safety, risk to personal safety, immediate and long-term loss of market share, political, corporate or personal embarrassment, loss of operational capability
o Likelihood damage or loss will escalate after a service disruption, and the times of the day, week, month or year when disruption will be most severe
o Staffing, skills, facilities and services necessary to enable critical, essential business processes to continue operating at a minimum acceptable level
o When minimum levels of staffing, facilities and services must be recovered
o The time within which all required business processes and supporting staff, facilities and services should be fully recovered; relative business recovery priority for each IT service

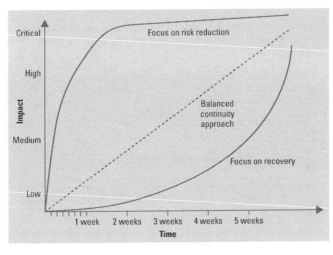

Business Impact Analysis (BIA) – graph of business impact

One key output of a BIA exercise is a graph of anticipated business impact caused by the loss of a business process or the loss of an IT service over time, as illustrated in SD Figure 4.22, which drives business and IT continuity strategies and plans. More preventive measures need to be adopted for those processes and services with earlier and higher impacts.

Risk Assessment

- Assessment of the level of threat and the extent to which an organization is vulnerable to that threat
- Can be used in assessing and reducing the chance of normal operational incidents and is a technique used by availability management to ensure the required availability and reliability levels can be maintained
- Key aspect of information security management

> **Risk Assessment**
>
> The initial steps of risk management: analyzing the value of assets to the business, identifying threats to those assets, and evaluating how vulnerable each asset is to those threats. Risk assessment can be quantitative (based on numerical data) or qualitative.

The second driver in determining ITSCM requirements is the likelihood that a disaster or other serious service disruption will actually occur. This is risk assessment – an assessment of the level of threat and the extent to which an organization is vulnerable to that threat.

Risk assessment can also be used in assessing and reducing the chance of normal operational incidents and is a technique used by availability management to ensure the required availability and reliability levels can be maintained. Risk assessment is also a key aspect of information security management.

Risk Assessment – examples of risks and threats

Adapted from SD Table 4.2: Examples of risks and threats

Risk	Threat
Loss of internal IT systems/ networks, PABXs, ACDs etc.	Fire, power failure, arson / vandalism, flood, aircraft impact, weather damage, environmental disaster, terrorist attack, sabotage, catastrophic failure, electrical damage, e.g. lightning, accidental damage, poor-quality software
Loss of external systems / networks, e.g. e-commerce, cryptographic systems	All of the above, excessive demand for services, denial of service attack, e.g. against an internet firewall, technology failure, e.g. cryptographic system
Loss of data	Technology failure, human error, viruses, malicious software, e.g. attack applets
Loss of network services	Damage or denial of access to network service provider's premises, loss of service provider's IT systems/networks, loss of service provider's data, failure of the service provider
Unavailability of key technical and support staff	Industrial action, denial of access to premises, resignation, sickness/ injury, transport difficulties
Failure of service providers, e.g. outsourced IT	Commercial failure, e.g. insolvency, denial of access to premises, unavailability of service provider's staff, failure to meet contractual service levels

Risk Assessment – risk assessment and management

SD Figure 4.15: Risk assessment and management

© Crown copyright 2011. Reproduced under license from the Cabinet Office.

SD Figure 4.15 shows that risk assessment involves identification and assessment of the level (measure) of the risks calculated from the assessed values of assets and the assessed levels of threats to, and vulnerabilities of, those assets. Risk is also determined by whether the business is more willing to accept risk or not.

Risk management involves the identification, selection and adoption of countermeasures justified by the identified risks to assets in terms of their potential impact on services if failure occurs, and the reduction of those risks to an acceptable level. Risk management is an activity associated with many other activities, especially ITSCM and information security management processes and the service transition lifecycle stage. All these risk assessment exercises should be coordinated versus separate activities. This approach using a formal method ensures coverage is complete, with sufficient confidence that:

o All possible risks and countermeasures have been identified
o All vulnerabilities have been identified and their levels accurately assessed
o All threats have been identified and their levels accurately assessed
o All results are consistent across the broad spectrum of the technology reviewed
o All expenditure on selected countermeasures can be justified

Formal risk assessment and management methods are now an important element in the overall design and provision of IT services. The assessment of risk is often based on the probability and potential impact of an event occurring. Countermeasures are implemented wherever they are cost-justifiable, to reduce the impact of an event, or the probability of an event occurring, or both. Risk assessment and management described here aligns in its essentials with an asset-focused approach required in ISO/ IEC 27001. Management of risk (M_o_R) provides an alternative generic framework for the management of risk across all parts of an organization – strategic, program, project and operational.

ITILFND05-05-47 State the purpose, objectives and scope for design coordination
(SD 4.1.1, 4.1.2)

Design Coordination Process – Purpose

o Ensure the goals and objectives of the service design stage are met by providing
   and maintaining a single point of coordination and control for all activities and
   processes within this stage of the service lifecycle

Design Coordination

The process responsible for coordinating all service design activities, processes and resources;
ensures consistent and effective design of new or changed IT services, service management
information systems, architectures, technology, processes, information and metrics.

Design Coordination Process – Objectives

o Ensure consistent design of appropriate services, service management information
   systems, architectures, technology, processes, information and metrics to meet
   current and evolving business outcomes and requirements
o Coordinate all design activities across projects, changes, suppliers and support
   teams, and manage schedules, resources and conflicts where required
o Plan / coordinate resources and capabilities to design new or changed services
o Produce service design packages from service charters and change requests
o Ensure good designs / SDPs are made / given to service transition as agreed
o Manage the quality criteria, requirements and handover points between the service
   design stage and service strategy and service transition
o Ensure that all service models and service solution designs conform to strategic,
   architectural, governance and other corporate requirements
o Improve effectiveness and efficiency of service design activities and processes
o Ensure all parties adopt a common framework of standard, reusable design
   practices: activities, processes and supporting systems, whenever appropriate
o Monitor and improve the performance of the service design lifecycle stage

Design Coordination Process – Scope

o Assisting and supporting each project or other change through all the service
   design activities and processes
o Maintaining policies, guidelines, standards, budgets, models, resources and
   capabilities for service design activities and processes
o Coordinating, prioritizing and scheduling of all service design resources to satisfy
   conflicting demands from all projects and changes
o Planning and forecasting the resources needed for the future demand for service
   design activities
o Reviewing, measuring and improving the performance of all service design
   activities and processes
o Ensuring that all requirements are appropriately addressed in service designs,
   particularly utility and warranty requirements
o Ensuring production of service designs and SDPs and handover to service transition

ITILFND05-05-47 State the purpose, objectives and scope for design coordination
(SD 4.1.1, 4.1.2)

In the service design processes specified in ITIL 2007 Edition (formerly known as ITIL V3), an overarching process to coordinate design was not included. The addition of this process in ITIL 2011 Edition is significant – it a recognition of the need for an overall process that orchestrates the components of design. Without this process, the components of the service design package may be completed (see the relevant section for a refresher on what those components are), but when assembled may end up being so many Frankenstein monsters.

The principle is simple: Let us have coordination so that design is efficient, effective, repeatable, and standardized.

Have a look back at the section that covers the components of the service design package and juxtapose these against the design coordination process on the facing page.

Think about your organization: do you have such an overarching process? Or are you focused each on his or her own patch, at lower levels, for example, application development and infrastructure engineering, with no overall assurance that a service will be produced with all components necessary for ongoing operation with sustained service level achievement?

Can you think of examples where coordination was complete and effective and what the impact was on the organization? What about examples where overarching coordination was missing, what happened in your organization?

ITILFND05-05-51 Explain the purpose, objectives, scope, basic concepts, process activities and interfaces for change management (ST 4.2.1, 4.2.2, 4.2.4.6, 4.2.6.4, 4.2.6.5), including types of change request (ST 4.2.4.3), change models (ST 4.2.4.5), remediation planning (ST 4.2.4.8), change advisory board / emergency change advisory board (ST 4.2.5.10, 4.2.5.11), lifecycle of a normal change (ST 4.2.5, Figure 4.2)

Change Management Process – Purpose

o Control the lifecycle of all changes, enabling beneficial changes to be made with minimum disruption to IT services

Change Management

The process responsible for controlling the lifecycle of all changes, enabling beneficial changes to be made with minimum disruption to IT services

Change

The addition, modification or removal of anything that could have an effect on IT services. The scope should include changes to all architectures, processes, tools, metrics and documentation, as well as changes to IT services and other configuration items.

Change Management Process – Objectives

o Respond to the customer's changing business requirements while maximizing value and reducing incidents, disruption and re-work
o Respond to the business and IT requests for change that will align the services with the business needs
o Ensure changes are recorded and evaluated, and authorized changes are prioritized, planned, tested, implemented, documented and reviewed in a controlled manner
o Ensure that all changes to configuration items are recorded in the configuration management system
o Optimize overall business risk – it is often correct to minimize business risk, but sometimes appropriate to knowingly accept a risk because of the potential benefit

Change Management Process – Scope

o Changes to all architectures, processes, tools, metrics and documentation, IT services and other configuration items
o Changes to all configuration items across the whole service lifecycle
o Changes to any of the five aspects of service design:
  1. Service solutions for new or changed services including functional requirements, resources and capabilities needed and agreed
  2. Management information systems and tools, especially the service portfolio, for management / control of services across the lifecycle
  3. Technology / management architectures needed to provide services
  4. Processes needed to design, transition, operate, improve services
  5. Measurement systems, methods and metrics for the services, the architectures, their constituent components and the processes

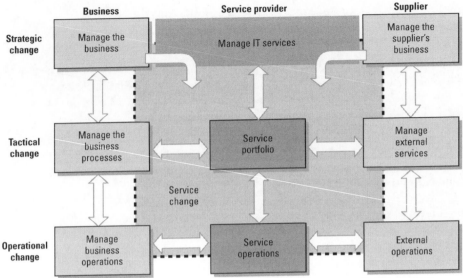

Figure 4.1: Scope of change management and release and deployment management for services

© *Crown copyright 2011. Reproduced under license from the Cabinet Office.*

ST Figure 4.1 shows the typical scope of a change management process for an IT organization and how it interfaces with the business and suppliers at strategic, tactical and operational levels. It covers interfaces to internal and external service providers where there are shared assets and configuration items that need to be under change management. Change management must interface with business change management (to the left in ST Figure 4.1) and with the supplier's change management (to the right in the figure). This may be an external supplier within a formal change management system, or the project change mechanisms within an internal development project.

The service portfolio provides a clear definition of all current, planned and retired services. Understanding the service portfolio helps all parties involved in the service transition to understand the potential impact of new or changed service on current services and other new or changed services.

Strategic changes are brought in via service strategy and the service portfolio management process in the form of change proposals. Changes to a service will be brought in via service design, continual service improvement, service level management and service catalogue management. Corrective change, resolving errors detected in services, will be initiated from service operation and may route via support or external suppliers into a formal RFC.

Change management is not responsible for coordinating all of the service management processes to ensure the smooth implementation of projects. This activity is carried out by transition planning and support.

Change Management Process – Change proposals

Change proposal

A document that includes a high level description of a potential service introduction or significant change, along with a corresponding business case and an expected implementation schedule. Change proposals are normally created by the service portfolio management process and are passed to change management for authorization. Change management will review the potential impact on other services, on shared resources, and on the overall change schedule. Once the change proposal has been authorized, service portfolio management will charter the service.

A change proposal should include:

o High-level description of the new, changed or retired service, including business outcomes to be supported, and utility and warranty to be provided
o Full business case: risks, issues, alternatives, budget, financial expectations
o An outline schedule for design and implementation of the change

Major changes that involve significant cost, risk or organizational impact will usually be initiated through the service portfolio management process. Before the new or changed service is chartered it is important that the change is reviewed for its potential impact on other services, on shared resources, and on the change schedule.

Change proposals are submitted to change management before chartering new or changed services in order to ensure that potential conflicts for resources or other issues are identified. Authorization of the change proposal does not authorize implementation of the change but simply allows the service to be chartered so that service design activity can begin.

A change proposal is used to communicate a high-level description of the change. This change proposal is normally created by the service portfolio management process and is passed to change management for authorization. In some organizations, change proposals may be created by a program management office or by individual projects.

Change management reviews the change proposal and the current change schedule, identifies any potential conflicts or issues and responds to the change proposal by either authorizing it or documenting the issues that need to be resolved. When the change proposal is authorized, the change schedule is updated to include outline implementation dates for the proposed change.

After the new or changed service is chartered, Requests for Change (RFCs) will be used in the normal way to request authorization for specific changes. These RFCs will be associated with the change proposal so that change management has a view of the overall strategic intent and can prioritize and review these RFCs appropriately.

Change Management Process – Interfaces

Integration with business change processes	Where appropriate, change management should be involved with business program and project management teams to ensure that change issues, aims, impacts and developments are exchanged and cascaded throughout the organization where applicable
Program and project management	Program and project management (usually based on PRINCE2 or PMBOK) must work in partnership to align all the processes and people involved in service change initiatives
Organizational and stakeholder change management	It is essential that organizational aspects of change management are properly considered and the change management process has appropriate interfaces with the people carrying out this work
Sourcing and partnering	Effective change management practices and principles must be put into place to manage these relationships effectively to ensure smooth delivery of service

Change management must work with transition planning and support to ensure that there is a coordinated overall approach to managing service transitions.

In order to be able to define clear boundaries, dependencies and rules, change management and release and deployment management should be integrated with processes used for organizational programs or projects, with supplier management and also with suppliers' processes and procedures. There will be occasions when a proposed change will potentially have a wider impact on other parts of the organization (e.g. facilities or business operations), or vice versa, and the change management process must interface appropriately with other processes involved.

The change management process must be tightly integrated with change evaluation. There should be clear agreement on which types of change will be subject to formal change evaluation, and the time required for this evaluation must be included in the overall planning for the change. Change management provides the trigger for change evaluation, and the evaluation report must be delivered to change management in time for the CAB (or other change authority) to use it to assist in their decision-making.

Change Management – integration with business change processes

Program and project management	Partner to align all processes and people involved in service change initiatives. Close alignment between change and program and project management is vital to ensure the change schedule is effective and changes are well managed. Change management personnel may attend project or program meetings, especially at initiation, to identify risks to IT services and other configuration items. For outsourced services, a key is how deeply change processes and tools are embedded into the supplier organization and where the release veto takes place. Conflicts arise if suppliers have responsibility for service availability.
Organizational and stakeholder change management	In some organizations there is a separate function that manages organizational changes; in others this aspect of change management may be carried out within the IT organization. It is always essential that organizational aspects of change management are properly considered and that the change management process has appropriate interfaces with the people carrying out this work.
Sourcing and partnering	Relationships cover internal and external vendors and suppliers and new or existing services. Effective practices and principles must be in place to manage relationships effectively for smooth service delivery. How well partners manage change must be determined and partner and sourcing relationships chosen accordingly. Sourcing and partnering arrangements should clearly define the level of autonomy a partner has in effecting change in their domain without reference to the overall provider. Providers must provide change management personnel and processes matched to business needs.

Where appropriate, change management should be involved with business program and business project management teams to ensure that change issues, aims, impacts and developments are exchanged and cascaded throughout the organization where applicable. This means that changes to any business or project deliverables that do not impact services or service components may be subject to business or project change management procedures rather than the IT change management procedures. However, care must be taken to ensure that changes to service configuration baselines and releases do follow the change management process. The change management team will, however, be expected to liaise closely with projects to ensure smooth implementation and consistency within the changing management environments.

The service portfolio management process will submit change proposals to change management before chartering new or changed services, in order to ensure that potential conflicts for resources or other issues are identified.

During the planning of different types of change requests, each must be defined with a unique naming convention. ST Table 4.3 provides examples of different types of change request across the service lifecycle. There are often specific procedures (e.g., for impact assessment and change authorization) for different change types.

Change Management Process – Change Requests: There are three service change types: standard, emergency, normal

Request for Change (RFC)

A formal proposal for a change to be made. It includes details of the proposed change, and may be recorded on paper or electronically. The term is often misused to mean a change record, or the change itself.

Standard Change

A pre-authorized change that is low risk, relatively common and follows a procedure or work instruction

Emergency Change

A change that must be implemented as soon as possible, for example to resolve a major incident or implement a security patch

Normal Change

Any service change that is not a standard change or an emergency change. Changes are often categorized as major, significant and minor, depending on level of cost and risk involved, and on scope / relationship to other changes. This categorization may be used to identify an appropriate change authority.

Example Types of Change Request by Service Lifecycle Stage

Adapted from ST Table 4.3: Example of types of request by service lifecycle stage

Type of change with examples	Work procedures	SS	SD	ST	SO	CSI
RFC to Service Portfolios – New portfolio line item – To predicted scope, Business Case, baseline – Service pipeline	Service Change Management	✓				
RFC to Service or service definition – To existing or planned service attributes – Project change that impacts Service Design – Service improvement	Service Change Management	✓	✓	✓	✓	✓
Project change proposal – Business change – No impact on service or design baseline	Project Change Management procedure		✓	✓		✓
User access request	User access procedure				✓	
– Operational activity – Tuning (within specifications) – Re-boot hardware on failure if no impact on other services – Planned maintenance	Local procedure (often pre-authorized)				✓	

Change Management Process – Change Models and Workflows

Change Model
A repeatable way of dealing with a particular category of change; defines specific agreed steps that will be followed for a change of this category. Change models may be very complex with many steps that require authorization (e.g. major software release) or may be very simple with no requirement for authorization (e.g. password reset).

Change models include:
- Steps to handle the change, including issues and unexpected events
- Order steps should be taken, with dependences or co-processing defined
- Responsibilities – who should do what (including identification of change authorities who will authorize the change and decide if formal change evaluation is needed)
- Timescales and thresholds for completion of the actions
- Escalation procedures – who should be contacted and when

Organizations will find it helpful to predefine change models – and apply them to appropriate changes when they occur. A change model is a way of predefining the steps that should be taken to handle a particular type of change in an agreed way. Support tools can then be used to manage the required process. This will ensure that such changes are handled in a predefined path and to predefined timescales. Changes that require specialized handling could be treated in this way, such as:
- Emergency changes that have different authorization, documented retrospectively
- Changes to mainframe software needing specific testing, implementation sequences
- Implementation of security patches for desktop Oss needing specific testing and guaranteed deployment to many targets, some of which may not be online
- Service requests that may be authorized and implemented with no further involvement from change management

These models are usually input to the change management support tools; the tools then automate the handling, management, reporting and escalation of the process.

Change Management Process – Remediation Planning

Remediation
Actions taken to recover after a failed change or release. Remediation may include back-out, invocation of service continuity plans, or other actions designed to enable the business process to continue.

- No change should be approved without explicitly addressing what to do if it fails
- There should be a back-out plan for every change
    1. Restores the organization to its initial situation
    2. Often by reloading of a baselined set of CIs
- If a back-out plan is not feasible, an alternative approach is required
    1. May require a revisiting of the change in the event of failure
    2. May be severe enough to require invoking the business continuity plan

Change Management Process – Change advisory board (CAB)

Change Advisory Board (CAB)
A group of people that supports the assessment, prioritization, authorization and scheduling of changes. A change advisory board is usually made up of representatives from: all areas within the IT service provider; the business; and third parties such as suppliers.

The change manager normally chairs the CAB; potential members include:

o Customer(s)
o User manager(s)
o User group representative(s)
o Business relationship managers
o Service owners
o Application developers /maintainers
o Specialists / technical consultants
o Services and operations staff, e.g. service desk, test management, ITSCM, ISM, capacity management
o Facilities/office services staff (Contractors' or third parties' representatives, e.g. in outsourcing)
o Other parties as applicable to circumstances (e.g. police if traffic disruptions are likely, marketing if public products could be affected)

A change advisory board (CAB) is a body that exists to support the authorization of changes and to assist change management in the assessment, prioritization and scheduling of changes. A CAB is often the change authority for one or more change categories, but in some organizations the CAB just plays an advisory role. In a large organization there may be many different CABs with a global CAB that is responsible for the most significant changes and other CABs supporting different business units, geographies or technologies. It is important that each CAB has full visibility of all changes that could have an impact on the services and configuration items within its control. For each CAB meeting, members should be chosen who are capable of ensuring that all changes within the scope of the CAB are adequately assessed from both a business and a technical viewpoint.

A CAB may be asked to consider and recommend the adoption or rejection of changes appropriate for higher-level authorization, and then recommendations will be submitted to the appropriate change authority. To achieve this, the CAB needs to include people with a clear understanding of the whole range of stakeholder needs. Some may be permanent members of the CAB, others will be invited to participate when needed for changes being discussed. It is important to emphasize that a CAB:

o Will be composed of different stakeholders depending on changes being considered
o May vary considerably in makeup, even across the range of a single meeting
o Should involve suppliers when that would be useful, for example:
  • The external service provider if a significant part of the service is outsourced
  • The hardware service provider when considering major firmware upgrades
o Should reflect both users' and customers' views
o Is likely to include the problem manager and service level manager and customer relations staff for at least part of the time

A practical tip is that a CAB should have stated and agreed evaluation criteria; this assists in change assessment, acting as a template / framework members use to assess each change.

change management process - CAB meeting standard agenda

○ Change proposals that have been received from service portfolio management
○ RFCs to be assessed by CAB members – in structured and priority order
○ RFCs that have been assessed by CAB members
○ Change reviews
○ Outstanding changes and changes in progress
○ Evaluation reports and interim evaluation reports received from the change evaluation process
○ Scheduling of changes and update of change schedule and PSO
○ Review of unauthorized changes detected through service asset and configuration management, to understand underlying issues and take corrective action
○ Failed changes, unauthorized, backed-out changes, or changes applied without reference to the CAB from incident management, problem management or change management
○ Change management wins/accomplishments for the period under discussion, i.e. a review of the business benefits accrued by way of the change management process
○ The change management process, including any amendments made to it during the period under discussion, as well as proposed changes

Advance notice of RFCs expected for review at the next CAB.
CAB meetings represent a potentially large overhead on the time of members. Therefore, all change proposals and RFCs, together with evaluation reports, the change schedule and PSO, should be circulated in advance and flexibility allowed to CAB members on whether to attend in person, to send a deputy or to send any comments. Relevant papers should be circulated in advance to allow CAB members (and others who are required by change management or CAB members) to conduct impact and resource assessments.

In some circumstances it will be desirable to discuss RFCs at one CAB meeting for more detailed explanation or clarification (before CAB members take the papers away for consideration) in time for a later meeting. A 'walkthrough' of major changes may be included at a CAB meeting before formal submission of the RFC.

CAB members should come to meetings prepared and empowered to express views and make decisions on behalf of the area they represent in respect of the submitted RFCs, based on prior assessment of the RFCs.

The CAB should be informed of any emergency changes or changes that have been implemented as a workaround to incidents and should be given the opportunity to recommend follow-up action.

Note that a CAB may be an advisory body only, depending on how the organization has assigned change authority. If the CAB cannot agree to a recommendation, the final decision on whether to authorize changes, and commit to the expense involved is the responsibility of management (normally the director of IT or the services director, service owner or change manager as their delegated representative).

Change Management Process – ECAB

o When the need for emergency change arises, i.e. there is no time to convene the full CAB, a smaller organization with authority to make emergency decisions is needed: the emergency change advisory board

Emergency Change Advisory Board (ECAB) A subgroup of the change advisory board that makes decisions about emergency changes. Membership may be decided at the time a meeting is called, and depends on the nature of the emergency change.

Emergency Change A change that must be introduced as soon as possible – for example, to resolve a major incident or implement a security patch. The change management process will normally have a specific procedure for handling emergency changes.

Change procedures should specify how the composition of the CAB and ECAB will be determined in each instance, based on the criteria listed above and any other criteria appropriate to the business. This is to ensure the composition of the CAB will be to represent business interests properly when major changes are proposed. It will also ensure that the composition of the ECAB will provide the ability, both from a business perspective and technical standpoint, to make appropriate decisions in any conceivable eventuality.

In an emergency situation it may not be possible to convene a full CAB meeting. Where CAB authorization is required, this will be provided by the emergency CAB (ECAB).

Emergency changes are sometimes required and should be designed carefully and tested as much as possible before use, or the impact of the emergency change may be greater than the original incident. Details of emergency changes may be documented retrospectively.

The number of emergency changes proposed should be kept to an absolute minimum, as they are generally more disruptive and prone to failure. All changes likely to be required should be foreseen and planned, bearing in mind availability of resources to build and test the changes. Occasions will occur when emergency changes are essential, so procedures must be devised to deal with them quickly, without sacrificing normal management controls.

The emergency change procedure is reserved for changes to repair an error in an IT service that is negatively impacting the business to a high degree. Changes intended to introduce immediately required business improvements are handled as normal changes, assessed as having the highest urgency. If a change is needed urgently (because of poor planning or sudden changes in business needs) this should be treated as a normal, high priority change.

Effectively, the emergency change procedure follows the normal change procedure except:

o Authorization will be given by the ECAB rather than waiting for a CAB meeting
o Testing may be reduced, or in extreme cases forgone completely, if this is considered a necessary risk to deliver the change immediately
o Documentation, e.g. updating the change record and configuration data, may be deferred, typically until normal working hours

Change management process- Emergency changes

Emergency change authorization
o Use documented, understood authorization for emergency changes
o Not all emergency changes will require the ECAB involvement
o Emergency change authorization must be formally agreed / documented

Emergency change building, testing and implementation
o Assign authorized changes to the relevant technical group for building
o Change and technical management ensure staff /resources are available
o Test as fully as possible; avoid implementing completely untested changes
o The less it is likely to fail, the less testing may be needed in an emergency
o Notify the business of risks and take responsibility for change decisions
o Change management ensures ineffective changes are swiftly backed out

Emergency change documentation
o It may not be possible to update all change records during urgent actions; temporary records are made during such periods, and all records are to be completed retrospectively, at the earliest possible opportunity; document an agreed time for completing updates when the change is authorized

Effectively, the emergency change procedure follows the normal change procedure except:
o Authorization will be given by the ECAB rather than waiting for a CAB meeting
o Testing may be reduced, or in extreme cases foregone completely, if this is considered a necessary risk to deliver the change immediately
o Documentation, e.g. updating the change record and configuration data, may be deferred, typically until normal working hours

When only limited testing is possible – and presuming that parallel development of more robust versions continues alongside the emergency change – target testing towards:
o Aspects of the service that will be used immediately
o Elements that would cause most short-term inconvenience
The business should be made aware of associated risks and be responsible for ultimately accepting or rejecting the change based on the information presented. Change management should give as much advance warning as possible to the service desk and other stakeholders, arranging for adequate technical presence to support service operation.
If a change, once implemented, fails to rectify the urgent outstanding error, there may need to be iterative attempts at fixes. Change management should take responsibility at this point to ensure that business needs remain the primary concern and that each iteration is controlled in the manner described in this section. Change management should ensure that ineffective changes are swiftly backed out. If too many attempts are made and fail, ask:
o Has the error been correctly identified, analyzed and diagnosed?
o Has the proposed resolution been adequately tested?
o Has the solution been correctly implemented?
In such circumstances, it may be better to provide a partial service to allow the change to be thoroughly tested, or to suspend service temporarily and then implement the change.

x`Change management process – Lifecycle of a Normal Change

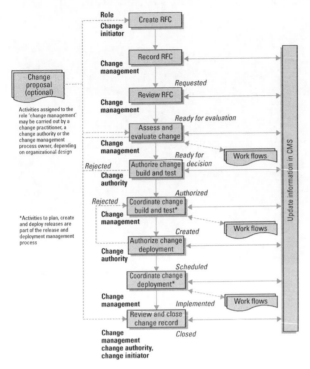

ST Figure 4.2 shows an example of a change to the provider services, applications or infrastructure. Examples of the status of the change are shown in italics. Change and configuration information is updated all the way through the activities. This example shows authorization for change build and test and change deployment. In practice there may be additional authorization steps, for example to authorize change design or change development.

Based on Cabinet Office Crown Copyright Material

Typical activities in managing individual changes are:

o Create and record the RFC
o Review the RFC
   1. Filter changes (e.g. incomplete or wrongly routed changes)
o Assess and evaluate the change
   1. Establish the appropriate level of change authority
   2. Establish relevant areas of interest (i.e. who should be involved in the CAB)
   3. Evaluate justification, impact, cost, benefits, risks, predicted performance
   4. Submit a request for evaluation to initiate activity from the change evaluation
o Authorize the change
   1. Obtain authorization/rejection
   2. Communicate the decision with all stakeholders, in particular the RFC initiator
o Plan updates
o Coordinate change implementation
o Review and close change
   1. Collate the change documentation, e.g. baselines and evaluation reports
   2. Review the change(s) and change documentation
   3. Ensure lessons learned details are recorded in the SKMS
   4. Close the change document when all actions are completed

Change management process – Interfaces within service management – between change and service asset and configuration management

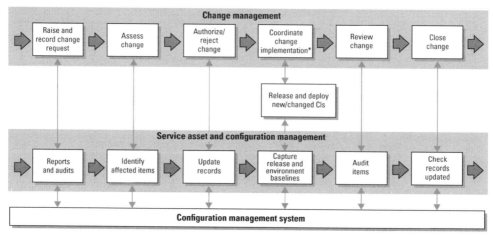

ST Figure 4.6 Interfaces between change management and service asset and configuration management

All service management processes may require change management, for example to implement process improvements. Many service management processes will also be involved in the impact assessment and implementation of service changes.

The configuration management system provides reliable, quick and easy access to accurate configuration information to enable stakeholders and staff to assess the impact of proposed changes and to track change workflow. This information enables the correct CI versions to be released to the appropriate party or into the correct environment. As changes are implemented, the configuration management information is updated.

The CMS may also identify related CIs that will be affected by the change, but not included in the original request, or similar CIs that would benefit from similar changes.

An overview of how the change management and service asset and configuration management processes work together for an individual change is shown in ST Figure 4.6.

Change Management Process – Interfaces with Service Transition

Problem management	Changes are often required to implement workarounds and to fix known errors; problem management is a major source of RFCs and contributor to CAB discussion
IT service continuity management	Update procedures and plans via change so they are current and stakeholders are aware; assess each change for impact on ITSCM; for a standard change do this when the change is authorized; for normal and emergency, in change assessment.
Information security management	Changes required by security will be implemented through change management; security is a key contributor to CAB discussion; assess each significant change for potential impact on ISM
Capacity management and demand management	Capacity management has an important role in assessing proposed changes including total impact on service capacity. Changes arising from capacity management are initiated as RFCs
Service portfolio management	Prioritizes, charters, and submits RFCs for strategic changes; change proposals are input to long-term planning and to change management for related RFCs. Some RFCs require analysis by the SPM process, potentially adding to the service pipeline

ITILFND05-05-61 State the purpose, objectives and scope for release and deployment management (ST 4.4.1, 4.4.2), including four phases of release and deployment (ST 4.4.5, Figure 4.23)

Release and Deployment Management Process – Purpose
o Plan, schedule and control the build, test and deployment of releases; deliver new business-required functionality while protecting existing services' integrity

Release and Deployment Management The process responsible for planning, scheduling and controlling the build, test and deployment of releases, and for delivering new functionality required by the business while protecting the integrity of existing services

Release One or more changes to an IT service that are built, tested and deployed together. A single release may include changes to hardware, software, documentation, processes and other components

There are different considerations that apply to the manner a release is deployed. The usual options are "Big Bang" versus phased, "push and pull", and automated or manual.

Release and Deployment Management Process – Objectives
o Define / agree release and deployment plans with customers, stakeholders
o Create and test release packages of compatible related configuration items
o Maintain integrity of release packages and constituent components in transition; ensure all release packages are stored in a DML and recorded accurately in the CMS
o Deploy release packages from the DML by an agreed plan and schedule
o Ensure all release packages can be tracked, installed, tested, verified and/or uninstalled or backed out if appropriate
o Manage organization and stakeholders during release, deployment activities
o Ensure new or changed services and enabling systems, technology and organization can deliver agreed utility and warranty
o Record and manage deviations, risks and issues related to new or changed service and take necessary corrective action
o Ensure there is knowledge transfer to enable the customers and users to optimize their use of the service to support their business activities
o Ensure skills and knowledge are transferred to service operation to deliver, support and maintain the service efficiently and effectively, to warranties and service levels

Release and Deployment Management Process – Scope
o Processes, systems and functions to package, build, test and deploy a release into live use, establish the service specified in the service design package, and formally hand the service over to the service operation functions
o All configuration items required to implement a release, for example:
   1. Physical assets such as a server or network
   2. Virtual assets such as a virtual server or virtual storage
   3. Applications and software
   4. Training for users and IT staff
   5. Services, including all related contracts and agreements

Release and deployment management is responsible for ensuring appropriate testing takes place, but actual testing is carried out as part of the service validation and testing process.

Release and deployment management is not responsible for authoring changes, and requires authorization from change management at various release lifecycle stages.

Four Phases of Release and Deployment

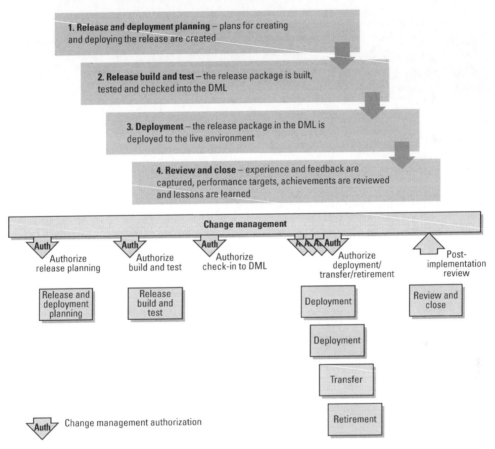

ST Figure 4.23: Phases of release and deployment management

© Crown copyright 2011. Reproduced under license from the Cabinet Office.

ST Figure 4.23 shows multiple points where an authorized change triggers release and deployment management activity. This does not require a separate RFC at each stage. Some organizations manage a whole release with a single change request and separate authorization at each stage for activities to continue, while other organizations require a separate RFC for each stage. Both of these approaches are acceptable; what is important is that change management authorization is received before beginning each stage.

ITILFND05-05-62 State the purpose, objectives and scope for knowledge management (ST 4.7.1, 4.7.2), including Data-to-Information-to-Knowledge-to-Wisdom (DIKW) & SKMS (ST 4.7.4.2, 4.7.4.3, Figure 4.36)

Knowledge Management Process – Purpose
o Share perspectives, ideas, experience and information
o Ensure that these are available in the right place at the right time to enable informed decisions; and to improve efficiency by reducing the need to rediscover knowledge

Knowledge Management

The process responsible for sharing perspectives, ideas, experience and information, and for ensuring that these are available in the right place and at the right time. The knowledge management process enables informed decisions, and improves efficiency by reducing the need to rediscover knowledge.

Knowledge Management is typically displayed within the Data-to-Information-to-Knowledge-to-Wisdom (DIKW) structure.
o **Data** – discrete facts about Events
o **Information** – comes from providing context to data
o **Knowledge** – tacit experiences, ideas, insights, values, and judgments of individuals
o **Wisdom** – the ultimate discernment of the material

The basis of Service Knowledge Management System is formed by a considerable amount of data in a central database or Configuration Management System (CMS) and the CMDB. The CMDB feeds the CMS, and the CMS provides input for the SKMS and so supports the decision-making process.

Knowledge Management Process – Objectives
o Improve the quality of management decision-making by ensuring that reliable and secure knowledge, information and data is available throughout the service lifecycle
o Enable the service provider to be more efficient and improve quality of service, increase satisfaction and reduce the cost of service by reducing the need to rediscover knowledge
o Ensure staff have a clear and common understanding of the value their services provide to customers and ways in which benefits are realized from use of services
o Maintain a service knowledge management system (SKMS) that provides controlled access to knowledge, information and data that is appropriate for each audience
o Gather, analyze, store, share, use and maintain knowledge, information and data throughout the service provider organization

Knowledge Management Process – Scope
o Knowledge management is a lifecycle-wide process relevant to all lifecycle stages
o Includes oversight of the management of knowledge, the information and data from which that knowledge derives

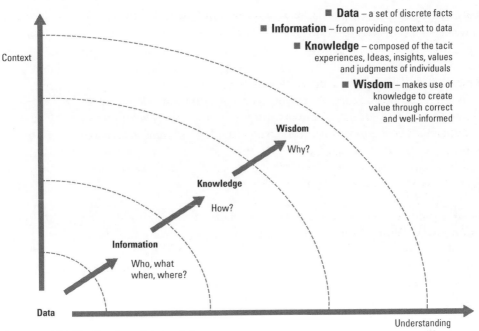

ST Figure 4.35: The flow from data to wisdom

Knowledge management is shown in Data-to-Information-to-Knowledge-to-Wisdom (DIKW).

Data is a set of discrete facts. Most organizations capture significant amounts of data in highly structured databases such as service management and service asset and configuration management tools/systems and databases.

The key knowledge management activities around data are the ability to:
Capture accurate data
o Analyze, synthesize and then transform the data into information
o Identify relevant data and concentrate resources on its capture
o Maintain integrity of the data
o Archive and purge data to optimize balance of data availability and resource use
o An example of data is the date and time at which an incident was logged

Information comes from providing context to data. Information is typically stored in semi-structured content such as documents, email and multimedia. The key knowledge management activity around information is managing the content in a way that makes it easy to capture, query, find, re-use and learn from experiences so that mistakes are not repeated and work is not duplicated. An example of information is the average time to close priority 2 incidents. This information is created by combining data from the start time, end time and priority of many incidents.

Knowledge is composed of the tacit experiences, ideas, insights, values and judgments of individuals. People gain knowledge both from their own and from their peers' expertise, as well as from the analysis of information (and data). Through the synthesis of these elements, new knowledge is created. Knowledge is dynamic and context-based. Knowledge puts information into an 'ease of use' form, which can facilitate decision-making. In service transition this knowledge is not solely based on the transition in progress, but is gathered from experience of previous transitions, awareness of recent and anticipated changes and other areas, which experienced staff will have been unconsciously collecting for some time. An example of knowledge is that the average time to close priority 2 incidents has increased by about 10% since a new version of the service was released.

Wisdom makes use of knowledge to create value through correct and well-informed decisions. Wisdom involves having the application and contextual awareness to provide strong common-sense judgment. An example of wisdom is recognizing that the increase in time to close priority 2 incidents is due to poor-quality documentation for the new version of the service, as shown in ST Figure 4.35.

SKMS, and relationship of the CMDB, the CMS, and the SKMS

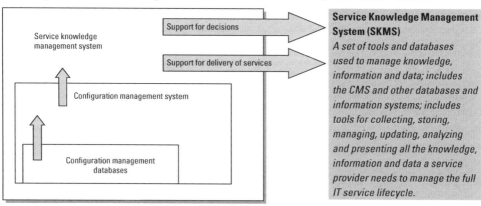

ST Figure 4.36: Relationship of the CMDB, the CMS and the SKMS

© Crown copyright 2011. Reproduced under license from the Cabinet Office.

In IT service management, knowledge management is focused within the service knowledge management system (SKMS), which is concerned, as its name implies, with knowledge. Underpinning this knowledge will be a considerable quantity of data, which will also be held in the SKMS. One very important part of the SKMS is the configuration management system (CMS). The CMS describes the attributes and relationships of configuration items, many of which are themselves knowledge, information or data assets stored in the SKMS. ST Figure 4.36 is a very simplified illustration of the relationship of the three levels, with configuration data being recorded within the CMDB, and feeding through the CMS into the SKMS. The SKMS supports delivery of the services and informed decision-making.

ITILFND05-05-62 State the purpose, objectives and scope for knowledge management (ST 4.7.1, 4.7.2), including Data-to-Information-to-Knowledge-to-Wisdom (DIKW) & SKMS (ST 4.7.4.2, 4.7.4.3, Figure 4.36)

Knowledge management may sound like a lofty title but the basic idea is right: Let us make sure when people make decision, take action and perform activities they have ready access to the knowledge they need to work efficiently and effectively. Let us decide to manage by fact, as this decision is the foundation from moving from best effort towards certainty when delivering and supporting services.

Further, let us make sure that we don't just provide raw data without any analysis to key stakeholders, especially customers and management – let us go the extra mile and analyze that data and provide insight into what it means. In other words, let us move up the knowledge "food chain" from dealing with data, to information, to knowledge, and ultimately, wisdom.

For examination purposes knowing that the basis for the SKMS is the CMS (tool) and CMDB (database, may be multiple physical and federated), and that the SKMS is the largest 'container', housing the CMS, CMDB and all other sources of knowledge about services.

If you think about what a services business needs, the SKMS makes sense. It is not enough to have documentation on the specifications for services and processes, etc. You also need someplace to store historical and other information on services; hence the SKMS.

For testing purposes, knowing the DIKW model
    Dumb
    Information
    Keeps
    Wearying

ITILFND05-05-63 State the purpose, objectives and scope for service asset and
configuration management (SACM) (ST 4.3.1, 4.3.2)

Service Asset and Configuration Management Process - Purpose

Ensure that the assets required to deliver services are properly controlled, and that
accurate and reliable information about those assets is available when and where it is
needed
o This information includes details of how the assets have been configured and the
relationships between assets

Service Asset and Configuration Management (SACM)
The process responsible for ensuring that the assets required to deliver services are properly
controlled, and that accurate and reliable information about those assets is available when and
where it is needed. This information includes details of how the assets have been configured and
the relationships between assets.

Service Asset and Configuration Management Process – Objectives

o Ensure assets under the control of the IT organization are identified, controlled
and properly cared for throughout their lifecycle
o Identify, control, record, report, audit and verify services and other CIs including
versions, baselines, components, attributes and relationships
o Account for, manage and protect the integrity of CIs through the service lifecycle
by working with change management to ensure that only authorized components
are used and only authorized changes made
o Ensure integrity of CIs and configurations required to control services by
establishing and maintaining an accurate and complete CMS
o Maintain accurate configuration information on the historical, planned and current
state of services and other CIs
o Support efficient and effective service management processes by providing accurate
configuration information to enable people to make decisions at the right time – for
example to authorize changes and releases, or to resolve incidents and problems

Service Asset and Configuration Management Process – Scope

o Management of the complete lifecycle of every configuration items (CIs)
  1. Ensures CIs are identified, baselined and maintained and changes controlled
  2. Ensures that releases into controlled environments and operational use are done
     on the basis of formal authorization
  3. Provides a configuration model of the services and service assets by recording
     the relationships between configuration items
o Interfaces to internal and external service providers where there are assets and
configuration items to be controlled, e.g. shared assets

ITILFND05-05-63 State the purpose, objectives and scope for service asset and
configuration management (SACM) (ST 4.3.1, 4.3.2)

One of the key points here with this process is that configuration management –
knowing what you have, your configuration, the components of your services, and
how they relate to one another – is not enough. There is a superset of assets that
must be recognized, maintained, protected, and managed to ensure consistent quality
service delivery and support.

For examination purposes, you should know what a CI is and the kinds of things that
can be classified as CIs, e.g., not just hardware and software, but also documents,
people, etc.

Does your organization use this concept and process, or something similar to it? How
is that working for you? What works well, and what does not?

ITILFND05-05-64 State the purpose, objectives and scope for transition planning and support (ST 4.1.1, 4.1.2)

Transition Planning and Support Process – Purpose
o Provide overall planning for service transitions and to coordinate the resources that they require

Transition Planning and Support
The process responsible for planning all service transition processes and coordinating the resources that they require.

Transition Planning and Support Process – Objectives
o Plan and coordinate resources to ensure that the requirements of service strategy encoded in service design are effectively realized in service operation
o Coordinate activities across projects, suppliers, service teams where required
o Establish new or changed services into supported environments within the predicted cost, quality and time estimates
o Establish new or modified management information systems and tools, technology and management architectures, service management processes, and measurement methods and metrics to meet requirements set in the design stage of the lifecycle
o Ensure all parties adopt a common framework of standard re-usable processes and systems for effectiveness and efficiency of integrated planning and coordination
o Provide clear and comprehensive plans that enable customer and business change projects to align their activities with the service transition plans
o Identify, manage and control risks, to minimize the chance of failure and disruption across transition activities; and ensure that service transition issues, risks and deviations are reported to the appropriate stakeholders and decision makers
o Monitor and improve the performance of the service transition lifecycle stage

Transition Planning and Support Process – Scope
o Maintaining policies, standards and models for service transition activities, processes
o Guiding each major change or new service through all service transition processes
o Coordinating efforts to enable multiple transitions to be managed at the same time
o Prioritizing conflicting requirements for service transition resources
o Planning budget and resources to fulfill future requirements for service transition
o Reviewing and improving performance of transition planning and support activities
o Ensuring that service transition is coordinated with program and project management, service design and service development activities
Transition planning and support is NOT responsible for detailed planning of the build, test and deployment of individual changes or releases; these activities are carried out as part of change management and release and deployment management.

ITILFND05-05-64 State the purpose, objectives and scope for transition planning and support (ST 4.1.1, 4.1.2)

A process is needed to ensure that the move to production to the live environment and production acceptance is planned and coordinated from design into operation. This process in ITIL is transition planning and support.

Without proper transition to production, services and systems can be hamstrung for their life in operation because of the way they were introduced; in typical poor transition scenarios, you see a flurry of changes, often emergency changes, required to get the service or system into production. The issue here is that what was tested in design and development is not then representative of what was put into product; it is likely that key changes have been made and updates have not be made accordingly to architecture diagrams, troubleshooting guides, and the like, a sure cause for issues throughout the life of the service or system.

A key point to remember is that service transition, while INVOLVED in service design, is not accountable for design, build, and test; these are the "pitching" aspects of a transition; it is useful to think of transition planning and support as "production acceptance", which is the "catching" part of a transition.

ITILFND05-05-71 Explain the purpose, objectives, scope, basic concepts, process activities and interfaces for incident management (SO 4.2.1, 4.2.2, 4.2.4.2, 4.2.5, 4.2.6.4)

Incident Management Process – Purpose

o Restore normal service operation as quickly as possible and minimize the adverse impact on business operations, ensuring agreed service quality levels are maintained

Incident Management

The process responsible for managing the lifecycle of all incidents. Incident management ensures that normal service operation is restored as quickly as possible and the business impact is minimized.

Incident

An unplanned interruption to an IT service or reduction in the quality of an IT service. Failure of a configuration item that has not yet affected service is also an incident – for example, failure of one disk from a mirror set.

Incident management is the process responsible for managing the lifecycle of all incidents. Incidents may be recognized by technical staff, detected and reported by event monitoring tools, communications from users (usually via a telephone call to the service desk), or reported by third-party suppliers and partners.

Incident Management Process – Objectives

o Ensure standardized methods and procedures are used for efficient and prompt response, analysis, documentation, ongoing management and reporting of incidents
o Increase visibility and communication of incidents to business and IT support staff
o Enhance business perception of IT through use of a professional approach to quickly resolving and communicating incidents when they occur
o Align incident management activities and priorities with those of the business
o Maintain user satisfaction with the quality of IT services

Incident Management Process – Scope

Scope includes any event which disrupts, or which could disrupt, a service, such as events communicated directly by users, either through the service desk or through an interface from event management to incident management tools. Incidents can also be reported and/or logged by technical staff, for example if they notice something untoward with a hardware or network CI staff may report or log an incident and refer it to the service desk. This does not mean that all events are incidents; many event classes are not related to disruptions, but are indicators of normal operation or informational.

Although both incidents and service requests are reported to the service desk, they are not the same. Service requests do not represent a disruption to agreed service, but are a way of meeting the customer's needs and may be addressing an agreed target in an SLA. Service requests are dealt with by the request fulfillment process.

Incident Management Process – Basic Concepts – Incident, Timescales, Incident Model

Incident
Unplanned interruption or reduction in quality of an IT service

Timescale
Time within which an incident of a particular type must be handled for all incident handling stages

Incident model
A way of predefining the steps that should be taken to handle an incident in an agreed way

An incident model should include:
o Incident handling steps in chronological order, with any dependencies or co-processing defined
o Responsibilities; who should do what
o Precautions to be taken before resolving an incident, e.g., backing up data or configuration files, or steps to comply with health and safety guidelines
o Timescales and thresholds for completing actions
o Escalation procedures; who should be contacted and when
o Any necessary evidence-preservation activities (particularly relevant for security- and capacity-related incidents)

Timescales must be agreed for all incident handling stages (these will differ depending upon the priority level of the incident), based upon the overall incident response and resolution targets within SLAs, and captured as targets within OLAs and UCs. All support groups should be made fully aware of these timescales. Service management tools should be used to automate timescales and escalate the incident as required based on predefined rules.

Incident models predefine 'standard' steps to apply in an agreed way to particular types of incidents when they occur, helping ensure incidents are handled in a predefined path and within predefined timescales. Incident models are useful since many incidents are not new – they involve dealing with something that has happened before and may well happen again. Incidents which would require specialized handling can be treated in this way (for example, security-related incidents can be routed to information security management and capacity- or performance-related incidents that would be routed to capacity management). The models should be input to the incident handling support tools in use and the tools should then automate the handling, management and escalation of the process. Incident models should be stored in the SKMS.

Incident Management Process – Basic Concepts – Major incident, incident status tracking

Major incident   Highest incident impact category; requires a separate procedure with shorter timescales and greater urgency

Status   Required field in many types of record indicating the current stage in the lifecycle of the associated incident, problem, configuration item, etc.

Incident status tracking field value examples:
- **Open** Incident is recognized but not yet assigned to a resource for resolution
- **In progress** Incident is in the process of being investigated and resolved
- **Resolved** A resolution has been put in place for the incident but normal state service operation has not yet been validated by the business or end user
- **Closed** The user or business has agreed that the incident has been resolved and that normal state operations have been restored

Major incident

A definition of what constitutes a major incident must be agreed and ideally mapped onto the overall incident prioritization scheme – such that they will be dealt with through this separate procedure. Where necessary, the major incident procedure should include the establishment of a separate major incident team under the direct leadership of the incident manager, formulated to concentrate on this incident alone to ensure that adequate resources and focus are provided to finding a swift resolution. If the service desk manager is also fulfilling the role of incident manager (say in a small organization), then a separate person may need to be designated to lead the major incident investigation team – to avoid conflict of time or priorities – but should ultimately report back to the incident manager.

If the cause of the incident needs to be investigated at the same time, then the problem manager would be involved as well, but the incident manager must ensure that service restoration and underlying cause are kept separate. Throughout, the service desk ensures all activities are recorded and users are kept fully informed of progress. While the service desk may be accountable for ensuring that the incident/ major incident record is always up-to-date, responsibility may also lie elsewhere (such as with other technical teams).

People sometimes use loose terminology and/or confuse a major incident with a problem. In reality, an incident remains an incident forever – it may grow in impact or priority to become a major incident, but an incident never 'becomes' a problem. A problem is the underlying cause of one or more incidents and remains a separate entity always!

Incident status tracking

Incidents should be tracked throughout their lifecycle to support proper handling and reporting on the status of incidents. Within the incident management system, status codes may be linked to incidents to indicate where they are in relation to the lifecycle.

Incident Management Process – Basic Concepts – Expanded incident lifecycle

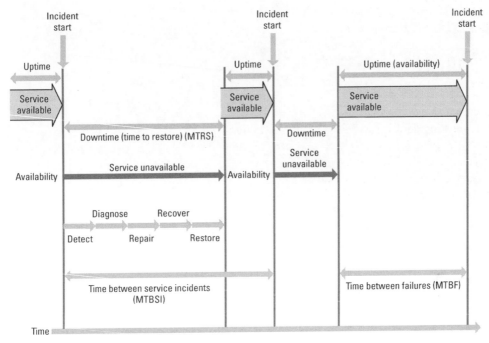

SD Figure 4.10: the expanded incident lifecycle

Expanded incident lifecycle *Detailed stages in the lifecycle of an incident. The stages are detection, diagnosis, repair, recovery and restoration. The expanded incident lifecycle is used to help understand all contributions to the impact of incidents and to plan for how these could be controlled or reduced.*

ITIL Service Design and ITIL Continual Service Improvement describe the expanded incident lifecycle which can be used to help understand all contributions to the impact of incidents and to plan for how these could be controlled or reduced

Incident Management Process – Activities, methods, techniques

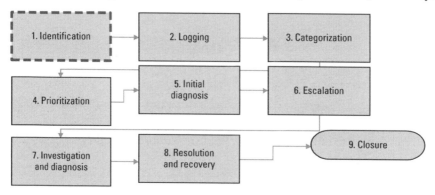

1. Incident identification
  o A user is impacted and contacts the service desk
  o A failure is detected on a key component that is monitored

While work cannot begin on an incident until it is known that an incident has occurred, it is usually unacceptable, from a business perspective, to wait until a user is impacted and contacts the service desk. As far as possible, all key components should be monitored so failures or potential failures are detected early and the incident management process can be started quickly. Ideally, incidents should be resolved before they impact users!

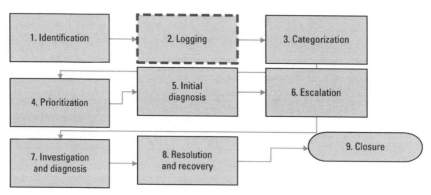

2. Incident logging, information may include:
  o Unique reference number
  o Category / sub-category
  o Urgency; impact, priority
  o Date/time recorded
  o Name/ID of person or group recording
  o Notification method - phone, email, etc.
  o User name/department/phone/location
  o Call-back method (phone, mail etc.)
  o Description of symptoms

  o Incident status – active, closed, etc.
  o Related CI
  o Assigned support group/person
  o Related problem/known error
  o Activities undertaken to resolve the incident and when these took place
  o Resolution date and time
  o Closure category, date and time

All incidents must be fully logged and date/time stamped, regardless of whether they are raised through a service desk telephone call, automatically detected via an event alert, or from any other source. All relevant information relating to the nature of the incident must be logged so a full historical record is maintained – and so if the incident has to be referred to other support group(s), they will have all relevant information to hand to assist them.

If the service desk does not work 24/7 and responsibility for first-line incident logging and handling passes to another group, such as IT operations or network support, out of service desk hours, then these staff need to be equally rigorous about logging of incident details. Full training and awareness needs to be provided to such staff on this issue.

As further activities to resolve an incident occur, the incident record should be updated with relevant information and details so a full history is maintained. For example, the categorization or priority may change after further diagnosis or escalation activities.

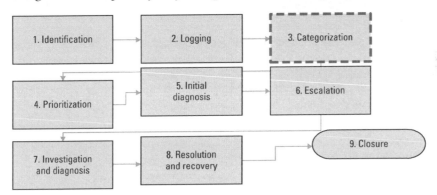

3. Incident categorization
o Allocate a categorization code so the exact incident type is recorded
o Used later to analyze incident types/frequencies for trends for use in problem, supplier management, etc.
o Incident categorization may change throughout the lifecycle of an incident. For example, upon discovery and logging of the incident, initial categories may reflect symptoms (e.g. 'service unavailable' or 'performance slow'). Upon later analysis, categories may reflect the actual CIs at fault such as 'server' or 'disk drive'.

Note that the check for service requests in this process does not imply that service requests are incidents. This is simply recognition of the fact that service requests are sometimes incorrectly logged as incidents (e.g. a user incorrectly enters the request as an incident from the web interface). This check will detect any such requests and ensure that they are passed to the request fulfillment process.

Sometimes the details available at the time an incident is logged may be incomplete, misleading or incorrect. It is therefore important that the categorization of the incident is checked, and updated if necessary, at call closure time (in a separate closure categorization field, so as not to corrupt the original categorization).

Incident Management Process – Multi-level categorization
o A multi-level categorization scheme can be used to categorize incidents
o The capability to track chosen categories as they change throughout the lifecycle of
   an incident may prove useful for potential improvements
o Multi-level categorization is available in most tools, usually to 3-4 levels

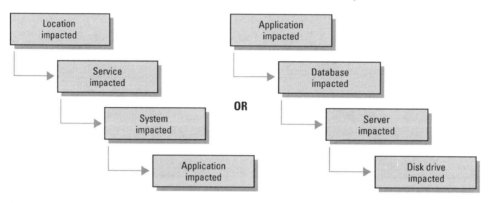

SO Figure 4.4 Multi-level incident categorization

© Crown copyright 2011. Reproduced under license from the Cabinet Office.

4. Incident prioritization
Prioritization is normally determined by the urgency of the incident (how quickly the
business needs resolution) and the level of business impact
o Impact is often the number of users affected, but loss of service to a single user can
   have a major impact
o Other factors contributing to impact:
   1. Risk to life or limb   4. Effect on business reputation
   2. The number of services affected   5. Regulatory or legislative
       breaches – may be multiple
   3. The level of financial losses

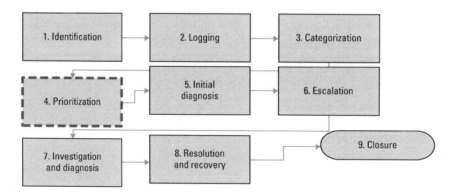

Incident Management Process – Simple priority coding system

An effective way of calculating impact and urgency and other elements and deriving an overall priority level for each incident is given in SO Table 4.1.

SO Table 4.1: Simple priority coding system

Urgency	Impact		
	High	Medium	Low
High	1	2	3
Medium	2	3	4
Low	3	4	5

Priority code	Description	Target resolution time
1	Critical	1 hour
2	High	8 hours
3	Medium	24 hours
4	Low	48 hours
5	Planning	Planned

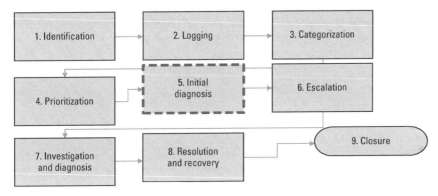

Based on Cabinet Office Crown Copyright Material

5. Initial diagnosis
o To try to discover the full symptoms of the incident and to determine exactly what is wrong and how to correct it
o If possible, the analyst resolves the incident while the user is on the phone and closes it if the resolution and recovery are agreed to be successful
o If they cannot resolve the incident while the user is still on the phone, but there is a prospect that the service desk may be able to do so, the analyst informs the user of the intent, supplies an incident reference number and attempts to find a resolution

Incident Management Process – Incident matching procedure

SO Figure 4.5: Example of an incident-matching procedure

© Crown copyright 2011. Reproduced under license from the Cabinet Office.

Incident matching procedure

A procedure for matching incident classification data against that for problems and known errors; successful matching gives efficient and quick access to proven resolution actions, reducing the time it takes to restore service back to users

Many incidents are regularly experienced and the appropriate resolution actions well known. However, a procedure is needed for matching incident classification data against that for problems and known errors. Successful matching gives efficient and quick access to proven resolutions, reducing the time to restore service to users. The classification and matching process allows incidents to be handled quicker and minimizes the need for escalation.

Effective use of incident matching ensures that incidents are not redundantly being investigated for resolution over and over each time. A procedure can be developed to help service desk and other support staff match incidents to find resolutions quickly where possible. An example of an incident-matching procedure is shown in SO Figure 4.5.

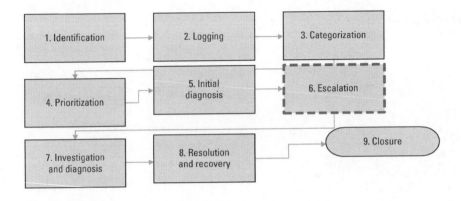

6. Escalation

Escalation

An activity that obtains additional resources when these are needed to meet service level targets or customer expectations; there are two types functional and hierarchic

Functional escalation

Transferring an incident, problem or change to a technical team with a higher level of expertise to assist

Hierarchic escalation

Informing or involving more senior levels of management to assist in an escalation

Functional escalation	Hierarchic escalation
As soon as it becomes clear that the service desk is unable to resolve the incident itself (or when target times for first-point resolution have been exceeded – whichever comes first), the incident must be immediately escalated for further support.	If incidents are of a serious nature (for example, high-priority incidents) the appropriate IT managers must be notified, for informational purposes at least.

The exact levels and timescales for both functional and hierarchic escalation need to be agreed, taking into account SLA targets, and embedded within support tools which can then be used to police and control the process flow within agreed timescales. The service desk should keep the user informed of any relevant escalation that takes place and ensure the incident record is updated accordingly to keep a full history of actions.

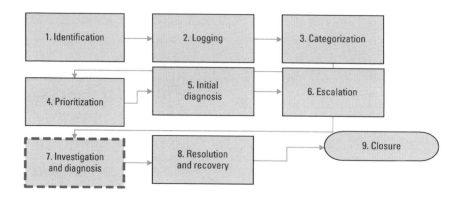

7. Investigation and diagnosis

o Establishing exactly what has gone wrong or is being sought by the user
o Determining the order of events
o Confirming the full incident impact of, e.g., number / range of affected users
o Identifying events that may have triggered it (e.g. a recent change?)
o Detailed knowledge searches looking for previous occurrences by searching incident/problem records and/or known error databases (KEDBs) or manufacturers'/suppliers' error logs or knowledge databases

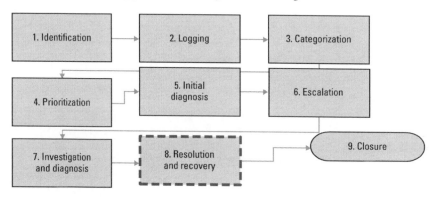

8. Resolution and recovery

When a potential resolution has been identified, this should be applied and tested. The specific actions to be undertaken and the people who will be involved in taking the recovery actions may vary, depending upon the nature of the fault, but could involve:

o Asking the user to undertake activities on their equipment
o The service desk implementing the resolution centrally using remote control software
o Specialist support groups being asked to implement specific recovery actions (e.g. network support reconfiguring a router)
o A third-party supplier or maintainer being asked to resolve the fault

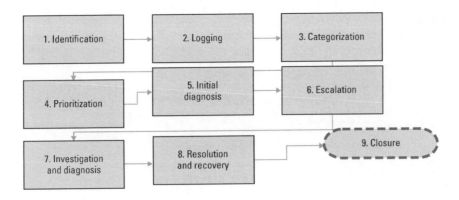

9. Closure

The service desk should check that the incident is fully resolved and that the users are satisfied and willing to agree that the incident can be closed. The service desk should also check:

o **Closure categorization** Check and confirm that the initial incident categorization was correct or, where the categorization subsequently turned out to be incorrect, update the record so that a correct closure categorization is recorded for the incident – seeking advice or guidance from the resolving group(s) as necessary.
o **User satisfaction survey** Carry out a user satisfaction call-back or email survey for the agreed percentage of incidents.
o **Incident documentation** Chase any outstanding details and ensure that the incident record is fully documented so that a full historic record at a sufficient level of detail is complete.
o **Ongoing or recurring problem?** Determine (in conjunction with resolver groups) whether the incident was resolved without the root cause being identified. In this situation, it is likely that the incident could recur and require further preventive action to avoid this. In all such cases, determine if a problem record related to the incident has already been raised. If not, raise a new problem record in conjunction with the problem management process so that preventive action is initiated.
o **Formal closure** Formally close the incident record.

Note that some organizations may choose to utilize an automatic closure period on specific, or even all, incidents (e.g. incident will be automatically closed after two working days if no further contact is made by the user). Where this approach is to be considered, it must first be fully discussed and agreed with the users – and widely publicized so that all users and IT staff are aware of this. It may be inappropriate to use this method for certain types of incidents, such as major incidents or those involving VIPs etc.

Incident Management Process – Interfaces with Service Design

Service level management	The ability to resolve incidents in a specified time is a key part of delivering an agreed level of service
Information security management	Providing security-related incident information as needed to support service design activities and gain a full picture of the effectiveness of the security measures as a whole based on an insight into all security incidents
Capacity management	Incident management provides a trigger for performance monitoring where there appears to be a performance problem
Availability management	Availability management will use incident management data to determine the availability of IT services and look at where the incident lifecycle can be improved

Incident Management Process – Interfaces with Service Transition

Service asset and configuration management	• Provides data used to identify and progress incidents and to assess the impact of an incident; also contains information on which categories of incident to assign to which support group • In turn, incident management can maintain the status of faulty CIs. It can also assist service asset and configuration management to audit the infrastructure when working to resolve an incident
Change management	• Where a change is needed to implement a workaround or resolution, it will be logged as an RFC and progressed through change management • In turn, incident management is able to detect and resolve incidents that arise from failed changes

Incident Management Process – Interfaces with Service Operation

Problem management	• For some incidents, it will be appropriate for problem management to investigate and resolve the underlying cause to prevent or reduce the impact of recurrence • Incident management provides reporting point for these • Problem management can provide known errors for faster incident resolution through workarounds to restore service
Access management	• Incidents should be raised when unauthorized access attempts and security breaches have been detected • A history of incidents should also be maintained to support forensic investigation activities, resolution of access breaches

ITILFND05-05-71 Explain the purpose, objectives, scope, basic concepts, process activities and interfaces for incident management (SO 4.2.1, 4.2.2, 4.2.4.2, 4.2.5, 4.2.6.4)

For examination purposes, here is what is important:
o You must be able to identify the verbatim definition of an incident from choices given
o You must be able to distinguish an incident from a problem or service request
o You must be able to recall that the Service Desk FUNCTION is not the same as the Incident Management PROCESS (the incident management process runs horizontally through an organization, and is participated in by many functions (departments), e.g., network operations, technical services, deskside support – along with the service desk); the service desk is at the head end of the incident management process but is not equivalent to the incident management process.
o You must know what an incident model is, and be able to chose the correct list of what it should include from a set of lists (choosing the verbatim / correct answer over plausible but not verbatim lists)
o You must know what a major incident is and how it is handled different
o You must understand the priority coding system – impact, urgency, priority
o You must be able to recall status field examples through the lifecycle, e.g., open, in progress, resolved, closed
o You must be able to recall the components of the expanded incident lifecycle; you should be able to pick the components off a list, the correct / verbatim list
o You should be able to choose correct key interfaces with other ITIL processes from a list
o You should be able to pick a set of steps in a list that are in the incident management process and distinguish it from a list that may be plausible but is not verbatim from the list specified in ITIL
Remember CIRCLED PI:
Categorization

Identification

Resolution and Recovery

Closure

Logging

Escalation

Diagnosis

Prioritization

Investigation

ITILFND05-05-72 Explain the purpose, objectives, scope, basic concepts, process activities and interfaces for problem management (SO 4.4.1, 4.4.2, 4.4.4.2, 4.4.5, 4.4.6.4), not section on problem analysis techniques (4.4.4.3)

Problem Management Process – purpose
o Manage the lifecycle of all problems from first identification through further investigation, documentation and eventual removal
o Minimize the adverse impact of incidents and problems on the business that are caused by underlying errors within the IT Infrastructure, and to proactively prevent recurrence of incidents related to these errors

Problem Management   The process responsible for managing the lifecycle of all problems. Problem management proactively prevents incidents from happening and minimizes the impact of incidents that cannot be prevented.

Problem   Cause of one or more incidents, not usually known when a problem record is created; problem management process is responsible for further investigation.

Problem Management Process – objectives
Prevent problems and resulting incidents from happening
Eliminate recurring incidents
Minimize the impact of incidents that cannot be prevented

Problem Management Process – scope
Problem management has both reactive and proactive aspects:

o **Reactive problem management** focuses on solving problems in response to one or more incidents
o **Proactive problem management** focuses on identifying and solving problems / known errors before further related incidents re-occur
o Conducting periodic scheduled reviews of operational logs and maintenance records and event logs targeting patterns and trends of warning and exception events
o Conducting brainstorming sessions to identify trends indicating underlying problems
o Using check sheets to proactively collect data on service or operational quality issues that may help to detect underlying problems

Problem Management Process – principles and basic concepts - Reactive and proactive problem management activities
The difference between reactive and proactive problem management lies in how the problem management process is triggered:

With **reactive problem management**, process activities will typically be triggered in reaction to an incident that has taken place. Reactive problem management complements incident management activities by focusing on the underlying cause of an incident to prevent its recurrence and identifying workarounds when necessary.	With **proactive problem management**, process activities are triggered by activities seeking to improve services. One example might be trend analysis activities to find common underlying causes of historical incidents that took place to prevent their recurrence. Proactive problem management complements CSI activities by helping to identify workarounds and improvement actions that can improve the quality of a service.

Problem Management Process – principles and basic concepts – Problem models

o Many problems will be unique and will require handling in an individual way, but it is conceivable that some incidents may recur due to dormant or underlying problems
   1. For example, where the cost of a permanent resolution will be high and a decision has been taken not to go ahead with an expensive solution but to 'live with' the problem)
o Besides creating a known error record in the KEDB to ensure quicker diagnosis, the creation of a problem model for handling such problems in the future may be helpful
   2. This is very similar in concept to the idea of incident or request models described in previous chapters, but applied to problems.

Problem Management Process – principles and basic concepts – Incidents versus problems

o An **incident** is an unplanned interruption to an IT service or reduction in quality of an IT service o Incidents do not 'become' problems o Incident management activities are focused on restoring services to normal state operations o It is quite common to have incidents that are also problems	o A **problem** presents a different view of an incident by understanding its underlying cause, which may also be the cause of other incidents o Problem management activities are focused on finding ways to prevent incidents happening in the first place

Problem Management Process – Activities, methods, techniques

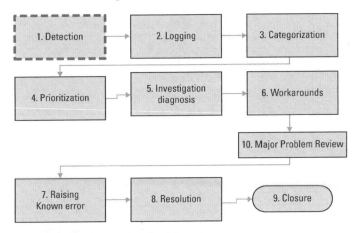

1. Detection - triggers

Reactive problem management	Proactive problem management
○ Suspicion or detection of a cause of one or more incidents	○ Analysis of incidents
○ Analysis of an incident by a technical support group	○ Trending of historical incidents
○ Automated detection of an infrastructure / application fault	○ Quality of service activities
○ Notification from a supplier or contractor that a problem exists	

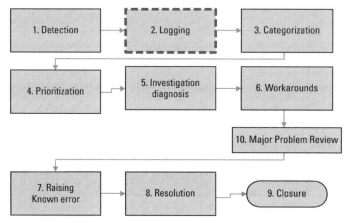

2. Logging
○ Record all relevant problem details for a full historic record
○ Date and time stamped to allow suitable control and escalation
○ Cross-reference to incident(s), recording details such as:
    1. User, service, equipment details
    2. Date/time initially logged
    3. Priority and category details
    4. Incident description, record numbers, other cross-reference
    5. Diagnostic and recovery details

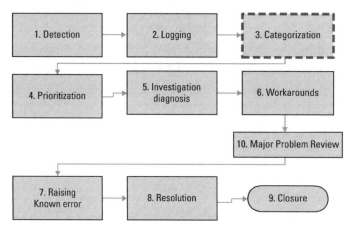

3. Categorization

Categorize Problems in the same way as incidents, using the same coding system, so the true nature of the problem can be easily traced in the future and meaningful management information can be had, and enables incidents and problems to be more readily matched.

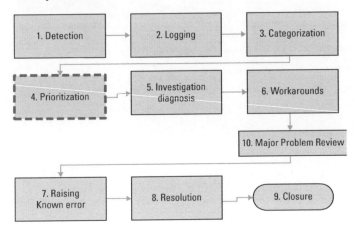

Based on Cabinet Office Crown Copyright Material

4. Prioritization

o Prioritization is normally determined by the urgency of the problem (how quickly the business needs resolution) and business impact

o Impact is often the number of users being affected, but loss of service to a single user can have a major impact

o Should also factor in problem severity
   1. Can the system be recovered, or does it need to be replaced?
   2. How much will it cost?
   3. How many people, with what skills, and how long to fix it?
   4. How extensive is the problem (e.g. how many CIs are affected)?

Problem Management Process – Simple priority coding system

Problems should be prioritized the same way using the same reasons as incidents. An effective way of calculating impact and urgency and other elements and deriving an overall priority level for each problem is given in SO Table 4.1.

SO Table 4.1: Simple priority coding system

Urgency	Impact			
		High	Medium	Low
	High	1	2	3
	Medium	2	3	4
	Low	3	4	5

Priority code	Description	Target resolution time
1	Critical	1 hour
2	High	8 hours
3	Medium	24 hours
4	Low	48 hours
5	Planning	Planned

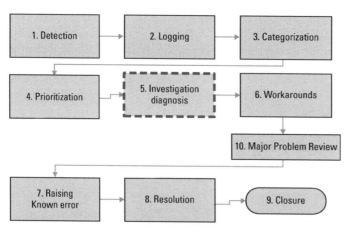

5. Investigation & diagnosis
o Diagnose root cause with an appropriate level of resources and expertise should be applied commensurate with the priority and associated service target
o Apply problem-solving techniques
o Use the CMS to help determine impact and pinpoint and diagnose the exact point of failure
o Use the KEDB for problem-matching techniques to see if the problem has occurred before and, if so, to find the resolution

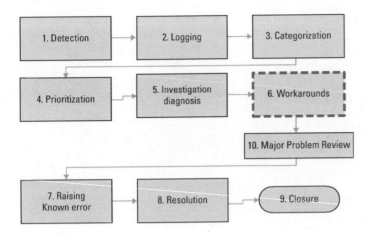

6. Workarounds
o Here we seek a workaround – a temporary way of overcoming the difficulties – to the incidents caused by the problem
o It is vital for work on a permanent resolution continue if justified
o When a workaround is found, it is vital that the problem record stays open and workaround details are documented in it

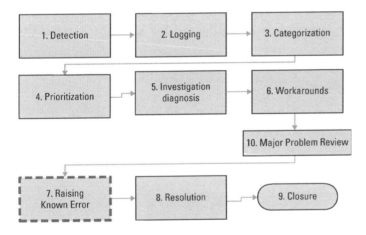

7. Raising an known error record
o A known error is a problem with a documented root cause and workaround
o Known error records should identify the related problem record and document the status of actions being taken to resolve the problem, its root cause and workaround
o All known error records should be stored in the known error database (KEDB)

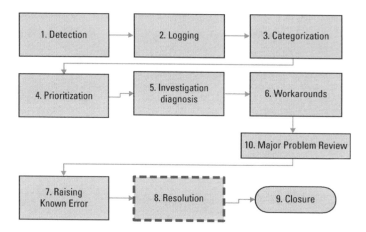

8. Resolution

○ Once a root cause is found and solution developed, apply it to resolve the problem
○ If a change is needed an RFC must be raised and authorized before applying the fix
○ Use an emergency RFC for very serious problems / urgent fixes
○ Some solutions are not justifiable and a decision may be taken to leave the problem record open but to use a workaround

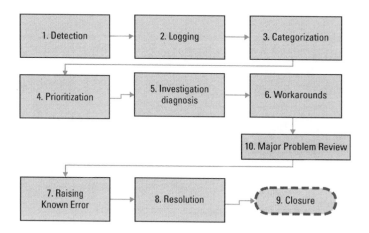

9. Closure

○ When a final resolution has been applied, the problem record should be formally closed – as should any related incident records that are still open.
○ A check must be performed here to ensure the record has a full historical description of all events – and if not, update the record
○ Status of any related known error record must be updated to show the resolution has been applied

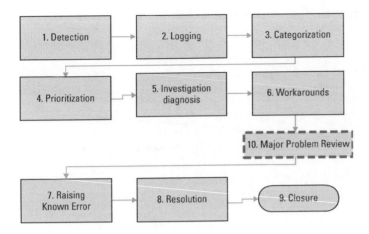

10. Major problem review
After every major problem, conduct a lessons learned review examining:
o Things done right and wrong
o What to do better in the future
o How to prevent recurrence
o Whether there is any third-party responsibility and if follow-up actions are needed

After every major problem (as determined by the organization's priority system), and while memories are still fresh, a review should be conducted to learn any lessons for the future. Such reviews can be used as part of training and awareness activities for support staff – and any lessons learned should be documented in appropriate procedures, work instructions, diagnostic scripts or known error records. The problem manager facilitates the session and documents any agreed actions.

Major problem reviews can also be a source of input to proactive problem management through identification of underlying causes that may be discovered in the course of the review.

The knowledge gained from the review should be incorporated into a service review meeting with the business customer to ensure the customer is aware of the actions taken and the plans to prevent future major incidents from occurring. This helps to improve customer satisfaction and assure the business that service operation is handling major incidents responsibly and actively working to prevent their future recurrence.

Problem Management Process – Interfaces with Service Strategy

Financial management for IT services	• Assists in assessing the impact of proposed resolutions or workarounds, and pain value analysis • Problem management provides information about the cost of resolving and preventing problems • Used as input into the budgeting and accounting systems and total cost of ownership calculations

Problem Management Process – Interfaces with Service Design

Availability management	• Involved with seeking reduced downtime and increased uptime • Much of the management information available in problem management will be communicated to availability management
Capacity management	• Some problems will require investigation by capacity management teams and techniques, e.g. performance issues • Problem management provides management information on the quality of decisions made during the capacity planning process
IT service continuity management	• Problem management acts as an entry point into IT service continuity management where a significant problem is not resolved before it starts to have a major impact on the business
Service level management	• Problem management contributes to improvements in service levels, and its information is used for some SLA review components • SLM provides parameters within which problem management works

Problem Management Process – Interfaces with Service Transition

Change management	• Problem management ensures resolutions/workarounds that require a CI change are given to change management via RFC • Change management tracks changes, advises problem management
Service asset and configuration management	• Problem management uses the CMS to identify faulty CIs and also to determine the impact of problems and resolutions
Release and deployment management	• Responsible for deploying problem fixes out to the live environment • Problem management will help resolve problems caused by faults during the release process
Knowledge management	• The SKMS can be used to form the basis for the KEDB and hold or integrate with the problem records

Problem Management Process – Interfaces with CSI

The seven-step improvement process	• Incidents and problems are a basis for identifying service improvement opportunities; adding them to the CSI register • Proactive problem management activities may identify underlying issues that if addressed, can contribute to increases in service quality and end user/customer satisfaction

ITILFND05-05-72 Explain the purpose, objectives, scope, basic concepts, process activities and interfaces for problem management (SO 4.4.1, 4.4.2, 4.4.4.2, 4.4.5, 4.4.6.4), not section on problem analysis techniques (4.4.4.3)

For examination purposes, here is what is important:
o You must be able to identify the verbatim definition of an problem from choices given
o You must be able to distinguish an incident from a problem or service request, and a problem from a known error, and know that a known error must have a workaround
o You must understand the priority coding system – impact, urgency, priority
o You must be able to recall status field examples through the lifecycle, e.g., open, in progress, resolved, closed
o You must recall that problem management has two aspects, reactive and proactive, and be able to classify an activity as belonging to one or the other
o You must be able to choose correct key interfaces with other ITIL processes from a list
o You should be able to pick a set of steps in a list that are in the problem management process and distinguish it from a list that may be plausible but is not verbatim from the list specified in ITIL

Remember CRIMPLED CoW
  Categorization

  Resolution

  Investigation & Diagnosis

  Major Problem Review

  Prioritization

  Logging

  Error, raising known

  Detection

  Closure

  (o)

  Workarounds

ITILFND05-05-81 State the purpose, objectives and scope for event management
(SO 4.1.1, 4.1.2)

Event Management Process – Purpose
o Manage events throughout their lifecycle
o Coordinate the lifecycle of activities to detect and make sense of events and determine appropriate control action

Event Management   The process responsible for managing events throughout their lifecycle. Event management is one of the main activities of IT operations.

Event   A change of state that has significance for the management of an IT service or other configuration item. The term is also used to mean an alert or notification created by any IT service, configuration item or monitoring tool. Events typically require IT operations personnel to take actions, and often lead to incidents being logged

Effective service operation is dependent on knowing the status of the infrastructure and detecting any deviation from normal or expected operation. This is provided by good monitoring and control systems, which are based on two types of tools:

Active monitoring tools – poll key CIs to determine status and availability; exceptions generate alerts that must be communicated to the appropriate tool or team for action.	**Passive monitoring tools** – detect and correlate operational alerts or communications generated by CIs.

Event Management Process – Objectives
o Detect all changes of state with significance for the management of a CI or IT service
o Determine the appropriate control action for events and ensure these are communicated to the appropriate functions
o Provide the trigger, or entry point, for the execution of many service operation processes and operations management activities
o Provide the means to compare actual operating performance and behavior against design standards and SLAs
o Provide a basis for service assurance and reporting; and service improvement

Event Management Process – Scope
o Configuration items (CIs)
   1. Some CIs are included as they must stay in a constant state (e.g. a switch on a network must stay on; tools confirm this by monitoring responses to 'pings')
   2. Some CIs will be included because their status needs to change frequently and event management can be used to automate this and update the configuration management system (CMS) (e.g. the updating of a file server)
o Environmental conditions (e.g. fire and smoke detection)
o Software license monitoring to ensure optimum/legal license utilization and allocation
o Security (e.g. intrusion detection)
o Normal activity (e.g. tracking use of an application or the performance of a server)

ITILFND05-05-81 State the purpose, objectives and scope for event management
(SO 4.1.1, 4.1.2)

What is important for the exam is to be able to distinguish between and incident,
event, and alert. You should know that not all events generate incidents (some are
merely informational, others are warnings, for example that a threshold may be
reached soon); and that not all incidents come out of events trapped by monitoring
tools (e.g., a user can call the service desk).

Do you have a separately recognized event management process in your organization
that monitors and controls services? Is it integrated into your incident system so that
events that warrant such treatment, for example, critical server down exceptions, are
auto-ticketed into the incident system and notifications generated?

Request Fulfillment Process – Purpose
o managing the lifecycle of all user service requests

Request Fulfillment

The process responsible for managing the lifecycle of all service requests

Service Request

A formal request from a user for something to be provided – for example, a request for information or advice; to reset a password; or to install a workstation for a new user. Service requests are managed by the request fulfillment process, usually in conjunction with the service desk. Service requests may be linked to a request for change as part of fulfilling the request.

Request Fulfillment Process – Objectives
o Maintain user and customer satisfaction by efficient and professional handling of all service requests
o Provide a channel for users to request and receive standard services for which a predefined authorization and qualification process exists
o Provide information to users and customers about the availability of services and the procedure for obtaining them
o Source and deliver requested standard service components (e.g. licenses, software)
o Assist with general information, complaints or comments

Request Fulfillment Process – Scope
o The process needed to fulfill a request will vary based on what is being requested, but can usually be broken down into a set of activities that have to be performed; for each request, activities must be documented in a request model stored in the SKMS
o It will be up to each organization to decide and document which service requests it will handle through the request fulfillment process and which will have to go through other processes such as business relationship management for dealing with requests for new or changed services
o Gray areas always prevent generic guidance from being usefully prescribed

Some organizations are comfortable handling service requests through their incident management process (and tools) as a particular type of 'incident' (using a high-level categorization system to identify those 'incidents' that are in fact service requests). Note, however, that there is a significant difference here – an incident is usually an unplanned event, whereas a service request is usually something that can and should be planned. Therefore, in an organization where large numbers of service requests have to be handled, and where the actions to be taken to fulfill those requests are very varied or specialized, it may be appropriate to handle service requests as a completely separate work stream – and to record and manage them as a separate record type. This is essential if reporting is desired that more accurately separates incidents from requests.

ITILFND05-05-82 State the purpose, objectives and scope for request fulfillment
(SO 4.3.1, 4.3.2)

There are things that are not incidents (something is broken) and are generally handled outside of the everyday change process. These things tend to follow a routine path and require information specific to the work to be done. These are service requests.

For examination purposes, it is important to distinguish between service requests, incidents, and changes; also, regardless of how your organization classifies them, the examples given in ITIL – password reset, new user workstation installation – if these examples are given you need to indicate that these are service requests, handled by the request fulfillment process, not changes or incidents.

Do you manage and track service requests under a separate workflow? Or does your organization group them in with incidents or changes? How is this handled? How, if at all, is reporting handled such that the different types – incidents, changes, service requests, and their associated volumes, are distinguished?

ITILFND05-05-83 State the purpose, objectives and scope for access management
(SO 4.5.1, 4.5.2)

Access Management Process – Purpose
o Provide the right for users to be able to use a service or group of services
o The execution of policies and actions defined in information security management

Access Management

The process responsible for allowing users to make use of IT services, data or other assets.
Access management helps to protect the confidentiality, integrity and availability of assets by
ensuring that only authorized users are able to access or modify them. Access management
implements the policies of information security management and is sometimes referred to as
rights management or identity management.

Access Management Process – Objectives
o Manage access to services based on policies and actions defined in information security management
o Efficiently respond to requests for granting access to services, changing access rights or restricting access, ensuring the rights provided or changed are properly granted
o Oversee access to services and ensure rights being provided are not improperly used

Access Management Process – SCOPE
o Execution of the policies in information security management, in that it enables the organization to manage the confidentiality, availability and integrity of the organization's data and intellectual property
o Ensures that users are given the right to use a service, but it does not ensure that this access is available at all agreed times – this is provided by availability management
o Executed by all technical and application management functions and is usually not a separate function; however, there is likely a single control point of coordination, usually in IT operations management or on the service desk
o Can be initiated by a service request

ITILFND05-05-83 State the purpose, objectives and scope for access management
(SO 4.5.1, 4.5.2)

Some organizations do not distinguish access management as a separate process, but it makes sense to do so, as generally these types of requests are handed by security groups. You can think of security management as the strategic process that sets the policies, and access management as the operational process that executes these policies on a day to day basis.

What does your organization do? Is there a separate group, role, or process for access management? Or is this done within each technology stream? Is the workflow for access management separated from incident and service request management, or does your organization make no such distinction? Either way, how is that working for you?

ITILFND05-05-91 State the purpose, objectives and scope for the seven-step improvement process (CSI 3.9.3.1, 4.1, 4.1.1, 4.1.2, Figure 3.4)

The seven-step improvement process – Purpose
o Define and manage the steps needed to identify, define, gather, process, analyze, present and implement improvements

Seven-Step Improvement Process
The process responsible for defining and managing the steps needed to identify, define, gather, process, analyze, present and implement improvements; the performance of the IT service provider is continually measured by this process and improvements are made to processes, services and infrastructure in order to increase efficiency, effectiveness and cost effectiveness. Opportunities for improvement are recorded and managed in the CSI register.

The seven-step improvement process – Objectives
o Identifying opportunities for improving services, processes, tools, etc.
o Reducing the cost of providing services and ensuring that IT services enable the required business outcomes to be achieved
o Identifying what needs to be measured, analyzed and reported to establish improvement opportunities
o Continually reviewing service achievements to ensure they remain matched to business requirements; continually aligning and re-aligning service provision with outcome requirements
o Understanding what to measure, why it is being measured and carefully defining the successful outcome

The seven-step improvement process – Scope
o Analysis of the performance and capabilities of services, processes throughout the lifecycle, partners and technology
o Continual alignment of the portfolio of IT services with the current and future business needs as well as the maturity of the enabling IT processes for each service
o Making best use of the technology that the organization has and looks to exploit new technology as it becomes available where there is a business case for doing so
o Organizational structure, capabilities of the personnel, and asking whether people are working in appropriate functions and roles, and if they have the required skills

Fundamental to CSI is the concept of measurement. CSI uses the seven-step improvement process shown in CSI Figure 3.4. All activities of the improvement process assist CSI in some way. It is relatively simple to identify what takes places but more difficult to understand exactly how this will happen. The improvement process spans not only the management organization but the entire service lifecycle. This is a cornerstone of CSI, the main steps of which are as follows:

1. **Identify the strategy for improvement** Identify the overall vision, business need, the strategy and the tactical and operational goals
2. **Define what you will measure** Service strategy and design should have identified this information early in the lifecycle. CSI can then start its cycle all over again

at 'Where are we now?' and 'Where do we want to be?' This identifies the ideal situation for both the business and IT. CSI can conduct a gap analysis to identify opportunities for improvement as well as answering the question 'How do we get there?'

3. **Gather the data** To answer the question 'Did we get there?', data must first be gathered (usually through service operations) from many sources based on goals and objectives identified. At this point the data is raw and no conclusions are drawn.

4. **Process the data** Here data is processed in alignment with critical success factors (CSFs) and KPIs specified. This means that timeframes are coordinated, unaligned data is rationalized and made consistent, and gaps in the data are identified. The simple goal of this step is to process data from multiple disparate sources to give it context that can be compared. Once data is rationalized we can begin analysis.

5. **Analyze the information and data** As we bring data more and more into context it evolves from raw data into information where we can start to answer questions on who, what, when, where and how as well as trends and the impact on the business; this step is often overlooked in the rush to present data to management.

6. **Present and use the information** Here the answer to 'Did we get there?' is formatted and communicated to the various stakeholders an accurate picture of the results of the improvement efforts. Knowledge is presented to the business in a form and manner that reflects their needs and assists them in determining the next steps.

7. **Implement improvement** Knowledge gained is used to optimize, improve and correct services and processes. Issues have been identified and now solutions are implemented –wisdom is applied to the knowledge. Improvements to improve the service or process are communicated and explained to the organization; then the organization establishes a new baseline and the cycle begins anew.

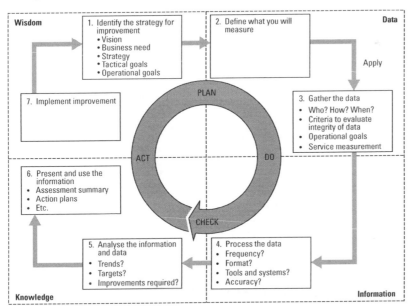

CSI Figure 3.4: The seven-step improvement process

CHAPTER 6
ITILFND06 FUNCTIONS (60M)

The purpose of this unit is to help you to explain the role, objectives and organizational structures of the service desk function, and to state the role, objectives and overlap of three other functions. The recommended study period for this unit is minimum 1 hour.

ITILFND06-06-1 Explain the role, objectives and organizational structures for the service desk function (SO 6.3, 6.3.1, 6.3.2, 6.3.3, Figures 6.2, 6.3, 6.4)

Service desk function – Role
The single point of contact for IT users on a day-by-day basis

- Handles incidents, escalates incidents to problem management staff, manages service requests and answers questions
- Provides an interface for other activities such as customer change requests, maintenance contracts, software licenses, SLM, service asset and configuration management, availability management, financial management for IT services, and IT service continuity management

Service Desk
The single point of contact between the service provider and the users. A typical service desk manages incidents and service requests, and handles communication with the users.

Service desk function – Objective
The primary aim of the service desk is to provide a single point of contact between the services being provided and the users. Specific responsibilities will include:
- Logging all incident/service request details, allocating category and priority codes
- Providing first-line investigation and diagnosis
- Resolving incidents/service requests when first contacted whenever possible
- Escalating incidents/service requests they cannot resolve within agreed timescales
- Keeping users informed of progress
- Closing all resolved incidents, requests and other calls
- Conducting customer/user satisfaction call-backs/surveys as agreed
- Communication with users – keeping them informed of incident progress, notifying them of impending changes or agreed outages etc.
- Updating the CMS under the direction and approval of service asset and configuration management if so agreed

Service desk function – Organizational structures

Type	Description
1. Local	Located "near" the user location
2. Centralized	One central physical location
3. Virtual	One central Service Desk accessible through the network from several locations
4. Follow-the-Sun	Two or more combined to provide 24-hour coverage
5. Specialized	Support by specialist groups

Service Desk Function – Organizational Structures – Local

Aids communication, gives a clearly visible presence; might not be an efficient use of staff if call volumes are low; why set up one?

o Language and cultural or political differences
o Different time zones
o Specialized groups of users
o Customized / specialized services that require specialist knowledge
o VIP / criticality status of users

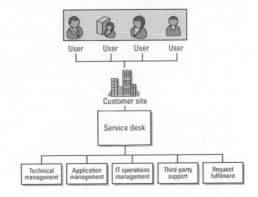

SO Figure 6.2: Local service desk

© Crown copyright 2011. Reproduced under license from the Cabinet Office.

Service Desk Function – Organizational Structures – Centralized

o Merged into one or few locations; fewer overall staff to deal with a higher volume of calls
o Retain "local presence" to handle physical support requirements
o Controlled and deployed from the central Service Desk

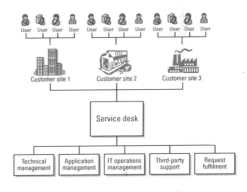

SO Figure 6.3: Central service desk

© Crown copyright 2011. Reproduced under license from the Cabinet Office.

Service Desk Function – Organizational Structures – Virtual

Single visible Service Desk which may actually be run by staff in multiple locations connected together; allows for "home working", secondary support group, offshoring, or outsourcingof Service Desk staff; CSFs: consistency and uniformity in service quality; adapting cultural terms

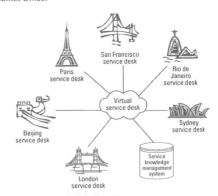

SO Figure 6.4: Virtual service desk

© Crown copyright 2011. Reproduced under license from the Cabinet Office.

TILFND06-06-2 State the role and objectives of the technical management function (SO 6.4.1, 6.4.2), the application management function (SO 6.6.1, 6.6.2) with application development (SO 6.6.6.1, Table 6.2), and the IT operations management function (IT operations control and facilities management) (SO 6.5.1, 6.5.2)

Technical management FUNCTION – ROLE

- o Custodian of technical knowledge and expertise related to managing the IT infrastructure; ensures that the knowledge required to design, test, manage and improve IT services is identified, developed and refined
- o Provider of actual resources to support the service lifecycle; ensures that resources are effectively trained and deployed to design, build, transition, operate and improve the technology required to deliver and support IT services

Technical Management

The function responsible for providing technical skills in support of IT services and management of the IT infrastructure. Technical management defines the roles of support groups, as well as the tools, processes and procedures required.

Technical management FUNCTION – OBJECTIVES

Help plan, implement and maintain a stable technical infrastructure to support the organization's business processes through:

- o Well designed and highly resilient, cost-effective technical topology
- o Use of technical skills to maintain the technical infrastructure in optimum condition
- o Swift use of technical skills to speedily diagnose and resolve any technical failures

Application management function – ROLE

- o Custodian of technical knowledge and expertise related to managing applications; ensures that the knowledge required to design, test, manage and improve IT services is identified, developed and refined
- o Provides the actual resources to support the service lifecycle; ensures that resources are effectively trained and deployed to design, build, transition, operate and improve the technology required to deliver and support IT services

Application Management

The function responsible for managing applications throughout their lifecycle

Application management function – objectives

- o Support the organization's business processes by helping to identify functional and manageability requirements for application software
- o Assist in the design and deployment of those applications and the ongoing support and improvement of those applications

Application Development versus Application Management

SO Table 6.2: Application development versus application management

	Application development	Application management
Nature of activities	One-time set of activities to design and construct application solutions	Ongoing set of activities to oversee and manage applications throughout their entire lifecycle
Scope of activities	Performed mostly for applications developed in-house	Performed for all applications, whether purchased from third parties or developed in-house
Primary focus	Utility focus Building functionality for their customer What the application does is more important than how it is operated	Both utility and warranty focus What the functionality is as well as how to deliver it Manageability aspects of the application, i.e. how to ensure stability and performance of the application
Management mode	Most development work is done in projects where the focus is on delivering specific units of work to specification, on time and within budget This means that it is often difficult for developers to understand and build for ongoing operations, especially because they are not available for support of the application once they have moved on to the next project	Most work is done as part of repeatable, ongoing processes. A relatively small number of people work in projects This means that it is very difficult for operational staff to get involved in development projects, as that takes them away from their ongoing operational responsibilities
Measurement	Staff are typically rewarded for creativity and for completing one project so that they can move on to the next project	Staff are typically rewarded for consistency and for preventing unexpected events and unauthorized functionality (e.g. 'bells and whistles' added by developers)
Cost	Development projects are relatively easy to quantify because the resources are known and it is easy to link their expenses to a specific application or IT service	Ongoing management costs are often mixed in with the costs of other IT services because resources are often shared across multiple IT services and applications
Lifecycles	Development staff focus on software development lifecycles, which highlight the dependencies for successful operation, but do not assign accountability for these	Staff involved in ongoing management typically only control one or two stages of these lifecycles – operation and improvement

IT operations management function – ROLE

○ Execute ongoing activities and procedures required to manage and maintain the IT infrastructure so as to deliver and support IT services at the agreed levels; includes:

IT operations control – oversees the execution and monitoring of the operational activities and events in the IT infrastructure	**Facilities Management** – management of the physical IT environment, typically a data center or computer rooms and recovery sites together with all the power and cooling equipment

IT Operations Management
The function within an IT service provider that performs the daily activities needed to manage IT services and the supporting IT infrastructure. IT operations management includes IT operations control and facilities management.

IT operations management function – Objectives

○ Maintenance of the status quo to achieve stability of the organization's day-to-day processes and activities
○ Regular scrutiny and improvements to achieve improved service at reduced costs, while maintaining stability
○ Swift application of operational skills to diagnose and resolve any IT operations failures that occur

IT operations management can be defined as the function responsible for the ongoing management and maintenance of an organization's IT infrastructure to ensure delivery of the agreed level of IT services to the business.

IT operations is the set of activities involved in the day-to-day running of the IT infrastructure to deliver IT services at agreed levels to meet stated business objectives.

IT operations control oversees execution and monitoring of operational activities and events in the IT infrastructure with the help of an operations bridge or network operations center.

Facilities management refers to the management of the physical IT environment, typically a data center or computer rooms and recovery sites together with all the power and cooling equipment. Facilities management also includes the coordination of large-scale consolidation projects, e.g. data center consolidation or server consolidation projects. In some cases the management of a data center is outsourced, in which case facilities management refers to the management of the outsourcing contract.

ITILFND06-06-2 State the role and objectives of the technical management function
(SO 6.4.1, 6.4.2), the application management function (SO 6.6.1, 6.6.2) with application
development (SO 6.6.6.1, Table 6.2), and the IT operations management function
(IT operations control and facilities management) (SO 6.5.1, 6.5.2)

It is important for the examination that you be able to:
o Distinguish between a process and a function
o List the four functions specified by ITIL:
   1. Service Desk
   2. Application Management
   3. Technical Management
   4. IT Operations
      Remember O-A-T-S

      (IT) Operations

      Application Management

      Technical Management

      Service Desk

o Distinguish between application development and application management
o Be able to cite that the IT operations management function includes two sub-
   functions: IT operations control (you can think of this as console monitoring in
   the datacenter) and facilities management (what you normally see in a data center
   – someone tending to power, air conditioning, changing filters, air flow, acquiring,
   moving, and consolidating facilities, etc.)

CHAPTER 7
ITILFND07
ROLES (45M)

The purpose of this unit is to help you to account for and to be aware of the responsibilities of some of the key roles in service management. The recommended study period for this unit is minimum 45 minutes.

ITILFND07-07-1 Account for the role and the responsibilities of the process owner
(SD 6.3.2), process manager (SD 6.3.3), process practitioner (SD 6.3.4), and service owner
(SD 6.3.1)

Process Owner – Role

o The process owner role is accountable for ensuring that a process is fit for purpose.
  This role is often assigned to the same person who carries out the process manager
  role, but the two roles may be separate in larger organizations. The process owner
  role is accountable for ensuring that their process is performed according to the
  agreed and documented standard and meets the aims of the process definition.

Process Owner

The person who is held accountable for ensuring that a process is fit for purpose. The process
owner's responsibilities include sponsorship, design, change management and continual
improvement of the process and its metrics. This role can be assigned to the same person who
carries out the process manager role, but the two roles may be separate in larger organizations.

Process Owner – Responsibilities

o Sponsoring, designing and change managing the process and its metrics
o Defining the process strategy
o Assisting with process design
o Ensuring that appropriate process documentation is available and current
o Defining appropriate policies and standards to be employed throughout the process
o Periodically auditing the process to ensure compliance to policy and standards
o Periodically reviewing the process strategy to ensure that it is still appropriate and
  change as required
o Communicating process information or changes as appropriate to ensure awareness
o Providing process resources to support activities required throughout the service
  lifecycle
o Ensuring that process technicians have the required knowledge and the required
  technical and business understanding to deliver the process, and understand their
  role in the process
o Reviewing opportunities for process enhancements and for improving the efficiency
  and effectiveness of the process
o Addressing issues with the running of the process
o Identifying improvement opportunities for inclusion in the CSI register
o Working with the CSI manager and process manager to review and prioritize
  improvements in the CSI register
o Making improvements to the process

Process Manager – Role

o The process manager role is accountable for operational management of a process.
  There may be several process managers for one process, for example regional
  change managers or IT service continuity managers for each data center. The
  process manager role is often assigned to the person who carries out the process
  owner role, but the two roles may be separate in larger organizations.

Process Manager – Responsibilities

o Working with the process owner to plan and coordinate all process activities
o Ensuring that all activities are carried out as required throughout the service lifecycle
o Appointing people to the required roles
o Managing resources assigned to the process
o Working with service owners and other process managers to ensure the smooth running of services
o Monitoring and reporting on process performance
o Identifying improvement opportunities for inclusion in the CSI register
o Working with the CSI manager and process owner to review and prioritize improvements in the CSI register
o Making improvements to the process implementation

Process Practitioner – Role

o A process practitioner is responsible for carrying out one or more process activities
o In some organizations, and for some processes, the process practitioner role may be combined with the process manager role; in others there may be large numbers of practitioners carrying out different parts of the process

Process Practitioner

A process practitioner is responsible for carrying out one or more process activities. In some organizations, and for some processes, the process practitioner role may be combined with the process manager role; in others there may be large numbers of practitioners carrying out different parts of the process.

Process Practitioner – Responsibilities

o Carrying out one or more activities of a process
o Understanding how their role contributes to the overall delivery of service and creation of value for the business
o Working with other stakeholders, such as their manager, co-workers, users and customers, to ensure that their contributions are effective
o Ensuring that inputs, outputs and interfaces for their activities are correct
o Creating or updating records to show that activities have been carried out correctly

Service Owner – Role

o The service owner is accountable for the delivery of a specific IT service. The service owner is responsible to the customer for the initiation, transition and ongoing maintenance and support of a particular service and accountable to the IT director or service management director for the delivery of the service. The service owner's accountability for a specific service within an organization is independent of where the underpinning technology components, processes or professional capabilities reside. It is possible that a single person may fulfill the service owner role for more than one service

Service Owner

A role responsible for managing one or more services throughout their entire lifecycle. Service owners are instrumental in the development of service strategy and are responsible for the content of the service portfolio.

Service Owner – Responsibilities

o Ensuring that the ongoing service delivery and support meet agreed customer requirements
o Working with business relationship management to understand and translate customer requirements into activities, measures or service components that will ensure that the service provider can meet those requirements
o Ensuring consistent and appropriate communication with customer(s) for service-related enquiries and issues
o Assisting in defining service models and in assessing the impact of new services or changes to existing services through the service portfolio management process
o Identifying opportunities for service improvements, discussing these with the customer and raising RFCs as appropriate
o Liaising with the appropriate process owners throughout the service lifecycle
o Soliciting required data, statistics and reports for analysis and to facilitate effective service monitoring and performance
o Providing input in service attributes such as performance, availability etc.
o Representing the service across the organization
o Understanding the service (components etc.)
o Serving as the point of escalation (notification) for major incidents relating to the service
o Representing the service in change advisory board (CAB) meetings
o Participating in internal service review meetings (within IT)
o Participating in external service review meetings (with the business)
o Ensuring that the service entry in the service catalogue is accurate and is maintained
o Participating in negotiating service level agreements (SLAs) and operational level agreements (OLAs) relating to the service
o Identifying improvement opportunities for inclusion in the continual service improvement (CSI) register
o Working with the CSI manager to review and prioritize improvements in the CSI register
o Making improvements to the service

ITILFND07-07-2 Recognize the responsible, accountable, consulted, informed (RACI) responsibility model and explain its role in determining organizational structure (SD 3.7.4.1, Table 3.2, not RACI-VS or RASCI)

RACI Model and Its Role in Determining Organizational Structure

RACI is an acronym for the four main roles of being:

1. **Responsible** The person or people responsible for correct execution – for getting the job done
2. **Accountable** the person who has ownership of quality and the end result. Only one person can be accountable for each task
3. **Consulted** the people who are consulted and whose opinions are sought. They have involvement through input of knowledge and information
4. **Informed** the people who are kept up to date on progress. They receive information about process execution and quality

A key characteristic of a process is that all related activities need not necessarily be limited to one specific organizational unit. Since services, processes and their component activities run through an entire organization, the individual activities should be mapped to the roles defined above. The roles and activities are coordinated by process managers. Once detailed procedures and work instructions have been developed, defined roles and activities must be mapped to existing staff. Clear definitions of accountability and responsibility are CSFs for any improvement activity. An authority matrix is often used to relate roles and responsibilities to processes and activities.

RACI models help define roles and responsibilities in processes and activities and identify who will take on each role. RACI models allow the user to understand exactly who, what, where, why, and when the appropriate individuals need to work together during service and process execution. Through RACI, issues are easily identified such as activities that have not been assigned to anyone or people taking on too many responsibilities.

Using the RACI model, there is only one person accountable for an activity, although several people may be responsible for executing parts of the activity. Accountable means end-to-end accountability for the process and it should remain with the same person for all activities of a process.

Developing an authority matrix can be challenging exercise but it's a crucially important one because the matrix clarifies to all involved which activities they are expected to fulfill and identifies gaps in service delivery and responsibilities. It is especially helpful in clarifying the staffing model necessary for improvement.

Using an authority matrix helps with two major activities that are often overlooked or hard to identify. One is that all the 'Rs' on an RACI matrix typically represent potential OLA opportunities. The second is that identifying roles that must be kept informed helps to expose communication and workflow paths. This can be very helpful when defining the communication procedures.

RACI Model – What It Looks Like

o Left column: activities, actions, decisions
o Top row: functional roles responsible for process or service
o Cells: RACI assignments

SD Table 3.2: An example of a simple RACI matrix

	Director service management	Service level manager	Problem manager	Security manager	Procurement manager
Activity 1	AR	C	I	I	C
Activity 2	A	R	C	C	C
Activity 3	I	A	R	I	C
Activity 4	I	A	R	I	
Activity 5	I	R	A	C	I

The RACI chart in SD Table 3.2 shows the structure and power of RACI modeling. The rows represent a number of required activities and the columns identify the people who make the decisions, carry out the activities or provide input.

Applying RACI to a process; only one person should hold end-to-end accountability for the process, typically the process owner. Similarly, there is only one person accountable for any individual activity, although several people may be responsible for executing parts of it.

Whether RACI or some other tool or model is used, the important thing is to not just leave the assignment of responsibilities to chance or leave it to the last minute to decide. Conflicts can be avoided and decisions can be made quickly if the roles are allocated in advance.

RACI Model – Steps to Create Chart

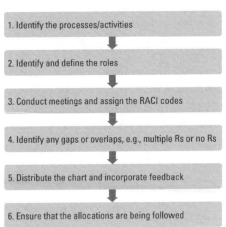

1. Identify the processes/activities
2. Identify and define the roles
3. Conduct meetings and assign the RACI codes
4. Identify any gaps or overlaps, e.g., multiple Rs or no Rs
5. Distribute the chart and incorporate feedback
6. Ensure that the allocations are being followed

RACI charting is an iterative process that you may have to revisit when there are changes to the service, process, service levels, and people in the organization.

RACI analysis should consider both role and activity perspectives

o **Role analysis** involves asking: o Many As: Are duties segregated properly? o Should someone else be accountable for some of these activities? Is this causing a bottleneck in some areas that will delay decisions? o Many Rs: too much for one function? o No empty spaces: Must this role be involved in so many tasks? o Does the participation type or degree fit this role's qualifications?	**Activity analysis** can indicate: o More than one A: only one role can be o No As: at least one A must be assigned o More than one R: too many roles responsible often means that no one takes responsibility. Responsibility may be shared, but only if roles are clear o No Rs: at least one must be assigned o Many Cs: Is there a requirement to consult with so many? What are the benefits and can the time be justified? o No Cs and Is: Are the communication channels open to enable people and departments to talk to each other and keep each other up to date?

Analysis of a RACI chart to identify weaknesses or areas for improvement should include considering both the role and activity perspectives.

It is important to understand the distinction between a formal function within an organization and the process roles that the individuals in that function are expected to carry out. Persons within a formal function may fulfill more than one specific service management role and carry out activities relating to more than one process. For example, an individual with a job title of 'network administrator' is responsible for carrying out incident management and capacity management activities. Although the network administrator may report to a different functional line manager, they are responsible for completing activities for the service desk function and capacity management process owners.

Developing an authority matrix can be a tedious and time-consuming exercise but it is a crucially important one. The authority matrix clarifies to all involved which activities they are expected to fulfill, as well as identifying any gaps in service delivery and responsibilities. It is especially helpful in clarifying the staffing model necessary for improvement.

RACI Model – Potential Problems
o Having more than one person accountable for a process means no one is accountable
o Delegation of responsibility or accountability without necessary authority
o Focus on matching processes and activities with departments
o Incorrect division / combination of functions; conflicting agendas or goals
o Combination of responsibility for closely related processes, such as incident management, problem management, service asset and configuration management, change management and release and deployment management; combining responsibilities can in some cases reduce the checks and balances that support good governance or could overload some persons filling a combined role

ITILFND07-07-2 Recognize the responsible, accountable, consulted, informed (RACI) responsibility model and explain its role in determining organizational structure (SD 3.7.4.1, Table 3.2, not RACI-VS or RASCI)

For examination purposes it is important to be able to:

o List the components of the RACI authority matrix – responsible, accountable, consulted and informed
o Identify from a list steps the RACI chart development, avoiding choice of a list of plausible but not verbatim activities
o Be able to identify potential problems surfaced by RACI charts, e.g., more than one person accountable, someone whose job it is solely to be informed (I'll take that job! ☺)

CHAPTER 8
ITILFND08 TECHNOLOGY AND ARCHITECTURE

The purpose of this unit is to help you to understand how service automation assists with expediting service management processes. The syllabus recommends that this unit is covered as part of the content in the other units.

Advantages of Service Automation

o The capacity of automated resources can be more easily adjusted in response to variations in demand volumes
o Automated resources can handle capacity with fewer restrictions on time of access; they can therefore be used to serve demand across time zones and after-hours
o Automated systems present a good basis for measuring and improving service processes by holding constant the factor of human resources; conversely, they can be used to measure the differential impact on service quality and costs due to varying levels of knowledge, skills and experience of human resources
o Many optimization problems such as scheduling, routeing and allocation of resources require computing power that is beyond the capacity of human agents
o Automation is a means for capturing the knowledge required for a service process; codified knowledge is relatively easy to distribute in the organization in a consistent and secure manner. It reduces the depreciation of knowledge when employees move within the organization or permanently leave

Automation can have particularly significant impact on the performance of service assets such as management, organization, people, process, knowledge and information. Applications by themselves are a means of automation but their performance can also be improved where they need to be shared between people and process assets. Advances in artificial intelligence, machine learning and rich-media technologies have increased the capabilities of software-based service agents to handle a variety of tasks and interactions.

When judiciously applied, the automation of service processes helps improve the quality of service, reduce costs and reduce risks by reducing complexity and uncertainty, and by efficiently resolving trade-offs. (This is the concept of Pareto efficiency, where the solution or bargain is efficient when one side of the trade-off cannot be better off without making the other side worse off.)

Service Management Areas that Benefit from Service Automation

Design and modeling	Service catalogue	Pattern recognition and analysis
Classification, prioritization, and routing	Detection and monitoring	Optimization

Demand for services can be captured from simple interactions customers have with items in an automated service catalogue. There is a need to hide the complexity in the relationships between customer outcomes and the service assets that produce them, and present only the information the customers need to specify the utility and warranty needed with respect to any particular outcome. However, customers need choice and flexibility in presenting demand.

It is possible to handle routine service requests with some level of automation. Such requests should be identified, classified and routed to automated units or self-service options. This requires the study of patterns of business activity that exist with each customer.

Degrading Effect of Variation in Service Processes

o Variation in the performance of individuals with time, workload, motivation and nature of the task at hand can be a disadvantage in many situations

o Variation in the knowledge, skills and experience of individuals can lead to variation in performance of processes

o Variations in processing times across service transactions, jobs or cycles can result in degradation of service levels, usually delays and congestion

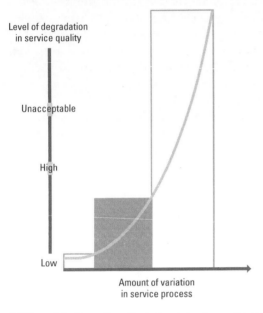

SS Figure 7.2: Degrading effect of variation in service processes

© Crown copyright 2011. Reproduced under license from the Cabinet Office.

Preparing for Automation – Guidelines

o Simplify the service processes before automating them; simplification alone can reduce variations as there are fewer tasks and interactions for variations to enter

o Clarify the flow of activities, allocation of tasks, need for information and interactions

o In self-service situations, reduce the surface area of the contact users have with the underlying systems and processes

o Do not be in a hurry to automate tasks and interactions that are neither simple nor routine in terms of inputs, resources and outcomes

Service Analytics and Instrumentation

Information only becomes knowledge when placed in the context of patterns and their implications. By understanding patterns of information we can answer:

o How does this incident affect the service?
o How is the business impacted?
o How do we respond?

Information is necessary but not sufficient for answering questions such as why certain data is the way it is and how it is likely to change in the future. Information is static. It only becomes knowledge when placed in the context of patterns and their implications. Those patterns give a high level of predictability and reliability about how the data will change over time.

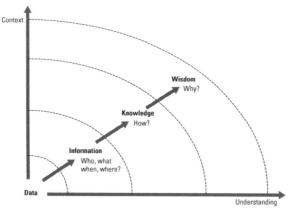

SS Figure 7.3: The flow from data to wisdom

© Crown copyright 2011. Reproduced under license from the Cabinet Office.

To understand things literally means to put them into a context. Service analytics involves both analysis, to produce knowledge, and synthesis, to provide understanding. This is called the DIKW structure (SS Figure 7.3).

Service analytics is useful to model existing infrastructure components and support services to the higher-level business services. This model is built on dependencies rather than topology – causality rather than correlation. Infrastructure events are then tied to corresponding business processes. The component-to-system-to-process linkage – also known as the service model – allows us to clearly identify the business impact of an event. Instead of responding to discrete events, managers can characterize the behaviour of a service. This behaviour is then compared to a baseline of the normal behaviour for that time of day or business cycle.

With service analytics, not only can an operations group do a better job of identifying and correcting problems from the user's standpoint, it can also predict the impact of changes to the environment. This same model can be turned around to show business demand for IT services. This is a high leverage point when building an on-demand environment.

This is as far along the DIKW structure as modern technologies allow. It is well understood that no computer-based technology can provide wisdom. It requires people to provide evaluated understanding, to answer and appreciate the 'Why?' questions. Moreover, the application of intelligence and experience is more likely to be found in the organizational processes that define and deliver service management than in applied technologies.

Instrumentation Techniques

Instrumentation
The term 'instrumentation' describes the technologies and techniques for measuring the behaviors of infrastructure elements. Instrumentation reports actual or potential problems and provides feedback after adjustments.

SS Table 7.1: Instrumentation techniques

Technique	Action
Asynchronous capture	Passive listeners scan for alerts
External source	Compile data from external sources, such as service desk tickets, suppliers or systems
Manual generation	Manually create or alter an event
Polling	Monitoring systems actively interrogate elements
Synthetic transactions	Simulate user experience by known transactions

© Crown copyright 2011. Reproduced under license from the Cabinet Office.

While data from element instrumentation is absolutely vital, it is insufficient for monitoring services. A service's behavior derives from the aggregate behavior of its supporting elements. While instrumentation can collect large amounts of raw data, greater context is needed to determine the actual relevance of any data. Information is the understanding of the relationships between pieces of data. Information answers four questions: Who, What, When and Where? This can be thought of as event, fault and performance management. The event management function refines instrumentation data into those that require further attention. While the line between instrumentation and event management can vary, the goal remains the same: create usable and actionable information.

Event Management Techniques

Event Management
The process responsible for managing events throughout their lifecycle. Event management is one of the main activities of IT operations.

SS Table 7.2: Event management techniques

Technique	Action
Compression	Consolidate multiple identical alarms into a single alarm
Correlation	See if multiple alert sources occurring during a short period of time have any relationship
Filtering	Apply rules to a single alert source over some period of time
Intelligent monitoring	Apply adaptive instrumentation
Roll-up	Compress alerts through the use of hierarchical collection structures
Verification	Actively confirm an actual incident

© Crown copyright 2011. Reproduced under license from the Cabinet Office.

A fault is an abnormal condition requiring action to repair; an error is a single event. A fault is usually indicated by excessive errors, and can result from a threshold violation or a state change. Performance, on the other hand, is a measure of how well something is working. The function of the operations group begins with fault management; as the function matures from reactive to proactive, the challenge becomes performance management. Fault management systems usually display topology maps with colored indicators. Typically they have difficulty with complex objects that span multiple object types/geographies. Context (transition from information to knowledge) makes the information useful for services.

Service analytics is useful to model existing infrastructure components and support services to the higher-level business services. The model is built on dependencies, not topology; causality, not correlation. Infrastructure events are then tied to corresponding business processes. The component-to-system-to-process linkage – also known as the service model – allows us to clearly identify the business impact of an event. Instead of responding to discrete events, managers can characterize the behavior of a service. This behavior is then compared to a baseline of normal behavior for that time of day or business cycle.

With service analytics, not only can an operations group do a better job of identifying and correcting problems from the user's standpoint, it can also predict the impact of changes to the environment. This same model can be turned around to show business demand for IT services. This is a high leverage point when building an on-demand environment.

This is as far along the DIKW structure as modern technologies allow. No computer-based technology can provide wisdom. It requires people to provide evaluated understanding, to answer and appreciate the 'Why?' questions. The application of intelligence and experience is more likely to be found in the organizational processes that define and deliver service management than in applied technologies. Section 9.1.4 outlines some of the challenges in measurement that can be addressed by service analytics.

ITILFND08-08-2 Understand how service automation assists with expediting service management processes (SS 7.1)

For the examination, you should be able to:

o Pick some of the advantages of service automation from a list, being careful to choose those that are verbatim from ITIL and not simply plausible
o Pick a correct list of the areas that benefit from service automation (what they are looking for here is that you understand and can cite a broad range of areas where automation can be applied to good effect)
o Distinguish between automation guidelines cited in ITIL (e.g., simplify before you automate) from others given as distractors
o Relate service analytics and instrumentation to the DIKW structure
o Pick instrumentation (e.g., polling) and event management (e.g., correlation) techniques from a list that includes distractors

CHAPTER 9
ITILFND09 COMPETENCE AND TRAINING (15M, NON-EXAMINABLE)

The purpose of this unit is to help you understand competence and training for ITIL. This unit is not examinable. The recommended period of study is 15 minutes.

Competence and skills for service management

Roles within ITIL service management all require specific skills, attributes and competences from the people involved to enable them to work effectively and efficiently. Whatever the role, it is imperative that the person carrying out that role has the following attributes:

○ Awareness of the business priorities, objectives and business drivers
○ Awareness of the role IT plays in enabling the business objectives to be met
○ Customer service skills
○ Awareness of what IT can deliver to the business, including latest capabilities
○ The competence, knowledge and information necessary to complete their role
○ The ability to use, understand and interpret the best practice, policies and procedures to ensure adherence

Delivering service successfully depends on personnel involved in service management having the appropriate education, training, skills and experience. People need to understand their role and how they contribute to the overall organization, services and processes to be effective and motivated. As changes are made, job requirements, roles, responsibilities and competencies should be updated if necessary.

Each service lifecycle stage depends on appropriate skills and experience of people and their knowledge to make key decisions. In many organizations, personnel will deliver tasks appropriate to more than one lifecycle stage. They may well find themselves allocated (fully or partially) from operational tasks to support a design exercise and then follow that service through service transition. They may then, via early life support activities, move into support of the new or changed services that they have been involved in designing and implementing into the live environment.

Examples of Attributes Required in Many of the Roles

Management skills	Both from a person management perspective and from the overall control of process
Ability to handle meetings	Organizing, chairing, and documenting meetings and ensuring that actions are followed up
Communication skills	An important element of all roles is raising awareness of existing processes to ensure buy-in and conformance; ability to communicate at all levels in the organization is imperative
Articulateness	Both written (e.g. for reports) and verbal
Negotiation skills	Required for several aspects, such as procurement and contracts
An analytical mind	To analyze metrics produced from the activity

ITILFND09-09-2 Competence and skills framework (SD 6.5.2)

Competence and Skills Framework

The Skills Framework for the Information Age (SFIA) is an example of a common reference model for the identification of skills needed to develop effective IT services, information systems and technology

It is constructed as a two-dimensional matrix:
o One axis divides the whole of ICT into 'skills'. Skills are grouped for convenience into subcategories or 'business roles'. Subcategories are grouped into five categories or work areas - strategy and planning, management and administration, development and implementation, service delivery and sales and marketing
o The other axis defines the level of responsibility and accountability exercised by ICT practitioners and users. Each of seven levels is defined in terms of autonomy, influence, complexity and business skills

Standardizing job titles, functions, roles and responsibilities can simplify service management and human resource management

Skills Framework for the Information Age (SFIA)
– an example of a common reference model for the identification of the skills needed to develop effective IT services, information systems and technology; The framework provides a clear model for describing what ICT practitioners do.
o SFIA defines seven generic levels at which tasks can be performed, with the associated professional skills required for each level
o A second dimension defines core competencies that can be combined with the professional skills
o SFIA is used by many IT service providers to identify career development opportunities

More information on SFIA can be found at www.sfia.org.uk

ITILFND09-09-3 Training (SD 6.5.3)

Training in Service Management

o Training in service management helps service providers to build and maintain their service management capability
o Training needs must be matched to the requirements for competence and professional development
o The official ITIL qualification scheme enables organizations to develop the competence of their personnel through approved training courses
o The courses help

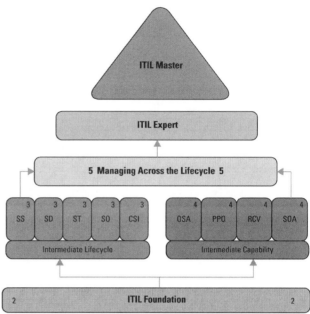

©APM Group-The Accreditor Limited 2011

students to gain knowledge of ITIL best practices, develop their competencies and gain a recognized qualification

The scheme has four levels:

ITIL Foundation	Aimed at basic knowledge of, and insight into, the core principles and processes of ITIL.
ITIL Intermediate	Based on two workstreams, one for the Service Lifecycle, and one for practitioner capabilities.
ITIL Expert	For individuals interested in demonstrating a high level of knowledge in ITIL in its entirety.
ITIL Master	Aimed at people who are experienced in the industry – typically, but not exclusively, senior practitioners, senior consultants, senior managers or executives, with five or more years' relevant experience. All candidates must hold the ITIL Expert qualification.

The scheme is based on a cumulative point system, for example, taking an ITIL Foundation course and passing the certification examination results in 2 point earned; 22 points are required to achieve ITIL expert certification. Students have a choice in which courses and examinations they take as long as the requisite number of points are earned. Further information on the ITIL qualification scheme can be found at the ITIL Official Site: http://www.itil-officialsite.com

ITILFND09-09-3 Training (SD 6.5.3)

Many practitioners need clarification on the role and content of the Intermediate Capability stream versus the Intermediate Lifecycle Stream.

The purpose and content of the Intermediate Lifecycle stream is straightforward. The Intermediate lifecycle stream consists of five individual certificates built around the five core OGC titles: Service Strategy, Service Design, Service Transition, Service Operation, and Continual Service Improvement

The Intermediate capability stream consists of four individual certificates focusing on detailed process implementation and management within cluster groupings of related content:
1. Operational Support and Analysis (OS&A) – covers Event, Incident, Request, Problem, Access, Service Desk, Technical, IT Operations and Application Management
2. Service Offerings and Agreements (SO&A) – covers Portfolio, Service Level, Catalogue. Demand, Supplier and Financial Management
3. Release, Control and Validation (RC&V) – covers Change, Release & Deployment, Validation & Testing, Service Asset & Configuration, Knowledge, Request Management / Service Evaluation
4. Planning, Protection and Optimization (PP&O) – covers Capacity, Availability, Continuity, Security, Demand and Risk Management

CHAPTER 10
ITILFND10 MOCK EXAM (120M INCLUSIVE OF REVISION)

The purpose of this unit is to help you to pass the ITIL Foundation exam. The recommended study period for this unit is minimum 2 hours inclusive of revision.

ITILFND10-10-1 Sit a minimum of one ITIL Foundation mock exam

The purpose of this unit is to help you with final preparation for taking the ITIL Foundation certification examination. Passing the examination requires knowing the Foundation level material as outlined in the syllabus, along with familiarity with the types of questions you will encounter. If you have been completing the questions in this study guide, along with the Sample Examinations successfully, you will be in good shape for the real examination.

Format of the examination

You must achieve a passing score in the Foundation Examination to gain the ITIL Foundation Certificate in IT Service Management.

Type	Multiple choice, 40 questions. The questions are selected from the full ITIL Foundation in IT Service Management examination question bank.
Duration	Maximum 60 minutes for all candidates in their respective language
	Candidates completing an examination: in a language that is not their mother tongue, **and** in a country where the language of the examination is **not a business** language in the country, have a maximum of 75 minutes to complete the examination and are allowed the use of a dictionary
Prerequisite	Accredited ITIL Foundation training is strongly recommended, but is not a prerequisite
Supervised	Yes
Open Book	No
Pass Score	65% (26 out of 40)
Distinction Score	None
Delivery	Online or Paper Based. Examination agent facility with a proof of education providers.
Supervised	Yes

Figure 10.1: Format of the examination

ITILFND10-10-1 Sit a minimum of one ITIL Foundation mock exam

Tips for taking the ITIL Foundation Examination

When preparing for the examination, be sure to get and take all available official sample examinations, and check your answers and rationale afterwards to ensure understanding. There are also some third-party sample examinations available that are worth having a look at, as well as flash cards and other study aids, many of which are free, and all of which can be had through a quick search of the internet. Also be sure to review the syllabus thoroughly, checking understanding of all required concepts, principles and models, and the glossary for definitions and acronyms required by the syllabus.

When taking the sample and actual examination

o Attempt to answer all 40 questions
o If you do not know the answer, guess, and mark the question for review
o The online version allows for marking and going back
o There are no trick questions
o There are also no patterns to how the answers are laid out
o All answers are to be marked on original examination paper
o Or if taken online, on the Web page

General test taking tips

o Skip and go back to a question you can't answer right away
o Do not forget to use a process of elimination
o Skip the preamble; it might be a misdirection, go right to the question; only read the preamble if it is necessary and useful to answer the question
o Watch for absolutes, for example, 'always', 'guarantees', 'never', 'only'
o For questions featuring lists: the least plausible answers are usually last on the list; start by comparing the last items on the list and use a process of elimination
o If stuck between two choices, ask: "What is most directly being managed here, and who is responsible for it?"
o Read questions carefully – do not miss the word 'NOT'!
o For testing purposes, take the ITIL view, rather than your own, and remember, it is always about the business

ITIL Books

Foundations of ITIL®V3

Now updated to encompass all of the implications of the V3 refresh of ITIL, the new V3 Foundations book looks at Best Practices, focusing on the Lifecycle approach, and covering the ITIL Service Lifecycle, processes and functions for Service Strategy, Service Design, Service Operation, Service Transition and Continual Service Improvement.

English €39.95 excl tax

ISBN 978 90 8753 057 0 (english edition)

ITIL® V3 Foundation Exam: The Study Guide

A complete and thorough explanation of all key concepts for ITIL V3 Foundation Exam, this title contains official sample exams and glossary of terms. Endorsed by APMG, it is definitely a great fold-flat format for class training or self-study.

English €22.50 excl tax

ISBN 978 90 8753 069 3 (english edition)

ITIL®V3 - A Pocket Guide

A concise summary for ITIL®V3, providing a quick and portable reference tool to this leading set of best practices for IT Service Management.

English €15.95 excl tax

ISBN 978 90 8753 102 7 (english edition)

ISO/IEC 20000

ISO/IEC 20000 - An Introduction
Promoting awareness of the certification for organizations within the IT Service Management environment.

ISBN 978 90 8753 081 5   (english edition)

English
€49.95
excl tax

Implementing ISO/IEC 20000 Certification - The Roadmap
Practical advice, to assist readers through the requirements of the standard, the scoping, the project approach, the certification procedure and management of the certification.

ISBN 978 90 8753 082 2   (english edition)

English
€39.95
excl tax

ISO/IEC 20000 - A Pocket Guide
A quick and accessible guide to the fundamental requirements for corporate certification.

ISBN 978 90 77212 79 0   (english edition)

English
€15.95
excl tax

Other leading ITSM Books

Metrics for IT Service Management
A general guide to the use of metrics as a mechanism to control and steer IT service organizations, with consideration of the design and implementation of metrics in service organizations using industry standard frameworks.

ISBN 978 90 77212 69 1

Six Sigma for IT Management
The first book to provide a coherent view and guidance for using the Six Sigma approach successfully in IT Service Management, whilst aiming to merge both Six Sigma and ITIL® into a single unified approach to continuous improvement. Six Sigma for IT Management: A Pocket Guide is also available.

ISBN 978 90 77212 30 1   (english edition)

The Service Catalog
Practical guidance on building a service catalog, this title focuses on IT community relationship with the business and users. Including useful templates on key documents such as OLAs and SLAs, this is definitive guide for all those delivering this tool.

ISBN 978 90 8753 571 1   (english edition)

Printed in Great Britain
by Amazon.co.uk, Ltd.,
Marston Gate.